T0311158

IN Writing will be enjoyable to the general reader for its obscure or previously suppressed stories using a well-researched behind-the-scenes point of view, as well as essays about more renowned people and issues that make up the fabric of our state's image. This is a celebration of Indiana, a state that, in my opinion, has suffered in the past from its collective inferiority complex.

RACHEL BERENSEN PERRY,
author of *William J. Forsyth: The Life and Work of an Indiana Artist*

Douglas Wissing's collection *IN Writing* is a revelation, an appealing insider's look at the often overlooked and unexpected history of a great swath of Indiana, its people, history, and lore. Though it begins and ends in Indiana, the reader will see how the rest of the world appears through the prism of the Hoosier state. Indiana is both a lens and a heart in Wissing's capable rendering.

WILLIAM O'ROURKE,
author of *Confessions of a Guilty Freelancer*

A Hoosier through and through, I love the way Doug Wissing reveals the quirks and marvels of our state and its people. I can't wait to give it to my "Flyover" friends with the inscription "I told you. We're way more interesting than you think."

BARBARA SHOUP,
author of *An American Tune: A Novel*

IN *Writing*

an imprint of
INDIANA UNIVERSITY PRESS • Bloomington and Indianapolis

Writing IN

UNCOVERING
the
UNEXPECTED
HOOSIER
STATE

DOUGLAS A. WISSING

This book is a publication of

QUARRY BOOKS
an imprint of
INDIANA UNIVERSITY PRESS
Office of Scholarly Publishing
Herman B Wells Library 350
1320 East 10th Street
Bloomington, Indiana 47405 USA
iupress.indiana.edu

and a co-publication with

INDIANA HISTORICAL SOCIETY PRESS
Eugene and Marilyn Glick
Indiana History Center
450 West Ohio Street
Indianapolis, Indiana 46202-3269 USA
indianahistory.org

© 2016 by Douglas A. Wissing

All rights reserved

No part of this book may be reproduced
or utilized in any form or by any means,
electronic or mechanical, including
photocopying and recording, or by
any information storage and retrieval
system, without permission in writing
from the publisher. The Association of
American University Presses' Resolution
on Permissions constitutes the only
exception to this prohibition.

The paper used in this publication meets the
minimum requirements of the American
National Standard for Information
Sciences–Permanence of Paper for Printed
Library Materials, ANSI Z39.48-1992.

Manufactured in the
United States of America

Library of Congress
Cataloging-in-Publication Data

Wissing, Douglas A., author.
   IN writing : uncovering
the unexpected Hoosier State /
Douglas A. Wissing.
   pages cm
   Includes index.
   ISBN 978-0-253-01904-2 (pbk. : alk.
paper) — ISBN 978-0-253-01910-3 (ebook)
1. Indiana—Description and travel. 2.
Indiana—Biography. 3. Indiana—History.
I. Title. II. Title: Indiana writing.
   F526.W78 2015
   977.2—dc23

                                    2015033430

1 2 3 4 5   21 20 19 18 17 16

"When we speak of place we often speak of our sense of it, its constant though peripheral presence. That is, there no such thing as a place, only our inscription of it we carry around in our own nervous systems."

MICHAEL MARTONE

CONTENTS

IN Writing

INTRODUCTION

THIS IS A BOOK ABOUT INDIANA IN ALL ITS GLORIOUS complexity: the sacred and profane; naughty and nice; saints and sinners; war and peace; small towns and big cities; art, architecture, poetry, and victuals. I've been around the world a few times, and contributed to big-city media like the *New York Times*, *Washington Post*, *BBC* and *CNN*, but I always tell people I'm as Hoosier as you get: a small-town boy descended from Quebecois fur-traders who paddled down to Vincennes in the 1700s and an Alsatian French Foreign Legionnaire who established a brewery there in the 1850s. So I am rooted in Indiana pure and simple. And no matter what I write, I always seem to swing back to the Hoosier state to explore the depths of who we are and what we do.

This is a book about the connections—sometimes unexpected—that bind us Hoosiers to the world. I've been learning that story since I was a kid standing by the Wabash River with my beloved grandfather Clarence Stout, Sr., who proudly celebrated our Hoosier-Creole heritage. He pointed upstream and explained our people came from up north in Canada. And then he pointed south and talked about how the wild boys of his youth used to paddle down to New Orleans to see what a real Creole city looked like. Connections. I've been seeing them since. Hoosiers contributing their talents and genius to the larger world: a famous Indiana-born explorer who introduced Tibet to America early in the twentieth century; courageous Indiana farmer-soldiers ardently trying to win the hearts and minds of twenty-first-century Afghan insurgents; Hoosier artisans' work pulsing with the aesthetics of far-away homelands; a famous modernist poet who had to leave to make his mark. Places that speak to the wider world: Columbus and its remarkable architecture; New Harmony and its enduring idealism; Indianapolis's gargoyles and its renowned Crown Hill cemetery. Then there's our celebrated Hoosier fare, offering quirky diversity to the world.

The essays in this book were selected from the million or so words I've written on Indiana in the course of producing hundreds of articles and a half-dozen books over the last twenty years. Excepting a new essay, "Jihadis in Indiana," all of the articles originally appeared in publications that include the *Los Angeles Times, New York Times, Indianapolis Star, Nuvo, Condé Nast Details, Traces, Indianapolis Monthly*, and the long-lost and lamented *artsindiana*. There are a few excerpts from my books.

The collection is not inclusive; it's not even representative. But hopefully these thirty-one chapters reflect some of Indiana's unexpected ways, and help us appreciate our remarkable state even more. So here it is, *IN Writing: Uncovering the Unexpected Hoosier State.*

Douglas A. Wissing
Bloomington, Indiana

Part 1
Saints and Sinners

Indiana-born entertainer Red Skelton left Vincennes in 1925 to join Doc Lewis's Patent Medicine Show. From there he entertained people in tent shows, showboats, circuses, dance marathons, vaudeville, radio, movies, and television.

Courtesy of Indiana Historical Society, General Picture Collection, M 411.

1

THE LAST VAUDEVILLIAN

RED SKELTON

IT WAS A BIG DEAL WHEN RED SKELTON CAME TO VISIT MY grandfather, Clarence Stout Sr., when I was a kid in Vincennes. There was not much going on down there in the mid-1950s, and Red was definitely the town celebrity. Red would show up in a vast car and disappear behind the pocket doors of my grandfather's wainscoted office that was hung with hundreds of autographed publicity photos of show-business greats and not-so-greats from the 1920s to the 1940s.

Besides being a composer and impresario, my grandfather managed the old Vincennes vaudeville theater, the Pantheon, when Red was a penniless, rubber-faced kid with a penchant for falling off stages for laughs. He told him, "Get out of Vincennes, Red, you've got too much talent," he later recounted as he puffed on his pipe.

Skelton took my grandfather's advice, and when Red died on September 17, 1997, at eighty-four years old, America and Indiana lost a clown, and a link to our development as a people. Skelton's career spanned a broad swath of entertainment history, from medicine shows to coast-to-coast broadcasts, from a traditional rural society to a fast-paced urban one.

It is a long way from the physical clowning of a medicine show to the arid cynicism of a Dennis Miller dialogue. Yet in his career, Skelton saw it all—moving from medicine shows to tent shows to showboats to burlesque halls to dance marathons to vaudeville stages to nightclubs to radio, movies, and, ultimately, twenty years of prime-time television.

He was born in Vincennes on July 18, 1913, hitting his cue for the first time, arriving "before his brothers got home from school," as his mother hoped. He grew up in poverty that marked him for life, his family "so poor they didn't have a pot to pee in, or a window to throw it out of," as a childhood friend recalled. Red had already run away from Vincennes once by the time my grandfather counseled it. Red left town with Doc Lewis's Medicine Show when he was just twelve, peddling patent medicine in Indiana, Arkansas, Illinois, and Missouri for the summer, before returning for another round of ill-fated schooling.

After a stint of street-corner entertainment and helping out at the Pantheon, he linked up with the John Lawrence Stock Company, a touring theater group playing "serious drama" under a tent, and he was off at fourteen into the world of entertainment. "Mom used to say I didn't run away from home," Skelton recalled. "My destiny just caught up with me at an early age." A week later, he and the touring group discovered his talent for comedy and his lack of talent for drama, and he found himself abandoned on the banks of the Missouri River in a fleabag hotel. As he pondered his fate, a stern-wheel showboat, *The Cotton Blossom*, churned around the bend, and quickly Skelton found himself afloat as an all-around entertainer. He traveled the Mississippi and Ohio Rivers for several seasons, taking pratfalls, performing in blackface in minstrel shows, and telling monologues and jokes.

Skelton's father worked as a clown for the Indiana-based Hagenbeck and Wallace Circus. Years later, Skelton encountered the circus putting up the big top in a river town, and he left the riverboat touring company to join the same circus as a walk-around clown, honing the physical comedy that became his stock in trade.

Red never really severed his Indiana connections. The circus brought him back through. He worked for a season with my grandfather's minstrel revue, playing a blackface mammy. Stock companies, carnivals, and the burlesque circuit brought him through Indiana.

As he honed his skills, he entertained the crowds at Depression-era dance marathons, where couples staggered around an arena till all but one dropped. When he later became a major star of radio, television, and movies, he never forgot his origins, returning time and again to refresh his roots, check out his birthplace, accept his awards, and establish a children's foundation, which still operates.

He was a complex man, paying the emotional price for his art. High-strung, suspicious to the point of paranoia, subject to career-threatening devolutions with the bottle, Skelton could be his own worst enemy. In many ways he was a mirror of Indiana: toting a vengeful pride born of insecurity, and sentimental to a degree found saccharine in the more sophisticated sections of the country—"corny" as only a son of the Corn Belt can be.

At his core, Skelton was a small-town, early-twentieth-century Indiana boy. Comedian Steve Allen saw "something about Red that was partly a little boy." Skelton's "Mean Widdle Kid" played out the willful churlishness in all of us. "I dood it," became a national phrase in the 1940s as his radio show took off. "I not pullin' de kitty's tail," he insisted as the pantomime cat clawed for escape, "I just holdin' on. He pullin.'"

His egalitarianism played out in his art. His characters such as Clem Kaddilehopper and Freddy the Freeloader are goofy, down-on-their-luck guys, but they comport themselves with the natural nobility of a democratic citizen. Like Charlie Chaplin's little tramp, Skelton's caricatures show us ourselves with a humor born of pathos. "To imitate a lunkhead without malice or derision is quite a feat—and Skelton brings it off everytime," wrote humorist Leo Rosten.

Performing was his "plasma," one biographer wrote. Skelton himself said, "People talk about stage fright, but what scares me is not so much the going on as the going off. I only come to life when people are watching." Though enormously wealthy after twenty years of prime-time television, canny investments, and even a burgeoning career as a painter, Skelton could not stop performing.

I met him in 1983, when he donated a rare book to Indiana University while in town to give a performance at the auditorium. He was a kindly senior citizen at the reception, gracious in his memories of my grandfather, "Oh, he was so important to me as a young man," he said. That night on the stage, though nearly seventy, he put down his cane and took off his knee braces to pratfall and silly around with his beloved characters until he had the audience of grandparents and college students howling in their seats. "The last vaudevillian," I thought, "He just can't help himself."

As always, Skelton said it best, "I love people. That's why I clown. It's simply that I love to make people laugh."

2

HUBRIS

BOBBY KNIGHT

WE WERE SITTING AT NICK'S BAR IN BLOOMINGTON, watching Indiana University lose by nearly fifty points when the doctoral candidate quoted Shakespeare, "Now is the winter of our discontent." There have been a lot of literary discussions about Bobby Knight through the years. "He's our own Shakespearean character," I have heard the lit majors say. A colossus astride the stage, fissured by his fatal flaw: Richard III, Iago, Julius Caesar. We debated the great characters, looking for clues to Knight as we sat at the Dylan Thomas booth, where the poet drank himself silly back in the 1950s. Indecisive Hamlet was never a choice, though often-prideful Macbeth was worked over pretty good. "Hubris," said one, dragging out the Greek tragedies' excessive pride that challenges the gods. "Who the gods destroy, they first make powerful," said another with an arched eyebrow.

When you live in Bloomington there is a certain unavoidable association with Knight, as befits being in the proximity of such an outsized character. Like it or not, it is what most people around the world associate with the town—Knight and the Kinsey Institute. I have had business deals go sour in Louisiana when the people learned where I was from. Knight is particularly unloved down there. I was hiking deep in a national park once, thrilled to escape a particularly clamorous bout of Knight-time fever, when a park ranger hailed me on the trail. "Was it true that Knight was going to go to New Mexico?" he asked.

Later in the year, I heard a pair behind me in the Paris airport lounge talking about Knight in French. I never turned around. A couple of years ago, I saw a Tibetan in a porkpie hat and an IU basketball t-shirt on the streets of Lhasa, Tibet. "Go Hoosiers," he said, although he knew no other English. When I met Jorgean and Angelique, a pair of hearty Germans, in Bangkok, they looked like a pair of sunburned zeppelins, having just returned from the islands off Southern Thailand. After they discovered I was from Indiana, Jorgean exclaimed, "Hooshers! Hooshers! I know! I know! Hoosher Dome! Reggie Miller! I know! Hooshers, I luf the Hooshers! Bobby Nutt! Great coach! Bobby Nutt! I know!"

"Uh, I think that's *Knight*," I told Jorgean.

"Embarrassed," the *Indiana Daily Student* headline read after last Sunday's game. "Humiliation Has a Number: The Hoosiers Lose by 48," the *New York Times* trumpeted. There is a truism in military strategy: Generals always fight the last war. The Germans sweeping up behind the Maginot Line facing the wrong direction is the classic example. Can Knight prosper one last time with his program? I hope so, though I am not sure. It struck me that the two most horrific losses the Hoosiers have endured have come in the last four years, including Minnesota beating us by fifty points in 1994.

As I pondered it all in Thomas's booth, his great exultation against mortality came to mind: "Do not go gentle into that good night," he wrote. "Old age should burn and rave at close of day. Rage, rage, against the dying of the light."

3

ODD BODKIN

THE PHONE RANG IN SHERIFF ROD JACKSON'S HOUSE ONE cold Wednesday night last January. Jackson was acquainted with the caller, a local named Donald Holtz, who had been in trouble with the law before. Holtz wanted the sheriff to know that someone was castrating men in Huntington, Indiana, and videotaping the operations. Holtz said he had scheduled himself for the procedure, but he and his fiancée were now having second thoughts.

A week later, the sheriff; the prosecutor's investigator, Janet Walters; three deputies; and two state policemen arrived at the Riverwood Ranch Apartments, a string of decaying roadside motor cabins from the 1940s. Edward Bodkin, a slight, middle-aged man with thinning grey hair and tinted aviator glasses, answered the door nude and sporting an extensive collection of genital jewelry. Offering no resistance, he led the men inside, where they found on a table beside the fridge nine small jars, each one containing a white ovoid lump floating in viscous liquid. The sheriff suggested that Bodkin find a dressing-gown.

Huntington (population: 18,523) is an old Wabash River town plunked down in the middle of corn-stubbled farmland. Located about seventy-five miles northeast of Indianapolis, out on the swells and swales of the prairie, Huntington is the hometown of former U.S. vice president Dan Quayle and boasts the country's only vice-presidential museum. Another major attraction? Thirteen exceptionally antique outhouses clustered on the outskirts of town. But that is all. In short, Huntington is not the kind of place you would expect to find a bunch of guys looking to be castrated.

Nevertheless, it was in Huntington that the darkest, most extreme edge of the body-modification underground surfaced—in the form of a fifty-six-year-old data-processing temp blinking in the media glare. In addition to jars of testicles and boxes of lurid letters, police confiscated several grisly videotapes of operations—evidence that at least five men had been castrated in Bodkin's previous residence, a peeling white clapboard apartment house just a few blocks west of the Dan Quayle Center and Museum. John Branham, the Huntington County prosecutor, charged Bodkin with practicing medicine without a license, a Class C felony. In lieu of the $50,000 bond, Bodkin remained in the Huntington County Jail.

Rumors depicted Bodkin as another homegrown sociopath like the serial-murderer Jeffrey Dahmer—even though Bodkin's "clients," as he called them, were consenting adults who had come to him for the surgery. The media trotted out all kinds of experts, who speculated about his private life. It was painful and humiliating, and he wanted to spare his clients the same exposure. So, a few days later, Bodkin sat down and told the authorities and the spinning tape recorder his story. "Uh, everyone has their own little idiosyncrasies, little fantasies," he began.

Bodkin is a cutter; he himself is not cut. He will not discuss his sexual "preference." But standard notions of "preference" do not really apply in the world he inhabits.

An only child, Bodkin lived on a farm near Kokomo, Indiana, until he was ten, when the family moved to nearby Russiaville. He studied voice and pipe organ at Chicago's Sherwood Conservatory of Music and played the organ at various Chicago churches.

Over the next couple of decades, Bodkin led a transient life, criss-crossing the Midwest, holding a variety of jobs (gardener, housepainter, clerk), and occasionally finding himself homeless. At the time of his arrest, he was temping at a Huntington fireplace factory. After hours, he rotated his nightly watering holes (Dad's, Poff's Place), drinking vodka and grapefruit juice and writing letters. He was a loner; following his arrest, most locals were only able to come up with the he-seemed-like-a-nice-guy platitudes that people spout when they realize they have been sharing the same space, breathing the same air, and maybe having a cup of coffee at the local diner with a fellow citizen who turns out to be a serial killer, a devil worshipper, or a guy who castrates people.

Bodkin grew up watching livestock castration on his parents' farm and so developed an intense interest in the procedure. At about the age of nine, he saw someone with an undescended testicle. "I thought that was neat," he said matter-of-factly. "It fascinated me from an appearance viewpoint. When I couldn't find anyone else [like that], I thought, 'Well, make your own.' That was my motivation to find someone who was willing."

Bodkin advertised his services in *Ball Club Quarterly* ("a communication network for those who have 'em and those who want 'em") and the bimonthly *Unique,* both of which are published by seventy-three-year-old Kenneth Schein. Schein distributes about a thousand copies of *Ball Club Quarterly* and two hundred of *Unique* from his California base—and is not given to philosophizing about the fixations and fetishes of his customers. "Ah, balls—some cut 'em off, some want to blow kisses at 'em," he summed up in his gravelly voice.

"Male, 45, interested in all aspects of voluntary castration," read a typical *Unique* advertisement. "Potentially seeking experienced and skilled cutter. Would also like to hear from any females interested in same matter." The key word here is "potentially"; according to Schein, a great many of the ads seem to be pure fantasy. "We've had some guys advertising in this magazine for twelve to fifteen years, looking for a cutter," he recalled.

And then there are the ones who are not just in it for the fantasy. Bodkin admits only to the five castrations—removing both testicles in four cases, one in the other (the man began to bleed profusely, forcing Bodkin to stop halfway through). He refuses to be specific about their individual motivations, and will only say generally that some subjects wanted to diminish their sex drive (either because they were former child molesters, gay men in denial, or both). One considered his testicles a distraction during anal intercourse. And at least one announced afterward that he was going to pursue a new lifestyle. Bodkin theorized that the man was planning to lead a life of total submission to his sadomasochism master, a woman.

Bodkin castrated his clients in exchange for the right to videotape the operations. Schein distributed the videos through his publications, selling them for $75 each, with Bodkin getting a piece of the profits. "His technique got immeasurably better as he went along," said Schein. At first, Bodkin used an orange-handled art knife, manicure scissors, a curved needle (also known as a "bodkin," coincidentally), and rusty needle-nosed pliers. "It looked like he worked on his car with them," noted investigator Walters. By the last castrations, Bodkin was using surgical equipment purchased from a veterinary supply company, and anesthetic.

There was another part to the deal: Bodkin got to keep "the trophies." These were the items on display in his kitchen: nine small jars labeled with the dates of the procedures, the subjects' initials, and either an L or an R. "It wasn't so much for me," Bodkin explained. "It appealed to a certain voyeuristic fascination . . . the different interests of my visitors. 'You have to have trophies,' they'd say. I have an active fantasy world, you know what I mean?"

Bodkin is not as odd as you think, or at least he is not alone. One body-modification website proprietor estimates that there are currently 100 cutters operating in the United States. Schein thinks that number is conservative, though he admits there is no way to be sure. What pass for statistics in this world are really just whispers on the Web: there's the Philadelphia-based doctor who performs surgical castration on transsexuals and eunuch fetishists for $750. Then there's the doctor down in Tijuana, Mexico, who averaged more than 100 castrations a year for six years at $3,000 a pop.

Bodkin exists on the edge of a subculture that is already on the edge. It all started with the first caveman to stick a bone through his nose, gathered momentum in the 1960s and 1970s with, in America, the self-proclaimed "modern primitive" guru-shaman Fakir Musafar, then blew up completely with the advent of the Internet.

Milling under the body-modification tent these days are the tattooed, the pierced (nipples, genitalia), the amputated (extremities, genitalia), the implanted (metal and coral, for horns and ridges), the injected (generally saline), and the bifurcated, truncated, and otherwise self-mutilated ("nullos" remove all their genitalia; "smoothies" lose the nipples, too). By imitating the ancient rituals of tribesmen from all over the world, practitioners aim to "reclaim" their bodies as their own, to transcend pain and achieve a state of grace.

"Body modification reflects culture," said Armando Favazza, professor of psychiatry and author of the seminal *Bodies Under Siege: Self-Mutilation and Body Modification in Culture and Psychiatry*. "Correctly done, body modification promotes physical healing, is spiritual and establishes order in a community. Musafar's modifications are ritualistic and aesthetic."

However, according to Favazza, mainstream modifiers such as Musafar disdain Bodkin and his ilk. "With these castrations, people have clearly gone over the edge," Favazza said. "There's nothing aesthetic; it's not ritualistic. It's gone deviant. It's S & M gone awry."

Bodkin's castration videos are elegant in simplicity, directed to a small, fervent audience's singular interest. There's not much character or plot development. The film consists of a pair of rubber-gloved hands performing their task in tight close-up: first cutting the scrotum along the natural seam in the middle ("Just follow the dotted line," Bodkin explained to prosecutors), sawing through the inner membrane, then tying off the artery in each testicle hanging bloody in the frame, severing the testicle, and suturing up the sac after swabbing out the inside with gauze and paper towels. The wounds are washed with contact-lens solution.

The final shot is two white objects on a green plastic tray, looking like fresh mozzarella balls or large oysters. "That's it. Took us one hour and 50 minutes," Bodkin's voice drones on the soundtrack.

To the psychiatry establishment, voluntary castration constitutes psychotic behavior. Medical literature dating back to the late nineteenth century diagnoses such patients as psychotic or intoxicated. Today, Favazza estimates, 100 to 200 castrations of this nature take place every year. It was not until 1954 that a case of self-castration not deemed psychotic even appeared on the books; such cases have since been categorized as gender-identity disorders.

Today, voluntary chemical or surgical castration is gaining acceptance as a means of treating repeat sex offenders; it is legal in seven American states, while several others have discussed legislation. Castrations are also legally performed for transsexuals, but only after they have endured a long waiting period and extensive counseling. But the reason why most men who undergo a bilateral orchidectomy (removal of both testicles) do so is cancer prevention. Up until a decade ago, it was a common treatment for prostate cancer, but most patients now opt for a chemical castration, taking medication that temporarily reduces testosterone.

"There are a number of side-effects to castration," said Doctor Michael Sarosdy, a urologist and cancer specialist based in Texas. Among them: loss of libido (though some men remarkably, do retain their sex drive), flaccid erections (or none at all), osteoporosis, hot flushes, decline in muscle mass, and loss of body hair. "They're certainly less aggressive," said Sarosdy. "There is a decline in the sense of well-being, like running out of gas."

Some eunuchs fight that feeling through hormone therapy. Marcel, for example, is a smoothie from Canada who had a castration, a penectomy, and scrotum and nipple removal. "I have always been fascinated by genital tortures, mutilation, and removal," he said. "My dick was just useful for urinating. I don't regret anything. My sex drive is still the same, because I take testosterone."

Others perceive castration as a means of experiencing total self-control. "To be castrated and not be male or feminine is about the best description I can communicate," said one eunuch on the Internet. "My goal is to be genderless but express myself mostly as female," said another. "My desire to be an 'it' is as serious as death!"

Trying to count castrati is not any easier than finding cutters; they are not exactly living out in the open. Bodkin says he corresponded with 200 or so, but most were in it for the fantasy. "Gelding," a eunuch living in Florida (who says he was castrated by two strangers in a night of extreme S & M), dispenses advice on the Net like a mother hen. "In the last three years, I've helped some 200 males get castrated through various means, including referral to doctors," he said. But, he added, arriving at an accurate count of the total population would be impossible. "The majority probably don't want it known to anyone," he said.

Over Janet Walters's desk is a sign that reads, "We work for God." The tall, blonde veteran investigator has been on the Bodkin case from the beginning. "He's a very pleasant man," she said. "I've spent hours talking to him"—about gardening, cooking, and his companion, a blind twelve-year-old Shih Tzu dog named Cuddles.

But the only person who really seems to have known Bodkin is not talking—although in the immediate aftermath of the arrest, Holtz had plenty to say to the media, much of it very involved. The pair first met in the 1960s, when, according to Holtz, Bodkin befriended Holtz's adoptive father and lived with them for a while in Michigan City, Indiana. They did not cross paths again until 1994, when the newly divorced Holtz moved in with Bodkin. During the many nights the pair spent getting drunk, Holtz said, Bodkin was pressing him to get castrated. Eventually he agreed. "We went barhoppin' and came home pretty much intoxicated," he told Court TV. "I was goin' through a divorce, and I wasn't goin' to use 'em no more . . . and I said, 'Why not?'" But Holtz got engaged again and started having second thoughts—which is when he made that late-night phone call to Sheriff Jackson.

Less than a week later, Holtz was married and Bodkin was arrested. On April 12 this year [1999], Circuit Court Judge Mark Mcintosh sentenced Bodkin to four years in jail, with two and a half years suspended and credit for sixty-nine days served. Bodkin's appearance at sentencing presented a stark contrast to his arraignment in February, when deputies made him wear a bulletproof vest. This time, he walked into the courthouse calmly and read his four-page statement: "I felt it prudent to spare the court unnecessary time considerations and graphic details regarding this case. Such details might be repugnant to some and a source of folly for others. . . . My activities were conducted at the specific request of the parties . . . to absolve emotional, psychological or physical needs . . . not merely the spurious fancy of some alternate lifestyle." Bodkin is counting the days until his October release from the Huntington County Jail, helping out with maintenance and answering his mail. The *Jerry Springer Show* asked him to be a guest, but he is not interested. ("They sent a director here, right to the jail," Sheriff Jackson said.) Bodkin figures he'll move to another town, though without Cuddles, since he consented to having the dog put down in February.

Bodkin is unrepentant about the acts that put him in jail. "I enjoy giving people happiness," he said. "If modification is going to bring this person happiness, I am willing to assist in their happiness." But asked whether he will continue to be a cutter, he quickly answers, "I can't—legally."

Meanwhile, Huntington will probably never be quite the same. The jokes still circulate, though perhaps not as much as in the days immediately following the arrest—when locals theorized that Bodkin was a Ball State University graduate, that Nut and Honey Crunch was his favorite cereal, and that the authorities were going to have to release him, since they could not find anyone with balls enough to testify against him.

Says Michael Sellon, the former director of the Dan Quayle Center and Museum, with a rueful laugh: "Huntington is now known for castrations, Dan Quayle, and an outhouse collection."

4

D.C. RIDDLE

AS U.S. SENATOR JOE LIEBERMAN'S CHIEF OF STAFF, CLARINE Nardi Riddle, BA 1971, JD 1974, sits at the epicenter of America's business.

"I always view myself as the air traffic controller for the Senator's office," she said with a laugh as she explained directing a high-velocity workplace staffed by dozens of "straight-A students."

Riddle tussles daily with the nation's pressing issues, from Iraq, homeland security, climate change, and energy policy, to the 22,000 constituent requests that come in *weekly*.

A gifted high-school student from Clinton, Indiana, Riddle came to IU already imbued with a sense of civic responsibility from Presbyterian youth work and an Italian American mother who held up Eleanor Roosevelt as a model.

"I've always had a burning desire to improve the social condition and solve the problems of the day," Riddle said.

While earning an honors degree in mathematics during the tumultuous Vietnam War years of 1967–71, she immersed herself in campus governance through numerous academic committees, the Student Foundation, and the Young Women's Christian Association. She served as a mediator between student radicals and university administration during the most incendiary days. In response, the university awarded Riddle the National Mortar Board Fellowship for Outstanding Undergraduate and the Herman B Wells Award for Outstanding Senior Student.

Energized by the potential for social change, Riddle entered the IU School of Law in Bloomington in 1971, one of a dozen women breaching the bastion of male professionalism. "It was a locker room culture that we [women] walked into," she said. "We worked hard to change that."

Riddle coordinated the Law School's Women's Caucus, which successfully addressed gender issues with the faculty. "We were heard," she said.

When one particularly chauvinistic professor persisted in sexist rampages, the women resorted to a direct approach: "We *hissed*," Riddle said. "We decided we weren't going to take it anymore."

During her final year of law school, Riddle was editor of the interdisciplinary law journal, *IUSTITIA*, and helped to write IU's first Title IX affirmative-action plan.

"Clarine creates forums for creative discussion and dialogue," IU law professor Patrick Baude said about her gift for mediation and conciliation. "Previously, there'd just been shouting. It was a different kind of lawyering."

In 1989, when Riddle was appointed Connecticut's youngest and first female attorney general, she became known as the "people's lawyer," using her office to champion environmental and consumer protection, while successfully arguing a case before the U.S. Supreme Court. She served as a Connecticut Superior Court judge from 1991 to 1993.

In 1999 the IU School of Law at Bloomington inducted Riddle into its prestigious Academy of Law Alumni Fellows, whose inductees include Birch Bayh, Wendell Willkie, and Hoagy Carmichael.

When Lieberman announced Riddle's appointment as his chief of staff in 2003, his press release trumpeted her "demonstrated commitment to public service" and "tremendous real-world experience," anticipating she would "accomplish great things."

For Riddle, it is yet another opportunity to help people find solutions to their problems.

As she said, "How do we move the ball forward and make the world a better place?"

In 1969 Congressman Alexander Pirnie of New York reaches into a container of draft numbers (center) as others look on, including retiring Selective Service Director Lieutenant General Lewis Blaine Hershey (left) and Deputy Director Colonel Daniel O. Omer (right) at the Selective Service Headquarters during the nationwide draft lottery in 1969.

Courtesy of Library of Congress.

5

THE HOOSIER GENERAL

LEWIS B. HERSHEY AND THE SELECTIVE SERVICE

PROTESTORS OVERRAN WASHINGTON, D.C., ON NOVEMBER 15, 1969. Deep in the tumult of the Vietnam War, it was the largest antiwar demonstration in U.S. history. Hundreds of thousands marched through the embattled capital. Tear gas hung like wraiths in the trees; the river of marchers crunched across glass broken by rampaging radicals. The whole panoply of dissenting America rallied at the National Mall—college students and Yippies, ministers and maidens, Ban the Bomb moms, Clean for Gene volunteers, draft resisters, vets with their fatigues and angry faces, Black Power activists, pacifists, patchouli-scented hippies and anarchists waving black flags, all milling on the Mall, sitting on the grass, lolling on bedrolls.

Through the vast crowd, an elderly general from Indiana meandered, marveling at how the world had changed. Indiana-born and Indiana-bred, General Lewis B. Hershey was the director of the Selective Service System, America's military conscription organization. The antiwar protestors reviled him.

A folksy Hoosier, Hershey had essentially encoded his midwestern belief system into America's military draft. Beginning in 1940, Hershey's organization drafted twenty million men and regulated the lives of hundreds of millions. Americans had generally accepted the draft, but anti-Vietnam War activists had changed that with unending agitation. Responding in kind, Hershey called the protestors "long-haired, runny-nosed, dirty-eared misfits," and tried to take away their deferments.

Wandering through the maelstrom on the Mall, however, Hershey was sanguine. "There are claims that 250,000 people were on the monument grounds," seventy-five-year-old Hershey wrote the next day to his son. Old soldier Hershey had reasons to be worried, but evinced few concerns, writing he "wondered whether we would be able to get out"—but only because of the throng rather than hostility. He reported the crowd was "good natured" and "all behaved very well." The antiwar march came at the penultimate moment for Hershey. After wielding immense power for nearly three decades, he had become another casualty of the unpopular war, dumped from his position by recently elected President Richard Nixon.

Hershey was born on September 12, 1893, on a small northeastern Indiana farm near Angola. His family was very poor—even cheap funerals were a burden. "There were many, many things we did not have," he wrote. But he always credited his success to the values and modalities he learned in Indiana. "First, we believed in work—hard work—and long working hours. Second, we learned early in life how important it is to rely on a person's word," Hershey said. "We took our neighbor's word at face value, because we knew his background and we believed there was validity to his word."

The Hersheys were pacifist Mennonites who migrated in 1708 from a Swiss Anabaptist hotbed to Pennsylvania's Mennonite and Amish settlements. In 1849 Hershey's grandfather migrated to another Amish center, Steuben County, Indiana, where the future leader of American military conscription was raised. While deeply committed to military service and not actively religious, Hershey was proud of his pacifist heritage, referring to himself as "the Mennonite General." Hershey was no stranger to war, as he grew up around Civil War soldiers whose battlefield memories defined their manhood. His uncle served at Chickamauga, was imprisoned at Andersonville, and had been blown up when the steamship *Sultana* exploded while repatriating Union soldiers. While visiting his uncle, young Hershey saw a circus for the first time, which commingled in his mind with another war. "Little kids were selling flag pins that opened up to read, 'The Hell with Spain, Remember the Maine,'" he remembered years later.

Schooling for Hershey was in the Hell's Point one-room schoolhouse, where the curriculum was rich in Victorian-era literature that emphasized duty, honor, and rural virtue. He did well, motivated by a love of learning and an intense dislike of farm work. Though most farm lads stopped their education at the eighth grade, Hershey enrolled in Fremont High School, where he graduated as class valedictorian. During his high school years, Hershey began courting a quietly confident young woman, Ellen Dygert, who came from a family of governors and diplomats. Beginning with walking to the post office and "going down to the train station to see the day's three trains come in," theirs was to be a lifetime relationship.

After Fremont, Hershey then took a special three-month education course at Tri-State College (now Trine University) in nearby Angola, Indiana. He wanted to teach, which he did that fall. But Hershey soon reentered Tri-State, financed by working as a deputy for his father, who had been elected sheriff.

While Steuben County had a large Amish population, it also had a strong martial tradition, sending more Union soldiers to the Civil War than any other comparable county. Angola sponsored an Indiana National Guard troop, Company B, First Battalion, Third Infantry Regiment. Attracted by the seeming opportunity for adventure, Hershey enlisted when he was seventeen. "I guess I got my interest in military training through debating the question," he later said. "We were all great for debates in northern Indiana, and then I joined the National Guard in 1911." In November 1913 a labor dispute prompted the governor to declare martial law in Indianapolis, and Hershey's unit was dispatched to help keep order. When Hershey led a small squad out to reconnoiter, he learned the locals did not appreciate the soldiers' presence, which caused him some apprehension. Years later Hershey told an awards dinner, "I didn't join the Guard to see the world—all I wanted to see was Indianapolis!"

In the chaos after the Mexican Revolution, President Woodrow Wilson ordered General Jack Pershing and 15,000 troops to the southern borderlands. The troops included several federalized National Guard units, including Indiana's. Before deploying, recently commissioned Lieutenant Hershey enthusiastically led local recruiting. But few volunteers enlisted, forcing his troop to march off shorthanded. Later, discussing military experience with his comrades, Hershey insisted that a patriotic tour of duty was essential to a full life, and that universal military service would fend off national "decadence." In his diary, he wrote that war would "remove many of the superficial things that have overcrowded our existence," as soldiers could "live like men" and learn "what real life is like after all."

After being posted to New Albany as a recruiter, Hershey again had little success, only enlisting four recruits in three months. He blamed the failure on "extreme individualism—all attention directed to the promotion of private fortunes and private interests." His days as a failed recruiter permanently tainted his views of a volunteer military. He felt the nation had to compel universal military training—or disarm.

Realizing a peacetime army appointment was unlikely, Hershey enrolled at Indiana University to pursue a graduate degree. But events in Europe changed his trajectory. As the United States edged toward involvement in World War I, Hershey organized an IU student drill team, but fulminated when only 130 men showed up. Thinking the president would federalize the National Guard, Hershey reenlisted in August 1917. Congress had already passed the Selective Service Act, requiring all men between twenty-one and thirty to register for military service, which Wilson called "mass volunteering."

Compulsory military service has a checkered American history. Seldom used in peacetime, wartime military drafts often ignited controversy. The U.S. military relied on a small, all-volunteer army through the nineteenth century until the Civil War brought conscription—along with widespread draft riots, including four days in New York City when a thousand people died. Union draftees could avoid conscription by hiring substitutes or paying a three-hundred-dollar commutation fee, so the conflict was often termed "a rich man's war but a poor man's fight." In the end, only a small percentage of Union soldiers were draftees or substitutes. Most were volunteers.

The United States did not truly rely on military conscription until World War I's Selective Service Act, which was spearheaded by a national preparedness movement. The nation generally accepted the new national draft, albeit a decentralized one run by local volunteers overseeing deferments and inductions. While 72 percent of U.S. soldiers serving in

World War I were draftees, the Selective Service draft ended with the war in 1918.

Hershey had a good war. He subsumed himself in military life, initially in dusty Western posts. His zeal and aptitude resulted in his captain's bars and a coveted slot at the School of Fires for artillery training. His graduation coincided with marriage to Ellen Dygert in the summer of 1918. As the climax to a seven-year courtship, Hershey made a military-connected proposal, asking for Ellen's hand by stating he wanted her to be the beneficiary of his army insurance. Though he lamely admitted it was a "rather sordid reason for speaking of matrimony," long-suffering Ellen accepted the offer.

Hershey arrived in France in October 1918, when the carnage was in its fourth year. In spite of 37 million civilian and military casualties, Hershey remained convinced of war's cleansing fire. He wrote, "I am a strong believer in the good that shall arise from the war, no matter how long it may be prolonged," and that military focus would supplant "the superficial things that have over-crowded our existence." Before he could get to the battlefield, however, the Germans surrendered. Unlike millions of delirious people celebrating Armistice, Hershey was crestfallen. Soon after his disappointment, he found a new military role. Instead of sailing back to Indiana, Hershey joined the American Expeditionary Headquarters in Brest, France, where he coordinated American army troop shipments.

Enamored with military life, Hershey determined to find a place in the regular peacetime army. In August 1920 Captain Hershey received his first regular army commission, despite what one reviewing officer called "a colorless record." For the next twenty years, Hershey was part of an under-resourced army not at war. In spite of the restrictions, Hershey used his skills at organization, administration, statistics, and persuasive language to continue to rise in position.

By 1936 Hershey was a forty-two-year-old captain with few advancement opportunities. Though a worldly, accomplished man, he presented himself as a homespun Hoosier, eager to charm with midwestern-tinged witticisms, akin to Kin Hubbard's wry Brown County aphorisms or fellow Hoosier Herb Shriner's self-deprecating jokes. Hershey began to prepare for civilian life after his military retirement. But first he took his family around the world, visiting Japan, Manchuria, China, Korea, the Philippines, Singapore, Ceylon, India, Egypt, Malta, France, and Italy, before heading to Washington, D.C., for what appeared to be his final assignment—with the U.S. Army General Staff personnel branch.

Events in Europe again radically changed Hershey's life. When he arrived in Washington in 1936, he was assigned as an executive officer to a U.S. military committee that was quietly promoting a new Selective Service bill. As Adolf Hitler went on the march, Hershey met important decision makers in Washington and across the country, including congressmen, local luminaries, army reserve commanders, and National Guard adjutant generals. An isolationist American public, however, remained opposed to war and wary of a draft, forcing Hershey's band to tread lightly. In 1939, as he organized conscription for the imminent war, Hershey told columnist Drew Pearson, "I am a Hoosier and an isolationist and I believe we should stay out of other people's troubles."

The French military collapse in the summer of 1940 roused powerful supporters of conscription to push for the Burke-Wadsworth Selective Service bill. While debating the bill, congressmen were repeatedly advised by a down-home, red-headed officer who knew the ins and outs of the draft. Through his testimony, Hershey continued to argue for local control. Neighbors should make the decision about who should serve and who should be deferred. Major Hershey was suddenly in the national limelight.

On September 16, 1940, newly promoted Lieutenant Colonel Hershey stood as Roosevelt signed the Selective Service Act, which only authorized the conscription of 900,000 men for a year's service in the Western hemisphere. On October 16, 1940, Hershey oversaw the registration of 16,400,000 young American men at 125,000 sites across the country. The first Selective Service director was University of Wisconsin president Clarence Dykstra. To utilize his expertise, Hershey was promoted to brigadier general and appointed deputy director to essentially run the draft. After Dykstra stepped aside, Roosevelt appointed Hershey director on July 31, 1941. The Japanese attack on the American fleet at Pearl Harbor galvanized Congress to remove the geographic restriction. On December 20, 1941, Roosevelt signed a new conscription law that required males from eighteen to sixty-five to register for duty for "the duration of the war and six months after its termination."

The Hoosier general ran a remarkable system that eventually inducted more than ten million men into World War II service. With Americans generally accepting the Selective Service, only 16,000 were convicted of draft evasion. The 6,443 local draft board offices operating in 1941 were essential. "The planning must be kept simple and provide what must be done in the community by the people of the community," Hershey insisted. Although the boards sometimes made capricious and inconsistent decisions, Hershey stood by them, saying, "I would rather have stupidity in the local boards than at National Headquarters."

V-J Day brought elation to Americans ready to lay down their arms and return to civilian life. The military draft was the last thing on most people's minds—except for Hershey, who never stopped lobbying for military conscription. To Hershey's consternation, the Selective Service authority expired in 1947. Hershey argued for on-going conscription, noting, "If men are to be men then the best of their wisdom and strength must continue to be used for the defeat of these enemies of human existence and happiness." Cold War tensions led Congress to enact a new draft law in 1948.

During the Korean War from 1950 to 1953, 1.5 million draftees were among the approximately 5.7 million American soldiers who served. While Hershey's Selective Service System continued to unfailingly meet the Pentagon's Cold War requirements, there was a rising anticonscription sentiment, evidenced by increasing numbers of conscientious objectors and draft-evasion cases, and popular antiwar movements such as the "Ban the Bomb" campaigns.

Hershey's son, Gilbert, a marine captain, fought in Korea, where he was seriously wounded in a mortar attack that left large fragments near his spine and jugular. He was quickly evacuated to a hospital ship, and then on to a hospital in Japan. As Gilbert was en route to Japan, a Washington correspondent filed a story about his father's reaction: "Hershey himself didn't want to talk about the matter. But aides said he was considerably upset by the news. 'You can tell it is bothering him, but he isn't making any outward show of his feelings,' one official said.

Despite his grief, the draft director remained on the job all day and kept all of his appointments."

Hershey's emotional reaction to his son's wounds was notable, because the general prided himself on his self-control. "I have tried in many cases to keep from showing my feelings, this has formed a habit that is gaining considerable strength," he wrote in his diary in 1916, when he was twenty-three. Somewhat of a prude, abstentious, even a vegetarian for years after he was married, Hershey preferred to control his impulses. While warm with his family and others, he might be considered repressed and emotionally distanced in today's parlance.

During his three decades as the head of the Selective Service System, Hershey oversaw the conscription of more than 20 million American soldiers for three major wars and countless Cold War brushfires. Over half a million American soldiers died in those three wars alone; almost double that number suffered wounds, many grievously. Millions of veterans suffered psychic wounds. In the extensive Hershey Archives, there is no record of the general visiting draftees in Walter Reed Hospital; no letters to wounded soldiers; condolences to the families of the fallen; anguished diary entries; or self-doubting letters about casualties. While there is ample documentation that Hershey attended the funerals of many important military commanders and civilian leaders, there is no record of his attendance at the funeral of even one dogface draftee who fell in the line of duty.

President Lyndon Johnson's massive escalation of the Vietnam War required immense draft calls. In 1964 there were 23,000 American "advisors" in Vietnam; by 1968 there were 543,000 troops on the ground. From 1964 to 1966, draft calls skyrocketed from 100,000 to 400,000. And while draftees were only about 16 percent of the total U.S. armed forces, they constituted 88 percent of the infantry riflemen in Vietnam. In 1965 more than 30 million men were registered with 4,061 local draft boards, comprised of approximately 40,000 community volunteers. Hershey was confident he could satisfy the Pentagon's omnivorous draft calls. The system was in a demographic sweet spot: the small Great Depression generation had timed out for military service, and the Selective Service could begin drafting the immense generation born after World War II.

Draft resistance, however, soared with the rising draft calls. An estimated 571,000 men illegally evaded the draft, with the government indicting 22,000. Tens of thousands of American men fled into Canadian and Swedish exile. Public support for Hershey's Selective Service System was collapsing.

The antiwar movement certainly seemed as if it could be dismissed in 1964, when twelve young men burned their draft cards in New York City. But after Congress passed the August 1964 Gulf of Tonkin Resolution and Johnson escalated the war, mass demonstrations began in the nation's capital and on college campuses. Then forty protestors staged a sit-in at the Ann Arbor, Michigan, draft board. The Selective Service retaliated by rescinding the deferments of seven student demonstrators. Hershey told a reporter, "We're old fashioned enough to believe that these whiskered kids were not acting for the national health, safety, and interest."

On October 26, 1967, Hershey promulgated a "Letter to All Members of the Selective Service," later known as "the Hershey Directive," which instructed draft-board members that they could cancel deferments of protestors alleged to have interfered with the military draft or recruitment. Through his decades-long suzerainty, Hershey essentially conferred on Selective Service board members police powers to suppress dissent. When the U.S. Supreme Court struck down the reclassifications, Justice William O. Douglas opined, "There is no suggestion in the current draft law that the Selective Service has free-wheeling authority to ride herd on registrants, using immediate induction as a disciplinary or vindictive measure."

Over the previous twenty years, Hershey had become accustomed to respect from the media, if not fawning deference. Now he saw the press as a baying chorus of critics undermining his beloved Selective Service. "There isn't anything new about cussedness," he said about dissent when he was a boy. "But if I'd shouted, 'Hell, no, I won't go,' there wouldn't have been any radio, television or newsmen around to hear my immortal words." In the face of the unrelenting criticism, he patronized: "A lot of kids are very frustrated. I feel sorry for them because some day, they'll be very sorry for some of the things they've done." Sometimes he was pugnacious: "'We had a saying on the farm in Indiana,' Hershey said, as he threw a left hook in the air, 'a man's liberty ends just before he comes to another man's nose,'" wrote a *New York Times* reporter.

Hershey was a complicated man. Dedicated to military ideals, he was wary of war. As far back as 1940 he argued that modern war would drive intelligent men insane. A career military officer, he steadfastly protected the rights of pacifists. Later in life he echoed the antiwar thoughts he uttered in 1939 when he was a middle-aged officer stealthily devising the Selective Service System. He said in 1966, "It's the same old story, I guess. We always get stuck with wars we didn't create. The diplomats get us into war and the armed forces get us out. Relations just keep getting worse and worse until the military has to take over." When he was seventy-seven, Hershey reflected, "I hate war, and didn't like sending boys off to die in three wars."

When Hershey found himself amidst the protesting multitudes on the Mall in 1969, he was already a walking dead man in Washington's power corridors. Hoping to quell campus unrest, Nixon ran on an anti-draft platform, claiming he would end conscription after "victory" in Vietnam. After his election, Nixon's advisers recommended he institute an all-volunteer military—and that he get rid of Hershey. The old general refused to succumb to political pressure and resign, saying he would only respect a direct order from the president. Nixon obliged him. On October 10, 1969, as the antiwar groundswell continued to rise, Nixon informed Hershey that he would be reassigned as a presidential manpower adviser—an essentially ceremonial post. As a sop, the president recommended Hershey's promotion to four-star general. Hershey was the only four-star general to never engage in combat.

However be-starred he was as he negotiated the crush of protestors on that clammy November day in 1969, Hershey was witnessing a profound transformation in American life; a sea change from his traditional rural Indiana ideals to a incessantly changing modernist mentality. Hershey was a man of his time, and his time had passed. Writing his family the next day, he ended his letter by incredulously repeating himself. "It was," he wrote, "certainly something I had not seen many times."

6

HERBIE WIRTH

HERBERT WIRTH WAS A BIRD OF A MAN, SCARCELY FIVE FEET tall, maybe a hundred or so pounds. Each day, six days a week, he headed out on his route, an elderly, stooped man with two shopping bags filled with his wares: kitchen towels, washcloths, potholders, bandannas, and an array of shoelaces in various hues. Everything was a quarter, except the fancy potholders a teenage neighbor girl crafted. They were fifty cents, but he did not take a commission. Door-to-door he would go with a smile, from Sixteenth Street to Broad Ripple. It was his neighborhood, where he lived in a small house his mother left him when she died in 1957. "I'm your neighbor," he would say to his customers in his high-pitched voice. Winter and summer, three times a year, he visited each door in his neighborhood, hurrying along in his polished shoes with his odd kind of shuffle-jog. He did it for more than twenty-five years, since 1944, when he was laid off at age fifty-seven from his job in a dry-goods store. Herbie, his customers called him.

Herbie was always polite, always smiling, happy to hear no, ready to hear yes, always ready to chat. For those who took the time, he told them he should have gotten married when he was young. It was a lonely life without a family. Not self-pitying, just telling the truth. Sometimes a housewife would say he was not without friends, all his neighbors knew him. Well, I do run into a lot of people in my work, he would say before heading to the next door.

Herbie knew Crown Hill well. Each Sunday in the warm months, he visited his mother's grave in Section 78, Lot 89 to leave a bouquet of flowers. Her headstone was a double one, with his name and birth date already inscribed. Knowing he was alone, he also took care of his funeral, paying Flanner and Buchanan $749.26 for a gray casket and the burial expenses. Not too many years later, *Indianapolis Star* columnist Tom Keating wrote a profound article about Herbie, who explained his sales psychology and philosophy of life. He understood his place in the social hierarchy, yet recognized his capacity to make the world a better place. "There won't be much of a dent in the world when I die," he told Keating, "but at least I can say I made an honest-to-God try to do what I did as a nice man."

On January 30, 1971, Herbie died of a heart attack in a north side supermarket, where he was waiting for the weekly shipment of his favorite bread. There was some initial concern about the funeral arrangements, but then folks learned that Herbie had taken care of things. He had specified that he did not want a service in a funeral home or church. He just wanted a graveside service at the cemetery—"And that some people be there." Keating again wrote about Herbie in the *Star*, telling his readers that the Crown Hill service for him would be at 10:00 on Wednesday morning, and the minister would be at the Thirty-fourth Street gate to meet anyone wishing to attend. "It would be a shame if no one showed up," Keating wrote.

People showed up. Droves of people showed up. Hundreds of cars. A thousand mourners. Rich and poor, black and white, young and old, hippie, soldier, and businessman, all gathered together at Crown Hill to remember a nice man. As it turned out, one of Crown Hill's largest memorial services was not for a statesman, a celebrity, or a plutocrat. It was for Herbie. Inspired by the outpouring of care, Historic Landmarks Foundation of Indiana director Robert C. Braun rushed to the Waiting Station tower, where the freshly re-roped cemetery bell had hung unrung for forty years. Braun began pulling the bell rope, tolling, tolling, for a half-hour tolling, till his hands were blistered, and then he tolled the slow, mournful death knell for one small man who succeeded in making the world a little better.

7

INNER VISION

AMISH HEALER

"IRIDOLOGY," GARY SAID, AS WE DROVE DOWN THE ROAD along the Ohio River. He is not a man for short words, so I looked at him expectantly. Above our heads, the highlands and bluffs of the Indiana shore rose abruptly green and rocky. Across a bottom field filled with yellowing soybeans, the pilothouse of a barge slowly moving upstream appeared to levitate at the field's edge.

"There's this Amishman, Reuben Schwartz, lives down by Tobinsport, on the river, he reads your eyes. Tells you what's wrong. People from all over come to see him. To get healed," Gary said. "Iridology is this science Reuben uses to look in your eyes and tell you what ailments you've got. 'Eyes don't lie,' he says. Then he tells you what herbs to take to fix it.

"He lives down there, no car. No groceries in Tobinsport, nothing there. Rows across to Clovesport, over in Kentucky, when he needs something. People bring him stuff, tomatoes and things to pay their bill."

Gary's blue eyes were dancing—he is one of those rare guys who knows the world, though he seldom travels beyond the sight of his Spencer County barn and dairy herd. "Once a year I go to Evansville for the day, the next year, Louisville. Got to get back by milking," he said. He is the fifth generation of his family to live on his farm in southern Indiana. A few years ago they had to add on to the house. "Too many books," his wife, Paula, said.

Gary was loose for the day, squiring me along the new Ohio River Scenic Route, pointing out every streambed and hamlet, weaving tales of yesteryear into last week. He was wearing a new t-shirt with his jeans and cowboy boots. It read "Older than Dirt," though it is only his memory that stretches back that far.

Reuben used to live up by Fort Wayne—good ground up there—with his seven sons. They're Old Order. One of his sons was a bishop. They don't have ministers, you know, they just get together and elect one. Anyway, he died in a sawmill accident, and suddenly there was a schism. Some of them wanted to modernize, buy cars, have electricity.

Reuben couldn't abide by it so he moved down here to the hills of Crawford County—that's the one with no traffic lights in the whole county. The Old Order are still into shunning. Reuben didn't want anything to do with them that left the faith as he saw it. Next thing you know he moved down here on the river and started healing people. Good soil down here.

Doctor from Jasper, he started losing all his patients to Reuben, thought he ought to come down and see for himself. So he drove down, signed in, no "Doctor," of course. Lot of people, long wait. Finally got in to see Reuben. He sat down. Reuben looks in his eyes and says, "You've got the worst case of hemorrhoids I've ever seen."

The road to Reuben's office, Indiana 166, is the end of the line, terminating in the sludge brown of the dammed and tamed Ohio River. A mile or so before the road's end, a small black and white handmade sign was nailed to a utility pole that read "Healing, Herbs." A half mile or so beyond that, a worse for wear aluminum house trailer with a new wooden porch was parked in a cornfield with a few cars in front of it.

Gary and I walked in with our other van mates: Sally, a well-spoken doyenne from Evansville, and Roger, a park ranger who looked like an overfed ferret and had an unfortunate fondness for puns. "Oh, how marvelous," Sally said at the sight of the orange gold shag carpeting and metal folding chairs in the low-ceilinged waiting room. A few metal shelves held sea salt and water purifiers beside a sign that read, "No Charge for Reading of Eyes. Donations accepted."

Everyone signed in except Gary, who looked like health personified. He sat stolidly, his red gimme cap bill at exact right angles to the wall, arms resolutely folded across his chest. Roger paced around the room, poking around with the stuff on the shelves and chatting up the other patients—a nervous, prosperous-looking retired couple and a blubbery bubba in a stretched-out green t-shirt, worn work boots, and a faded sawmill cap who confided to Roger he had "bad wind," speaking, as it turned out, about his weak lungs. Later, a pair of backwoods punkers came in. He had a shaved head and a sailor-striped shirt; she had her hair up in Bam-Bam style. Sally sat composed and prim on her folding chair, probably mentally reviewing her top ten Junior League meetings.

I was cynicism on legs. In the foothills of the Himalayas in back-country Yunnan, I once tracked down a Chinese herbalist, the infamous Doctor Ho. He had received some notoriety in the early 1980s from an article written about him by Bruce Chatwin. I found Doctor Ho in a dirt street village inhabited by the Bai tribe, whose tiny women wore enormous textile headdresses that gave them the appearance of being clipper ships under full Technicolor sail.

When I arrived at his mud house after a fifteen-mile ride on a wobbly Chinese bicycle from the nearest town, Lijiang, there were several people waiting outside, some Chinese, some Western. The rusty old screen door flung open and a very smiley Chinese man, about forty, swept out. "Welcome, welcome," he said in a thick accent that reminded me of Tatoo in Fantasy Island. "I am Doctor Ho's son. You must see Doctor Ho's book."

He brought out an enormous scrapbook filled with adoring letters from people all over the globe claiming cures for a variety of ailments from menstrual pains to high blood pressure to general ennui. Doctor Ho was a star. He'd parlayed a little bit of press into being one of the wealthiest guys in that part of southwestern China. (OK, the per capita income for the area was about $300 a year, but still.)

Now and again, someone would emerge from the house clutching bundles of herbs, gushing profuse thanks to Doctor Ho, a wizened guy with a wispy white beard. He dressed in a white lab coat with a wool sock hat that corkscrewed like the Cat in the Hat's. He glanced over at the group waiting under an old mulberry tree like an American dermatologist assessing the take in the waiting room.

The deal was that Doctor Ho took your "pulses," and based on the information he divined, prescribed Himalayan herbs to cure what ailed you. At no cost. Donations only.

I was absurdly healthy while traveling overland through Asia (and am in general), so I was curious what dire aliments and miraculous Himalayan herbs Doctor Ho was going to discover for me. After a lengthy wait, and watching lots of gushing, toting patients, I was ushered in, expecting the full treatment.

Doctor Ho took a quick look at me, and said in broken English, "Many people come, sick. I help. Some come, healthy. You good chi," referring to the Chinese concept of overall health and harmony, as he made a cusp around his face with his hands. "You no need. Go." I gave him some Chinese money anyway, probably from relief.

But as I pedaled away, the rickety screen door flew open and Doctor Ho burst out, calling to a passing pair of travelers, "Hello, I am Doctor Ho."

Reuben Schwartz is a small, solid man. Salt-and-pepper hair, cut with bangs and little flips at his ears, and a longish beard frame his face in the Amish fashion. Wide suspenders hold up utilitarian dark gray woolen pants, worn with a heavy navy blue shirt.

He has a hunched intent quality that erupts into an open friendly manner.

As I sat on a stool in his tiny examining room, Reuben picked up a flashlight and an eight-power lens, a photographers' loupe used to view slides. After a second of peering in my left eye he said, "You've got a hernia—a problem with your left testicle."

"Not that I know of," I stammered, taken a bit aback. "I don't have any problem picking up heavy things."

He looked again, then switched to my right eye. "Bad back?" he ventured.

"Uh, it went out a few years ago, but seemed to heal up OK."

He went back to the left eye that started the testicle problem. "Sure you don't have a testicle problem? Pain? Trouble of any kind?"

"No," I insisted. Reuben looked at me unconvinced. "Really, I've got two sons and everything," I said.

"Childhood injury? Climb over a fence and fall?" he asked. I wracked my brain, figuring we would never move beyond my left testicle. Suddenly I remembered, "Well, I did fall on my bicycle crossbar once when I was about ten." Reuben nodded sagely.

"Healed up well," he said, and I heaved a sigh of relief.

He continued looking in my eyes, and then said, "You take better care of yourself than most people I see." I asked how he could tell. "Oh, it's easy," he said as he pulled out pictures of eyes. "See these close tight fibers in this eye. It shows a fast healer, good constitution. See the lesions in this eye, sick, almost dead," as he pointed to an eye that looked disconcertingly unhealthy to me, almost on an atavistic level. Oh yeah, the eyes do not lie.

Iridology seemed a codification of the innate sense of health that we discern when we meet someone. But Reuben could be incredibly precise with his diagnoses, detecting digestion, cardiac, respiratory, and gland trouble in the color, texture, and intricate designs of the eye. Indeed, most of his patients came to him after medical technology failed them. "We see 100 to 120 people a week," he said, "from every state in the union, every continent."

There was a cardboard box with a mixture of small currency on the table. When I put five dollars in, Reuben seemed absolutely uninterested.

As I came out to the waiting room, the sawmill guy was regaling Roger with his ills. Roger was rapt. "Yep, last summer, when I had Pneeeu-monia, they fixed me right up with some LW. Give it to horses, too, when they got bad wind."

Sally went in and emerged, as I did, with a roughly clean bill of health and just a few herbal recommendations for our elimination systems, a pick me up, so to speak.

Roger, who was starting to affect the frantic woebegone look of a constipated hound, went in. After a long while, he came out, shaken. "Look at that," he said, holding up a long list of maladies, and an herbal prescription beside each one. "He knew every problem I've got, sinus, liver, thyroid—just looking in my eyes. Said I was starting to get a kidney stone. He knew all my parents' problems too." He looked down at the paper, and then back at us: "Man, I got to get to a doctor."

Part 2
Complicated Places

8

A FAIR OF THE HEART

STATE FAIRS ARE THE CONFLUENCE OF THE GARISH AND THE profound, a carnivalesque celebration of life amidst the drive for recognized excellence. Regal princesses with tiaras pass through the neon-lit Midway throngs. Burly farmers herd Brobdingnagian boars. Kids nap beside their brushed and curried heifers who gaze with long lashes at their resting guardians. Barkers howl the wonders of the sideshow; ladies quite alluring give a desultory bump. A swain with his first sideburns wallops the carnival game, trying to win a stuffed bear for his admiring sweetheart. Trailed by her two apple-cheeked boys, a young mother proudly paces through the crowd with a blue ribbon carefully placed across her prize pie.

The smells of corndogs and elephant ears mingle with the electric scent of cotton candy. Wood smoke, sopped sauce, and cooking pork chops waft from the barbecue stands. An unmistakable tang announces the animal buildings.

Cattle low, calves bawl, pigs grunt and squeal. A shiny show horse whinnies on its way to the barn. Over the thump of rock music drifting from the racketing amusement rides, the loudspeaker blares out a twang that can only come from that one particular place on the planet, announcing Hell Drivers and Rooster Crowing Contests, prize-winning pickles, the Ugly Lamp Competition, and the next heat in the pig races.

Bennie Zebelle of Muncie, Indiana, poses with a basket of tomatoes in the Agriculture Building at the 1947 Indiana State Fair.

Carolyn East, the granddaughter of Russell East, president of the 1933 Indiana State Fair board, enjoys cotton candy at the fair.

Sleek goats prance past hawk-eyed judges. Nervous vintners await the wine-tasting results like so many expectant grandparents.

There are more than 3,200 fairs in North America these days, a living thriving link to our agrarian heritage. It's a tradition that stretches back to biblical times, when people congregated in places such as Tyre to enjoy approximately the same things we do now: the fruits of farmers' and artisans' labor leavened with a fair share of effervescent entertainment.

When English settlers staged their first fair in Windsor, Nova Scotia, in 1765, they were by no means the earliest American fairgoers. The Aztecs had been frolicking at great fairs in what was to be Mexico City long before the Spanish Conquistadors came to gawk. In 1807 a New England farmer named Elkanah Watson organized the first fair in the United States by herding his prized sheep under an old elm tree in Pittsfield, Massachusetts. Carney rides and greasy festival food were only a few decades behind.

Today millions attend state fairs; 3.4 million in Texas alone. Across the country, families hurry to the endlessly spinning Ferris wheels, the

4-H Club member Lowell Harton from Rushville, Indiana, poses with his champion Chester white barrow at the 1932 Indiana State Fair.

All images courtesy of Indiana Historical Society, J. Allen and Son Collection, P 490; Gift of Center for Agricultural Science and Heritage.

rocketing roller coasters, and the chance to vicariously join our agricultural forebears in the appreciation of fine animals and verdant harvests. It is also a chance to revel in the unique quirks that make the place our own. Whether we wolf down our mile-high biscuits in Mississippi, Navaho tacos in Arizona, pumpkin pie in Vermont, burgoo in Kentucky, Iowa corn on the cob, or enchiladas in California, we know we are home when we go to the state fair.

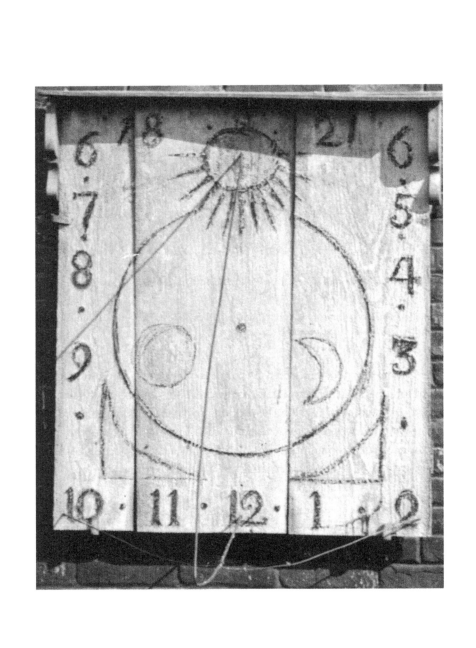

9

A SURPRISING UTOPIA

THIS PLACE COULD BE JUST ANOTHER SMALL HOOSIER TOWN basking on the banks of southern Indiana's Wabash River. It has a Victorian main street, cornfield-bordered basketball courts, and Kiwanis Club meetings on Thursdays. But turn down a shady street and utopia shimmers in the soft midwestern light.

Austere nineteenth-century frame houses with beautiful gardens reside alongside massive Germanic brick buildings resonating with a sense of hope and order. Pioneer-era log cabins cluster near the Modernist Atheneum, an angular porcelain-clad, steel-paneled building that looks dynamic enough to lift off. Gregorian chants, Shaker hymns, and Tibetan mantras waft from a formal garden. Visitors wind through sacred labyrinths.

Utopian communities are rife in quixotic America, but New Harmony is one place where the dreamers were both deeply sacred and steadfastly secular—and the modern manifestation is as idealistic and vital as its forebears.

In the early nineteenth century, when most of Indiana was still a vast, untamed forest, New Harmony was the home of two celebrated,

An 1821 sundial originally used on a private home by the Harmony Society. After a fire destroyed the house, the sundial found a new home on the south wall of Community House Number 2.

Courtesy of Indiana Historical Society.

dramatically different utopian experiments—"a chimera in the wilderness," historian Anne Taylor, author of *Visions of Harmony: A Study in Nineteenth-Century Millenarianism,* called it.

Fueled by the extraordinary minds drawn here, this little outpost was a center of American intellectual life far into the nineteenth century. After a sleepy hiatus, the town was revived in the 1960s, when the wealthy descendant of one of the original communalists embarked on a binge of historic renovation and cutting-edge architectural construction, as well as a plethora of spiritual undertakings.

Think of Williamsburg, Virginia, and Sedona, Arizona, humming together in some kind of paranormal convergence—that is New Harmony today.

For decades, I have wandered New Harmony's peaceful lanes, where history is wrought in stone and timber, and world-changing dreams have become reality. I often come seeking tranquillity but instead find myself stimulated by the idealism in this little river town.

The German Harmonists who founded New Harmony in 1814 were celibate Christians. Under their charismatic leader, Father George Rapp, the Harmonists built an American frontier marvel: an engineered brick town that had an orchestra and the largest library west of Pittsburgh and was surrounded by two thousand acres of tended fields, vineyards, and orchards. Lemon, orange, and fig trees thrived in portable greenhouses. "They made the wilderness smile," wrote one traveler of the time.

Then, in 1825, wealthy industrialist and social reformer Robert Owen bought out the Harmonists and established New Harmony's second utopian society. This one embraced progressive ideas and rejected religion completely.

Attracted by the vision of an intellectual haven in the virgin wilderness, some of the era's leading minds—including renowned zoologist Thomas Say, progressive education luminary Marie Duclos Fretageot, and the father of American geology William Maclure—traveled to New Harmony by keelboat, a vessel that came to be known as "The Boatload of Knowledge." Although their utopian dream died in its infancy, many Owenites settled in the village.

Their scientific inquiry and radical ideas, including progressive education, labor unionism, abolitionism, and feminism had a broad and lasting influence on America.

In the post-Civil War era, industrialization and urbanism eventually drained the town of much of its intellectual capital, as many descendants of the original utopians moved out.

New Harmony slept for nearly a century before Texas heiress Jane Blaffer Owen, who married Robert Owen's great-great-grandson, Kenneth Dale Owen, began reinvigorating the town by mixing historic preservation and modern architecture with cerebral and spiritual exploration.

"New Harmony was a buried stream. All we had to do was to get it to flow again," Owen told me in her southern accent. At ninety-one she still buzzed around New Harmony in her signature golf cart and wide woven sun hats. Owen talked to me of New Harmony as an epicenter of peace and serenity. "I agree with Dostoyevsky: 'Beauty will save the world,'" she said.

I decided she might be on to something as I walked around the town's gardens waving with blossoms and the leafy streets chockablock with elegant, finely proportioned buildings and listened to talk at the village tables as New Harmonites debated how they can change the world.

New Harmony today is still a tiny place—its 850 residents number about the same as the Harmonists who started the village—and visitors will find a few centuries compressed into a few blocks.

One morning last fall, I explored a lane at the edge of town, sauntering past a brown cornfield asymmetrical on a hillside, its striated rows as graphic as a Vincent Van Gogh painting.

The trail wound through a bower of trees to a low bluff above the Wabash River. On the far bank of the river, egrets and herons stood like sentinels. Forest birds called out as rising fish dotted the river with circles. Low hills lay gauzy in the morning mist, the trees tinged with the promise of fall. As I sat on a sandstone ledge, I felt like I was back in the 1820s, when America was young and fresh, and Indiana was the Western frontier.

Within a few minutes' walk, I was back in modern times, strolling down North Street to see the Roofless Church, architect Philip Johnson's 1960 paean to pan-denominational spirituality. Inspired by the thought that only the sky was a big enough roof for people of all faiths, Johnson designed a sublime brick-walled garden. In the middle of it, he set a tall, shingle-clad dome in the shape of an inverted rose, honoring the Harmonists' golden rose symbol.

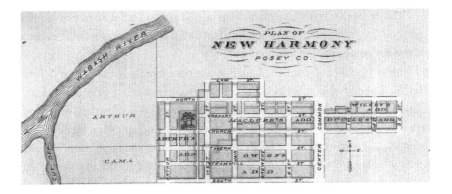

A view of New Harmony, Indiana, taken from the *1876 Illustrated Historical Atlas of the State of Indiana.*

Courtesy of Indiana Historical Society, Map Collection.

Adjacent to the church, architect Richard Meier's small Modernist Pottery Studio stands as a counterpoint to the nearby rustic log cabins and the spare Harmonist David Lenz House. Just down the street, Meier's dramatic Atheneum/Visitors Center drew architectural raves when it opened more than two decades ago. Alluring interior ramps lead to a small theater, where a short film informs visitors about New Harmony.

As I stood on the Atheneum's upper floor overlooking the river, I mused on a scale model of New Harmony in 1825, the year Robert Owen took possession, imagining the awkward exchanges between the pious Harmonists and the iconoclastic Owenites. It must have been like a band of Harvard hippies taking over a Shaker village.

Across the street, a blond woman in shorts entered the shady environs of the Cathedral Labyrinth and Sacred Garden. The space replicates the perimeter and labyrinth of the great twelfth-century cathedral at Chartres. The maze allows walkers to untangle their own quandaries as they solve the knot of the labyrinth. I watched the woman slowly negotiate the polished forty-two-foot granite circle, turning this way and that, and finally emerge quietly with a smile.

In 1818 the Harmonists built the massive stone Rapp-Owen Granary barely a block away from the Atheneum, not too many years before they sold New Harmony to Owen and left for new challenges in Pennsylvania.

Gateway to a Rappite Cemetery in New Harmony, Indiana.

Courtesy of Indiana Historical Society.

Within a few years of its founding, Owen's utopian endeavor collapsed in acrimony. Unlike the industrious Harmonists, there were too many brainy Owenite chiefs and not nearly enough workers.

Several of Owen's cerebral colleagues who remained after the collapse, including Maclure and Say, made this little outpost on the Wabash River a hub of America's natural sciences for several decades in the nineteenth century.

Owen's two sons also settled in New Harmony, educator Robert Dale Owen, who helped form the Smithsonian Institute, and David Dale Owen, the first geologist hired by the federal government to classify public lands. In the 1830s, David Dale Owen began to use the Rapp-Owen Granary as his laboratory. Today, the granary has been reborn as a stunning hall and performing space.

My stomach was rumbling as I headed up Main Street, past the brooding redbrick Community House Number 2, a gender-segregated

Harmonist dormitory. During the Owen period, it served as a school run by Parisian innovator Fretageot.

Crossing Church Street, I was in the middle of New Harmony's Victorian commercial district, an exuberance of gingerbread and Italianate- and Gothic-styled small-town mercantilism. But unlike many near-abandoned midwestern downtowns, New Harmony's Main Street is thriving. The town has a hardware store, grocery, and cinema, along with two art galleries, antique shops, a bookstore, and a variety of eateries.

I stepped into the Main Cafe, where the breakfast crowd sat at pushed-together tables under the high, pressed-tin ceiling. As I ate my ham and eggs and half order of biscuits and gravy, the talk turned to the state of the union—natural disasters, the high price of gas, a boy coming home from Iraq in a coffin.

I watched the veteran waitresses hustle between ruddy farmers, businessmen in white short-sleeve shirts, and a small detachment wearing t-shirts that proclaimed EMT and coroner.

It struck me that New Harmony is an authentic place, where a farmer is a farmer, a waitress is a waitress. It gives the town an honesty and immediacy that is absent in some parts of the country.

People put roots here or endeavor to come back when they can. Descendants of the Owenites still populate the town, along with folks drawn here by the utopian hope of New Harmony. They are often pragmatic visionaries who keep New Harmony's dream of a better tomorrow alive.

Sherry Graves is the great-great-great-granddaughter of Robert Owen and directs the Working Men's Institute, itself a living legacy of Maclure's determination to educate the masses.

"When I think about new people," Graves said, "I think they are people who walk to the beat of a different drummer."

Author's Note: Jane Blaffer Owen died in 2010.

The Eero Saarinen-designed North Christian Church in Columbus, Indiana.

10

ARCHITECTURE AND COMMUNITY

THE ROAD TO HOPE, INDIANA, IS LOCATED DOWN COUNTRY highways and lanes, past silos and barns and near-iconic rows of deep-green tasseled corn. At the edge of town a weathered, hand-lettered sign reads, "Hope—A Surprising Little Town." Hope is an old Moravian settlement. A half mile from the spacious town square, the tall nineteenth-century Moravian church and rectory are austere talismans, structures that speak of enduring values and continuing care. Nearby, the local elementary school vibrates to another aesthetic, a high-spirited contemporary building of masonry stripes and welcoming porticos that extends out to the gamboling children.

The town square has an almost small-town Texas air, with streets wide enough to turn around a horse and team. In the center of the square, the grassy park is dotted with a few small buildings and a white-painted Victorian gazebo. Across the way, the diminutive Irwin Union Bank and Trust branch office is an icon of modern architecture—a rust-red brick building with a dramatic tentlike roofline that appears to levitate over a band of clerestory windows. The renowned architect Harry Weese designed the building in the 1950s to blend into the vintage square while introducing a vibrant new idea into the community.

One recent hot summer Sunday, townsfolk gathered on the square to listen to the tinkle of carousel music and dedication speeches for their new branch library. It is a low-slung brick building spanning the space between the Weese building and an old feed mill next door. The cantilevered metal awning on the front of the library mixes intellectual contextualism with sheer practicality, continuing the line of the neighboring feed mill's west-facing awnings. The library's sloping roofline seems a cross between a section of a Bedouin tent and a parasail ready to catch the wind of the next century.

Inside the building, an immense curved beam defines the roofline. The taut detailing and spare aesthetic that speaks of Manhattan is in counterpoint to the bright colors of the children's books and the happy Hoosier faces.

"We wanted to be a good neighbor to Weese," said library architect Deborah Berke, a New Yorker and Yale professor universally described as tall and elegant. Berke spent months shuttling between New York and Hope, showing her ideas to the local library board and making sure the library met the town's needs. The board included a cross section of the town. "There was a music teacher; a hog farmer. I was impressed by their intelligence and insight for good architecture," she said. "On top of that there was the window of the land."

"This is a real town that has existed for a long time. It's not a show-place, it's a town," added Berke's project architect, Stephen Brockman. "We wanted to make a nice building, a nice library. It wasn't about Deborah's ego."

This is remarkable, given Berke's status as America's hot architect, the designer of choice for everyone from Calvin Klein (she recently finished the plans for his ultrachic boutiques) to Wall Street tycoons. She made her name in the 1980s designing homes and commercial buildings for the highly touted "new" town of Seaside in Florida and became the media darling with profiles in *Vogue, New York, Metropolitan,* and a host of trend-setting architectural publications. She's on the path toward the Pritzker Architecture Prize—architecture's version of the Nobel.

So what is she doing in a small Indiana town designing a branch library? Or for that matter, what are these lodestones of contemporary architecture doing in an agricultural village out on the prairie?

Hope happens to be in Bartholomew County, with the modernist architecture Mecca of Columbus as the county seat. And Columbus and Bartholomew County have become very savvy about dealing with world-class architects. After all, they have been doing it for a while.

Since the 1940s, they have engaged in a remarkable experiment in modern living, hiring the best international architects to design their public and commercial buildings and meld them into the fabric of their nineteenth-century towns. Columbus, a town of 35,000, boasts more than fifty buildings that represent the honor roll of modern architects— Weese, Eero and Eilel Saarinen, Cesar Pelli, Kevin Roche, I. M. Pei, Robert Venturi, and Richard Meier, to name a few. This is a Petrie dish, where the idea that good architecture can improve the human condition is still being tested.

The downtown piazza between Pei's public library and Eilel Saarinen's landmark First Christian Church centers on Henry Moore's monumental paean to Stonehenge, *Large Arch,* a twenty-foot high bronze of primal organic simplicity. The Museum of Modern Art's sculpture garden has a small one; Columbus, Indiana, has got the big one. In the Commons, the shopping and community center designed by Pelli, surrealist Jean Tinguely's enormous *Chaos I*—constructed of seven tons of industrial detritus that he scavenged from the local salvage yards—loops, turns, and ceaselessly whirls in an incessant pattern of self-creation. He has said it is his favorite piece.

Eero Saarinen's last work sits at the edge of town—the one he said he wanted to tell Saint Peter about. The North Christian Church's hexagonal walls spring from the mounded earth in a dynamic thrust that narrows to a thin spire that scribes the sky; a needle that plays the whirling heavens. Saarinen—famous for his luminous, shimmering gateway to the West, the Saint Louis Arch—left us with the North Christian Church as an unerring sign of the way home.

Venturi designed one of the fire stations. Robert A. M. Stern designed the hospital. Roche designed the austere local post office on the tidy Victorian main street near Zaharakos Confectionery, where they have been serving ice cream from their rococo onyx soda fountain since the Columbian Exhibition. It is just down the street from the turn-of-the-century Irwin Bank, with the elaborate iron detailing. The modernist architecture is mixed into a town with fourteen buildings on the National Historic Register, representing a catalog of nineteenth- and early-twentieth-century styles: Italianate, Greek and Colonial Revival, Queen Anne, Prairie, and Shotgun.

Small wonder the first postmodernist, Weese, explored the readaptation of the vernacular here in the 1950s, integrating folk architecture into his designs. Columbus folks love their old buildings, and restored structures stand proudly all over town. Roche deferred to Columbus when he wrapped his 1983 stark white Cummins Engine Company Corporate Headquarters around the nineteenth-century red-brick Cerealine Building, leaving the Italianate commercial building that defined the Columbus skyline intact and embraced by the new structure.

The buildings for the most part are modest structures—no marble-clad monuments to towering piles of lucre. They are relatively small structures, formed of affordable materials, consonant with a midwestern sensibility—albeit highly evolved.

The American Institute of Architects named Columbus as the sixth most architecturally significant city in the United States, behind only the megalopolises of New York, Chicago, Los Angeles, Boston, and Washington. Three of the town's architects have won the Pritzker Architecture Prize. In 1994 the world's top architects trooped to the little town on the prairie to have the Pritzker awards ceremony.

But the local folks are not in thrall to architectural dictates. When the local doge and scion of Cummins Engine, Yale- and Oxford-educated J. Irwin Miller, envisioned the unique community foundation in the 1950s that pays the architects' fees for the public buildings, he recognized the locus or the design had to spring from the citizenry. The program has engendered a particularly activist community that is not shy about sharing its thoughts.

"We told them, 'No flat roofs. And the windows have to open.'" Fire Station Number 6 Chief Gary Burriss said about the design process on his station with Boston-based William Rawn and Associates Architects. "Some of these other architect-designed Fire stations, they've got fixed windows with closed-loop heating and cooling—the same air endlessly recycled. Can you imagine what it's like nine or ten years later with ten guys in there all the time?" Irate citizens sent Venturi packing when he proposed pastel-colored light posts throughout the town. One critic blustered, "What does he think this is—Crayola City?"

As the decades have rolled on, architecture has become a defining focus of Columbus and the surrounding county, engendering a pride of place and empowerment that coalesces with deep local history and roots.

But modern architecture in Columbus is a far cry from the planned New Urbanism towns that are springing up around the country—places such as Disney's Celebration, California's Laguna West, Kentlands in Maryland, and the first of the faux towns, Seaside in Florida.

Seaside was built in the 1980s as the first new-planned town since the 1960s. It was designed along the tenets of New Urbanism as promulgated by urban planners and architects Elizabeth Plater-Zyberk and Andres Duany. Meant to foster community vitality and access to the beach, it is a tightly platted pastiche of pastel-colored houses in various historical styles, mainly Victorian. Like many of the New Urbanism towns, there is a retrograde architectural sentimentality here, as though the ubiquitous picket fences and front porches can substitute for the rancorous polity and policy of a true democratic town.

"Seaside is not a real place," Berke said. In spite of designing sixteen houses and two commercial buildings in the town, Berke terms herself "the loyal opposition." Seaside is a town of second homes and absentee owners who fly in for a bout of recuperative play acting far away from the distressing business of real civic life. Not surprisingly, Seaside was the set for the movie *The Truman Show,* where the town was portrayed as an elaborate television set masquerading as an authentic place.

The New Urbanists hope to re-create through deed restrictions and architectural review boards and massive amounts of corporate capital what evolves over long periods of time in real communities: a sense of civic intimacy. In the 1990s the Disney Corporation decided to bring one of Walt Disney's dreams to life, a planned community. But Celebration near Orlando is a far cry from Uncle Walt's vision—he wanted a Town of Tomorrow. Until the economic realities set in, Disney thought EPCOT, the futuristic amusement ride, would be his community for future-seeking urbanists. Instead, Celebration is another of the coarsely capitalistic New Towns, replete with the iconography of regressive nostalgia. "We wanted it to be a real town," Disney's planner Tom Lewis said. But they got something else instead. There may be back alleys and porches and eight harmonious, rigorously tasteful designs in Georgian, Colonial, and Victorian to choose from, but Celebration is missing the crazy guy with the funny designs on his peeling clapboards or the lady with the surfeit

In 1971 crews placed the Henry Moore Arch, standing twenty feet tall and weighing five-and-a-half tons, in the plaza in front of Columbus's Cleo Rogers Public Library.

All images courtesy of Indiana Historical Society, Irwin-Sweeney-Miller Family Collection, M 1003.

of lawn art or the arty couple who are just too busy to bother with their yard. Celebration, and the other New Urbanism towns, is missing the sheer exuberant, messy life of a real town.

"There's real civic life in Columbus," Berke said. "It's a community for people who don't want to live in a sugar-coated place. It's a great opportunity to do fulfilling work because it is a real place." Columbus and Hope are like a lot of other Indiana towns and neighborhoods that nurture a rich community life: Madison and Jasper, Garfield Park and Cottage Home in Indianapolis, Terre Haute's Farrington's Grove, Bloomington's Prospect Hill, the West Washington neighborhood in South Bend, and Old Richmond's German Village. There are dozens of examples throughout the state, places where humans have worked together for many decades to form and develop a nurturing community as a special place on the earth. It takes time and lots of diverse energies to make a real democratic place. Force-fed hothouse towns are not an adequate substitute.

By the end of the Hope Library dedication, Berke was beginning to wilt. It was ninety-four sultry degrees and she had flown directly to Indiana from her vacation in Spain. The townsfolk were happy—she had incorporated all of their concerns. The toilets flushed, the bookshelves seemed right, the back steps were designed so the skateboarders would be thwarted—at least until they worked out even more bone-threatening moves.

The gazebo was empty, and smiling people sauntered through the leaf-dappled commons toward their cars. Berke looked around the intact little square with its hardware store and jewelry shop and minuscule R. F. D. Museum and its small cafes serving the truckers that cruise through town. She gazed at the town's prim gingerbread Victorians and the upright red-brick churches. And she talked about the steadfastness of the Moravian architecture and its influence on her design. You could see her traveling up the road to the old church sheltered in the grove of trees at the edge of town. Looking at the new library, she talked about how pleased she was that the town appeared to like its new library. And then she turned to me and smiled. "What do you think?" she said.

11

THE SONG OF INDIANA

WHAT IS THE SONG OF INDIANA? PERHAPS IT'S A COLE PORTER or Hoagy Carmichael tune, a song by John Mellencamp, or "Moonlight on the Wabash." Maybe it is a Gregorian chant from the Saint Meinrad monks or a Tibetan chant from Bloomington or a Bean Blossom bluegrass lament or a Shipshewana Amish hymn. Or maybe it's the jingle of the reins as the draft horses pull through the fields or the murmur of a brook or the shush of Lake Michigan waves, the pushy cry of a red-winged blackbird, the heart-rend of a whippoorwill, or the chuff of a train; the silence of a Quaker service or the scream of an Indy racecar. Or maybe it is all these things.

I have driven from one end of this great state to the other, zigzagging across the dimples and folds and flatlands of Indiana, winding down countless country lanes. And I can testify there is a lot of Indiana to experience. The glint of the dawn on the Ohio River, the sugar powder hills of the dunes, canal boats, vintage cars and old-time trains, fireflies dotting a summer field into a pointillist canvas, and forests ablaze with autumn color stretching to the horizon. The smell of new hay, old wine, and campfires flickering on a cool evening.

Ah, Indiana. Here's to your rivers and roads and endless prairies. To your expansive forests and deep lakes. To your layers of history and the energy of your many cultures. And especially to your people, who twang out their greetings and take the time to tell you how to get there.

Indiana is a long state, stretching from the pine forest lands near Lake Michigan down to the cypress bogs of the Wabash River and the lower Ohio River. Across its 36,000 square miles, an almost unimaginable diversity thrives: hardwood forests and fecund wetlands, glades, barrens, savannas, and immense prairies.

There are several distinct natural regions in the state. The southern hill country is a rumpled swath of limestone hills and forest ravines. Caves, rushing streams, and dense forests are part of the ecology and culture of the region. With sprawling floodplains and unique aquatic life, the watersheds of the major southern Indiana rivers—the lower Ohio, the Wabash, and the White—are themselves a distinct natural region. The southern lowlands in the southwestern section of the state are bottomlands where rich agricultural land coexists with teeming wetlands and the state's best oil and coal deposits. It is the hottest part of the state, and the one closest to America's Deep South in both climate and culture.

The central flatlands display quite graphically the impact of glaciation, in some places lying flat as a poker table on the landscape, in others, rolling in swells and swales like a kindly sea. The Kankakee Swamp that stretched for 5,300 square miles across northwestern Indiana is just a memory, but a collection of state wildlife preserves along the Kankakee River give a hint as to the wonder of the wetlands. Lakeland in Indiana's northern belt is pocked with hundreds of kettle lakes, liquid memories of the ice blocks left by retreating glaciers. The Calumet Region's dunes at the Lake Michigan lakeshore are among the most diverse environments in the world, where the tenets of ecology were parsed out by pioneering biologists two generations ago. Diversity—there is diversity here in Indiana.

Prehistoric man found Indiana a nice place to make a home. The state is blanketed with evidence of their exuberant lives—mounds and mussel banks, millions of potsherds, arrowheads for a hundred thousand hunters. And their descendants roamed the state from one end to the other—the Miami, Delaware, Potawatomi, and Iroquois, to name a few. When the Europeans found the land, they came in the droves that have never ended. First the French hunters and trappers, then the British "long knife hunters," followed by the settlers of northern Europe, and then the great waves from eastern and southern Europe that peopled the burgeoning industrial cities. In one way or another, they are all still here, and they make Indiana what it is.

The first European settlements were along the rivers of southern Indiana—the Ohio, Wabash, and Whitewater—and accordingly the towns with the longest history and finest vintage architecture are found there. The canal boom of the 1830s left a string of port towns along its path that are intact memories of a short-lived boom, when the commerce of the world floated to their docks. The first great national road ran straight as a die across the belly of the state, and towns such as Centerville still tell the story. The coming of the silver railroad tracks changed the face of Indiana, withering the river and canal towns and accelerating the development of hundreds of others. Dozens of small Hoosier towns still radiate out from their time-worn stations—sometimes poignantly empty, more often converted to shops and visitor centers.

When the automobile arrived, Indiana took to it with a passion. Hoosiers pioneered the infant industry, creating many of the nation's early models, along with legendary ones such as Cord, Auburn, Stutz, and Duesenberg. The mythic brick racetrack in Speedway, Indiana, and the near-ubiquitous car museums across the state live to tell the tale. That and the small-town root beer stands, the post–World War II motor hotels now used as transient housing, and the swooping 1950s-style signs that hang on the fronts of buildings that are a hundred years older. They tell the story of an Indiana on wheels, too.

Driving is easy here. With a few exceptions, the routes in this book are on paved roads, mainly highways. I have aimed down the two-lanes for the most part, leaving the big highways for those in a hurry.

Most of the drives in this book are day trips, though any of them lend themselves to overnight jaunts or saunters that can last a week. There are plenty of delights for those who take the time to explore a bit.

The weather in Indiana is classified as temperate-continental, but any native will tell you that is only part of the story. "Hang around awhile if you don't like the weather," they say, "it'll change soon." And they are right. The mid-latitude westerly wind belt that passes over Indiana, and the jet stream and hemispheric storm track associated with it, guarantee lots of different things happening weatherwise, often in a short period. In general, there is about a ten-degree shift in annual average temperatures from the north (48 degrees) to the southwest (57 degrees).

What the north and south have in common is humidity. The great waves of moisture that boil up from the Gulf of Mexico ensure this is a well-watered place, essential for our dense forests and rich agricultural lands, though somewhat wilting for humans at times. Indiana gets almost forty inches of rain a year, with the south getting most of its precipitation in the winter, the central and north in the early spring. For all, the driest month is October.

While there are ample reasons to visit the state throughout the year, spring and fall are particularly inviting. In the spring, the blooming redbuds and dogwood turn the forests into ethereal landscapes. Fall foliage is almost iconic, with hundreds of thousands of acres on fire with reds, oranges, purples, and yellows—exotic biotic changes happening for our viewing pleasure. Indian summer in Indiana is a special time after the first frost. Days are warm and sunny with low humidity, the nights cool and crisp—another ideal time for touring.

Part 3
Culinary Delights

Shapiro's customers were often dazzled by the wide array of products offered for sale, including salmon, sardines, caviar, coffee, and kosher deli meats. According to Max Shapiro, over the years the American public had come to look at kosher deli food "just like pizza or Mexican food. I guess we helped educate them."

12

'COOK GOOD, SERVE GENEROUSLY, PRICE MODESTLY'

THE SHAPIRO'S STORY

THE SOUTH MERIDIAN BUSINESS DISTRICT, THE BEATING heart of Indianapolis's Jewish neighborhood, bustled on Sundays in 1915, revivified after Saturday Sabbath, when hundreds of Jewish immigrants walked past shuttered stores to the five synagogues clustered in the little enclave. Stretching south from Washington Street to Morris Street between Capitol Avenue and Union Street, the district was a densely populated city space that rang with the calls of Yiddish, the German-Hebrew language of the middle European Ashkenazi Jews, and murmurs of Ladino, the southern European Sephardic Jews' ancient Spanish-Hebrew language, mixing with the argot and dialects of their German, Irish, and African American neighbors.

The streets and sidewalks in the old industrial neighborhood pulsed with new Americans who had hailed from across the Russian Empire's Pale of Settlement that stretched from the Baltic regions down to the Ukraine, along with Galician Jews from Austria and Sephardic Jews from the Ottoman Empire. Traditional men with the long beards of the *shtetls*, or "little villages," as the cloistered Jewish communities of the Pale were known, rubbed shoulders with Jewish dandies dressed in the latest New York styles. Women herding their families down the boardwalks passed peddlers' pushcarts, horse wagons, and establishments catering to their trade: dry goods and drugstores, shoe shops, hardware stores and junk shops, barbers, laundries, theaters and dance halls, bakeries, coffee roasters, kosher meat, fish and poultry markets, as well as numerous grocery stores—including a fairly new one at 808 South Meridian Street. Run by Russian immigrants from Odessa, Louis and Rebecca Shapiro had some of their eight children helping out in the store, with the youngest ones safely ensconced in the apartment above.

The Shapiros were determined marketers, selling only the best kosher goods and fresh produce from the City Market. Louis had a reputation as an artistic grocer, arranging his wares in the most appealing way. Rebecca worked with their clientele, gently offering this delicacy, suggesting that menu option, with many of the goods delivered by the Shapiro kids in a horse cart. Each morning for their customers' sensory delight the Shapiros scattered aromatic spices on the grocery's wooden floors. "It smelled so good," ninety-eight-year-old Shapiro daughter Sylvia Gorfain remembered about her childhood days in the store. "People stood in line."

Almost a century later, people are still standing in line at the Shapiros's celebrated delicatessen at 808 South Meridian Street. Nurtured by decades of perseverance and sacrifice, the Shapiros's little business has grown into a beloved Indiana—nay, international—institution. But the Shapiros's path from pushcart to culinary pantheon, from struggling immigrants to honored Hoosiers, ultimately mirrors the courageous rise of refugees from Old World ghettos and *shtetls* into the mainstream of American life.

The origins of Indianapolis's Jewish community reached back to the mid-nineteenth century, when immigrants from Britain and Germany arrived in the booming little railroad town. Among the first Jewish immigrants to Indianapolis was said to be Moses Woolf, a Plymouth, England, shopkeeper who followed his girlfriend, Blumie, to America. A friend of his, Alexander Franco, wrote from Indianapolis, "There's a shortage of tradesmen, and a considerable need for dealers in small articles." With a small stock of notions and clothing, Woolf and his now-bride Blumie moved to Indianapolis. A number of the early arrivals worked in the needle trades, some eventually prospering with companies such as Kahn's Tailoring, L. Strauss and Company, and the William H. Block Company. The original Jewish settlers were primarily members of the Reform synagogue, the Indianapolis Hebrew Congregation, which began on November 20, 1856, with fourteen men, including two who came by horse and wagon from Kokomo and Knightstown. Two years later, the congregation purchased a three-and-a-half-acre plot of land at south

Meridian and Kelly Streets for a cemetery, which is still in use. By 1870 there were about five hundred members of the city's Jewish population.

Violent pogroms in the Russian Empire began in 1881, unleashing an enormous wave of Jewish emigration from eastern Europe. Spurred by discrimination, deadly riots, and conscription, the massive Jewish exodus lasted until U.S. immigration laws changed in 1924. Before the migration ended, more two million Jewish immigrants entered America, most settling in crowded Eastern industrial cities. Aided by organizations such as the Industrial Removal Office and Hebrew Immigrant Aid Society, a small number of Jewish immigrants relocated to the cities of the Midwest, the Shapiros among them. By 1907, there were about 5,500 members of the Indianapolis Jewish community.

Once in Indianapolis, the new immigrants initially organized themselves by national groups, reflected in the south side's synagogues. Sharah Tefilla was the first synagogue, or *shul*, in the neighborhood. Founded in 1870, it was known as the *polische shul* because of its Polish members. The group met for years in rented rooms, before purchasing a building at 352 South Meridian Street in 1882. As prosperity seeped into the community, Sharah Tefilla built a new synagogue, an imposing classical structure with white ionic columns. Located at Merrill and Meridian Streets, the synagogue opened in 1910. The second middle European synagogue, the Hungarian Hebrew Ohev Zedeck Congregation, began in 1884, meeting in rented rooms at the verge of the south side. With a reputation for being insular, the Hungarians lived in tight clusters on east New York and Ohio Streets and College Avenue. In 1899 the congregation purchased the original Indianapolis Hebrew Congregation building at Market and East Streets. Russian Orthodox Jews founded Knesses Israel in 1899. The *russische shul*, as it was known, was first housed on the northwest corner of Eddy and Merrill Streets, but four years later built a new synagogue across the street. By 1923 the congregation was meeting in its new building at 1023 South Meridian Street. Galician immigrants organized the United Hebrew Congregation in 1910, ostensibly to break the pattern of "old country" connections. Located at Union and Madison, it became known as the Union *shul*, also referred to as the *frantzische* (French) *shul* because its moderate Orthodox members were more restrained than those of the more demonstrative Orthodox temples, where loquacious-

ness and enthusiastic *davening* (prayer) was the norm. Russian Orthodox Jews founded Ezras Achim in a ramshackle building at 708 South
Meridian Street in 1910. Called the peddlers' *shul* for the vendors who
formed much of the congregation, it was the last synagogue formed by
the Yiddish-speaking Ashkenazim from eastern Europe.

Southern European Sephardim, Ladino-speaking descendants of
Iberian Jews expelled from Spain in the fifteen century, began arriving in
Indianapolis in 1906. Jacob and Rachel Toledano were the first, emigrat-
ing from Monastir (now Bitola) in Macedonia, then part of the Ottoman
Empire. Others from Monastir followed, along with Sephardim from
Salonica, Canakkale, Aleppo, and other Levantine cities. In 1913 the Sephardim organized the Congregation Sepharad of Monastir, which initially held services at the Jewish Federation's Communal Building at 17
West Morris Street. The group purchased an old Lutheran church in the
Sephardic neighborhood at Morris and Church Streets in 1919. With the
language barrier, early relations between the Ashkenazi and Sephardic
communities were often strained. There was even more tension between
the established German Jewish community that was comfortably situated on the city's north side, and the aspiring new arrivals on the south
side. It was to be a discomfiting relationship that played out over decades.

Prior to leaving for America, Louis was a grain broker and grocer in
Odessa, the Russian Empire's flourishing Black Sea port. According to
family lore, Louis, inspired by the glittering promise of the New World,
named his store the American Grocery Company. While traveling the
hinterlands contracting for grain, Louis stayed with Jewish families, as
Jews were not permitted to stay in many hotels. It is said that on one of
these visits, Louis fell in love with a young orphan girl who lived with her
uncle. Waiting until she was of age, Louis returned to ask her hand. Thus
was born a lifelong partnership between Louis and Rebecca.

The Shapiros' hometown of Odessa was a great center of Jewish
life. Over a third of the population of 403,000 in 1897 was Jewish, who
were an important part of the city's economic vitality. But in reaction to
Russia's nineteenth-century drive to Westernize, a conservative Pan-
Slavic agitation convulsed the country—with the traditional pariahs,
the Jews, as its focus. The Odessa Jews suffered a pogrom in 1871, with a
cataclysmic one in 1881. Bloody brawls continuously erupted in the city.

Jew-baiting was endemic. Each Easter, the Jewish community heard rumors of another impending riot. In 1900 another vicious pogrom swept Odessa. But when Tsar Nicholas II issued his October Manifesto in 1905 that liberalized civil rights and liberties, the Slavs unleashed a paroxysm of rage against the Jews, most violently in Odessa. The storm broke on October 18, 1905, when rival political crowds clashed. Thousands of Jews joined liberals celebrating the new laws, while conservative Russians demonstrated in support of church and the tsar. Russians began to attack Jews and loot their homes and businesses. The next day, armed left-wing students and Jews confronted an extreme right-wing rally. Shots rang out, and a young boy carrying an icon slumped to the ground, dead. After the riots finally subsided three days later, police reported that the mobs had killed at least four hundred Jews and injured another three hundred. (Police also reported a hundred Russian deaths.) More than 1,600 Jewish residences and buildings were ravaged. Unofficial sources reported far higher casualties and damages. According to family history, Louis suffered a broken arm during the riot, and the American Grocery Company was destroyed. Louis and Rebecca decided it was time to go.

The Shapiros and their six children landed at Ellis Island in 1906, initially intending to open a grocery in Brooklyn. But at the urging of the Industrial Removal Office, the Shapiros were soon headed to Lafayette, Indiana, to assist a junk dealer named Spector, who had sponsored them. (Shapiro lore says Spector was particularly interested in the Shapiro family with their five sons, as combined with his male sons they could make up a Lafayette *minyan*, the requisite ten men for Orthodox liturgical ceremonies.) The IRO was a paternalistic organization run by German Jews, who hoped to disperse the hordes of immigrant Jews into the hinterlands to prevent the creation of neoghettos in the East Coast cities where the new arrivals congregated. Fearful that the unassimilated immigrants from the Pale might spur further anti-Semitism, endangering the earlier Jewish arrivals' hard-won social positions, the IRO endeavored to settle them elsewhere. In the end, more than 80,000 people were transferred to more than a thousand towns across the country.

But Louis had a short career as a junk dealer. In his book about the IRO, *Dispersing the Ghetto*, Oberlin College Anthropology professor and Indianapolis native Jack Glazier recounted the tale told by Fanny Sha-

piro Katzow, the oldest Shapiro daughter and the family historian. The
first day Louis went on the job with Mr. Spector, they knocked on a door
asking if the woman had any scrap to sell. After negotiating a price for
a few items in the backyard, the men went around to load their wagon.
Spector tossed the pieces in his wagon and proceeded to load up some
other things. When Shapiro protested, Spector retorted, "Now you're
learning the junk business."

The Shapiros were soon in Indianapolis, arriving in June 1906. With
the five hundred dollars they had brought from Odessa, the Shapiros
opened a small store. But the little business could not provide a living
for the family, so while Rebecca ran the grocery, Louis took work at the
downtown Star Store, where a falling dry-goods box injured his throat.
The worst was yet to come. During his medical treatment, doctors discovered Louis suffered with tuberculosis, which required months of
treatment at the National Jewish Hospital for Consumptives in Denver.

"My mother had to support six kids," Sylvia recounted. "She had a
wagon, and she went door to door selling pound bags of ground coffee."
Rebecca would buy freshly ground coffee from a south side wholesale
roaster, hauling her goods to her customers with a pushcart. "She had
such a big clientele, when my father came back to Indianapolis, he immediately bought a horse and wagon," noted Sylvia. An early picture shows
the properly dressed Louis with his oldest daughter, Fanny, beside him
in the wagon with a handsome gray in the traces. The elegant lettering
on the wagon read, "Teas and Coffees. L. Shpiro. 1032 S. Illinois St. 9965
both phones."

In 1912 the Indianapolis City Directory recorded a big move: It listed
"Shapiro, Louis, grocer 808 S Meridian," a location that has remained
Shapiro's to this day. After operating out of the Illinois Street location
until 1911, the Shapiros were forced to move when the floor collapsed in
the building that served as both their warehouse and residence. But at
last the Shapiros had their own grocery, and an apartment above for their
growing family. Sylvia was born in 1911—"my American daughter," Louis
proudly announced.

The Shapiros had moved to the center of Jewish commerce in Indianapolis. "South Meridian was a beautiful shopping street," Sylvia
reminisced. "It was gorgeous. There was a corner drugstore, then a bar-

bershop, a Chinese laundry, bakery, tailor, ice cream parlor, coffee factory, movie house. There was everything, you know."

Shapiro's was clearly a family business. With the parents working long hours, the children pitched in to help. Son Max, later to be the business's guiding force, remembered sweeping the store at five years old, as did daughter Sylvia, who also recalled helping out at age five. So Rebecca could concentrate on the growing business, daughter Fanny quit school to raise the two youngest daughters, Sylvia and her sister, Belle. Never to have children herself, Fanny became the favorite Shapiro aunt and a lifelong part of Shapiro's Delicatessen. "Aunt Fanny was *the* backbone," said Sylvia's daughter, Oberlin College professor Phyllis Gorfain. As America entered World War I, the military snapped up the two oldest sons, Harry and Joe. They were destined never to return to the business. Abe and Max headed for the coasts for some seasons away from the Indianapolis store, Abe for a culinary career in New York, Max for the sunny chic of California. Isadore—Izzy—the sixth of the Shapiro children, stayed home to oversee the take-out counter.

Louis, with his penchant for modernism, kept his business au courant. Always orderly and clean, the Shapiros served the best kosher meats, Vienna Beef and Wilno sausages among them, brands they continued to feature into the twenty-first century. Delicacies, some imported; some like "Shapiro's Famous Mustard, a little goes a long way," stood stacked in perfect ziggurats and columns, their labels aligned like modern art pieces that augured Andy Warhol.

The 1920s brought prosperity to many south side Jewish families, accelerating the movement north to newer Jewish neighborhoods. But Shapiro's remained a lodestone for the Indianapolis Jewish community. Indianapolis native Fran Julian recollected being a little girl in the mid-1920s when she drove with her mother from the north side to Shapiro's. Peering over their car's radiator cap, she listened to her mother laud Shapiro's quality. "If mother wanted good corned beef and good rye bread, Shapiro's was the place," Julian said. "I remember Mr. Shapiro had white hair and a white moustache, slicing the tongue and corned beef. He had all these sons. It was a thriving business."

But the 1920s also brought a malignant element to power in Indiana: the Ku Klux Klan. Along with their virulent hatred of African Americans and Catholics, the Klansmen stoked anti-Semitic fires. In 1925 Indiana governor Ed Jackson, a well-known Klan member, incongruously spoke at the dedication of a Conservative synagogue. With flag-waving bombast and condescension, he spoke out against "hyphenated Americans": "I do not like adjectives or hyphens to differentiate one person from another, but rather I like to refer to all [of] them as American citizens." Jackson was voicing the strong nativist pressure to assimilate, which the Jewish community had to negotiate to maintain their culture. But Louis, imbued as he was with his love of America, took umbrage at the appropriation of "Americanism" by the voices of conservative reaction. To protest the Klan message, Louis made his beloved deli into a shrine of hyphenated America. He remodeled the store into an Art Deco wonderland of swoops and glazed tile, as sleek and modern as the Chrysler Building, as hygienic as an Eli Lilly and Company laboratory. And on the marquee of his fashionable new/old store, in place of the American Grocery Company, he proudly emblazoned "Shapiro's Kosher Foods" in a streamlined font, accompanied by giant Stars of David that trumpeted to the world that *this* was a Jewish American place.

Max and Abe were back home as the Great Depression tightened its grip on the country. Max was now dapper in a Hollywood kind of way, the perennial leading man of the deli. Abe came back from New York as an award-winning chef with a metropolitan palate, honed in some of Gotham's best delis. He began to use his big-city deli ideas to nudge the Shapiro offerings to new levels. The repeal of Prohibition in Indianapolis on April 7, 1933, gave the Shapiros a grand opportunity. Max told an *Indianapolis Star Magazine* reporter in 1983, "Then Prohibition ended, we started selling beer at ten cents a bottle. Three bottles for a quarter. Well, pretty soon customers wanted something to eat with their beer, so we started selling sandwiches—kosher corned beef, pastrami, you know." Corned beef sandwiches were a dime, salami sandwiches a hefty twenty-nine cents. The first kitchen fare the Shapiros served was Rebecca's spaghetti and meatballs. The family is still disputing who developed the recipe for the Shapiros' signature corned beef—Rebecca or Abe? However it went, the Shapiros had a winning team. Louis and Rebecca were around to add gravitas, Abe directed the kitchen, Izzy ran the take-out counter, Fanny opened the place and kept the ducks in a row, and Max

perfected his bon vivant counter act. "Try our beans," he would call to
an undecided customer. "We get good reports on our beans."

In the 1930s Louis and Rebecca designated Max as the heir apparent
for the Meridian Street store. He was astute, committed, and unmarried,
ready to devote himself to the business. At the time, Louis had a plan to
open a chain of Shapiro's around Indianapolis, each managed by one of
his children. Indeed, the Shapiros had a north-side deli for a time, run
by Fanny. But the south side location continued to prosper, particularly
with the 1940s and 1950s growth of nearby Lilly, truck terminals, and
other industries that brought customers into the deli. With an adjacent
parking lot, the downtown office trade could also catch a quick meal.
In 1940 Shapiro's opened a cafeteria, which kept the lines moving at a
good clip. It was the era when gentiles joined Shapiro's primarily Jewish
clientele. As Sylvia said, "Everybody came."

Acclaim began to come to the Shapiros. A 1945 *Food Store Review,*
an in-house publication of the B. Manischevitz Company, lauded Shapiro's as "the most popular food store in the city," calling Max "one of
the most shrewd merchandisers in the business." Louis was still hale
and hearty at seventy-five, "lending moral support" to his three sons.
Their ten employees were serving 1,200 to 1,500 customers a day in their
gleaming temple of Kosher-style gastronomy. According to the article,
the cafeteria provided 60 percent of their revenues, with groceries sup-
plying the balance.

Louis passed away in April 1949, and Rebecca suffered a stroke the
following summer that left her bedridden until her death in September
1956. It left Max to be the public face of Shapiro's. He still maintained
his debonair style, glorying in his vacations to such hotspots as Miami
Beach in the 1940s and Acapulco in the early 1960s. Later in life, Max
married a couple of times, but never had children. His second wife, Ann
Selig Shapiro, perfected many of Shapiro's famous desserts, including
the strawberry cheesecake. Abe and Fanny continued to carry enormous
responsibilities behind the scenes, Fanny diligently working in the store
into her eighties. She passed away in April 1990.

An ethnic revival that began in the 1970s inspired many to redis-
cover the joys of traditional eateries, Shapiro's among them. Proto-food-
ies began to search the place out. Sandwiches were $1.25 to $1.85 in the

1970s, rising to $2.95 for a towering corned-beef sandwich by 1984 when the Shapiro's were doing $3 million a year in business. The deli was on the march. When the longtime Passo's Pharmacy on the corner burned, Shapiros expanded into the space, making the deli four times the size of the original store. An extensive remodeling left Louis's Art Deco styling behind in favor of a 1980s fern-bar look, though large photos of Louis and Rebecca overlooked the dining room, centered between the columns that delineated the original eighteen-foot-wide grocery. The deli's new plate-glass windows were cutting-edge energy efficient, drawing an admiring article in *Glass Digest,* a trade publication. Likewise, when the adjacent Regen Bakery closed in the 1980s after decades of crafting venerable Jewish rye, Max cannily expanded the parking lot. Louis would have been proud—the Shapiros were still all about progressive ideas.

In the mid-1980s, a new Shapiro face began to show up in the news. Brian Shapiro was a fresh-faced, twenty-five-year-old Indiana University Law School graduate. Max, now in his late seventies, decided that his nephew, Brian, was going to take over. Brian's father Mort, an investment banker, was also involved with the business. Encouraged by the deli's success, Mort and Brian convinced Max to open a second store, this one in the far north side Jewish neighborhood along Eighty-sixth Street. Max was reticent: "Why should I open up a second restaurant when I haven't got the first one off the ground?" But a sprawling new Shapiro's began to take shape in a suburban strip mall. In a 1983 *Star Magazine* article, Max touted Brian's leadership potential, "He's almost ready. He just needs a couple of years to mature to run the place like a Shapiro." The reporter concluded, "You can bet Max will be there to make sure he does."

He did not have the chance; Max died a year later, in October 1984. Honors had come to Max in the previous few years. Beyond the numerous news articles, Shapiro's was listed as one of the one hundred Indiana landmarks of historic significance in the Indiana State Museum. His name was in the museum's time capsule. Purdue University's School of Engineering and Technology recognized him as the 1984 "Food Service Executive of the Year." Obituaries and columns in the local press lamented Max's passing, one noting "He would smack his two eager hands together in a clap that said, 'To life!'"

Brian inherited a growing concern, with all of the challenges associated with it. His accounting and law background served him well, and Shapiro's many longtime employees pitched in with the transition. Brian's relentless Shapiro work ethic undoubtedly helped him continue the restaurant's ethos of excellence. "One of the keys to the Shapiro's success is that they are hard workers. Enormously hard workers," Phyllis said. "They have enormous pride in this place. True, true devotion to the store and the quality, serving with great pride and integrity."

The Shapiros's mixture of innovation and tradition began to draw national attention. In 1988 Jane and Michael Stern, famous for their *Roadfood* books that celebrated American regional and ethnic eateries, featured Shapiro's in their syndicated "Taste of America" series, spreading the word of the Indianapolis deli around the land. In their book, the Sterns rhapsodized that "the corned beef sandwich takes you straight to deli heaven," going on to write, "The meat is lean, but not too lean, succulent enough so that each rosy slice, rimmed with a halo of smudgy spices, glistened under the florescent lights of the dining room." A *USA Today* article in 1988 compared Shapiro's corned beef to be equal to the legendary Carnegie Deli's sandwich, and the next year another *USA Today* piece declared Shapiro's served "the finest corned beef sandwich in the world."

Gastronomes from around the world made pilgrimages to the deli. Shapiro's became a must stop for celebrities. Television and film stars such as Dick Van Dyke, Elizabeth Montgomery, Jim Nabors, Priscilla Presley, Dennis Miller, Richard Simmons, and Jennifer Aniston visited. Sports figures such as Andy Granatelli, Bobby Knight, Rik Smits, Reggie Miller, Larry Brown, and Lebron James chowed down. Generations of politicians have held court, including Evan Bayh, Mitch Daniels, Bart Peterson, Bill Hudnut, and Rudy Guiliani among them.

But the successes were balanced with heartbreak and new challenges. A week before Christmas in 1989, a robbery at the Eighty-sixth Street store turned into the senseless murder of forty-four-year-old manager Fred Vanek, who had been a Shapiro's employee for twenty-five years. He was shot six times for refusing to open the safe. Donald J. Robertson later pled guilty to murder and received a ninety-two-year sentence.

Louis Shapiro set a high standard for his descendants. "Keeping that name going is important to me," Max once said. "Shapiro's has set a high standard here [in Indianapolis], and we value our reputation more than money."

All images are courtesy of Max Shapiro Inc.

By 1999, when Brian's father, Mort, died, the Eighty-sixth Street store was rundown and dispirited. But Brian was scouting for a better place, which became the lavish Shapiro's on Rangeline Road in Carmel, a $3 million neo-Georgian brick suburban deli with all of the bells and whistles, which opened in 2002. As before, everybody came. In 1997 the Shapiro's revered downtown bakery moved into an old brick cooper's building behind the deli, under the direction of classically trained Danish baker, John Poulsen.

Shapiro continued to prosper in the twenty-first century. Almost 2,500 people a day thronged their three locations, which now included a deli at the Indianapolis International Airport. *USA Today* continued to sing the deli's praises, including Shapiro's among the nation's ten best Jewish delis. Shapiro's was the oldest of any of the landmarks listed.

Each workday as it has for almost a century, the south side Shapiro's still serves as a gathering place. The line forms, first past the jeweled desserts with their siren call. Then the freshly made salads. Carl Caudill, the twenty-five-year veteran on the meat slicer, calls out to yet another gray-haired patron, "Young man! What will you have?" The hairnet-clad ladies on the steam table keep the queue moving, dispensing potato latkes and matzo ball soup with practiced alacrity. Busboys hurtle around the dining room, clattery and resonant with tables of kibitzing people: starched shirts talking business, jeans arguing sports, elderly friends exchanging old jibes, a table of huddled politicos, a shy-eyed couple offering each other snippets of their sandwiches, and small-town tourists regaling in the shared energy of the communal *shtetl*, the dense life of the modern city. No secrets here in this room of neighbors, this meeting space of citizens.

Amidst the ordered tumult, Brian talked about the challenges his fourth-generation business faced in a fickle marketplace devoted to the latest internet-driven food fad, riven by consolidations that eliminate longtime purveyors and personnel who march to distinctly different drummers. "You know, we're a dinosaur. We make stuff. We actually make stuff. We serve a lot of people a day," he said. "We try to maintain that good homemade food. It all comes down to maintaining your product to maintain loyalty. That's what wins." Really, his summation was not that much different from Louis Shapiro's original philosophy that is hand-painted on an old sign sitting on the deli case: "Cook good, serve generous, price modestly, and people will come."

13

SHE'S THE CHEESE

THE NEW YORK THEATER CROWD BUZZED IN MANHATTAN'S Picholine Restaurant, a celebrated redoubt of Provencal-inspired gourmet dining. Edith Piaf's laments drifted in the air past French tapestries and walls the color of Mediterranean terra cotta. Waiters in dark suits hovered over the tables, dispensing the latest epicurean advice to the elegant diners.

At table after table, necks craned in anticipation as Max McCalman wheeled up his heavily loaded serving trolle. A slender man with a boyish thatch of hair, McCalman is Picholine's *maître fromager*, the cheese master in charge of selecting and bringing to perfection the greatest cheeses in the world. He nodded to the diners and began to extol the virtues of the dozens of spectacular cheeses that stood chockablock on his rolling cheese board, what he called "a kaleidoscope of cultured milk." The artisan-made cheeses reflected what the French call *terroir*, an ineffable combination of geography, climate, animal genetics, and human culture that inextricably link a food to the particular land and people that produced it.

There was a pumpkin-red Mimolette from Flanders, promising butterscotch and caramel flavors in its rock-hard flesh. A Spanish Queso de la Garrotxa tasted of rosemary and thyme, reflecting the Catalonian goats' hillside diets. A Colston-Bassett Stilton the color of ancient blue-streaked gold stood imperious beside some of France's best soft cheeses, such as smelly Burgundian Epoisses and nutty-tasting Sainte-Maure de Touraines *chèvre* (goat cheese) from the Loire Valley.

Tucked among the array of the world's best cheeses, a small white ball of goat cheese that looked like a tiny dimpled moon awaited its share of accolades. It was Capriole Farms' Wabash Cannonball, the pride of the Kentuckiana hills. "It's a staple of our cheese board," McCalman said. "It's a wonderful launching point to a cheese tasting. It has a clean fresh flavor, kind of a good morning greeting kind of taste." The Wabash Cannonball is also a cheese that is redolent of a special place above the Falls of the Ohio, and a very special cheese maker—Judy Schad.

For a long time now, Schad has been gathering acclaim to her farm in the green and rumpled hills near Greenville, Indiana. She began making cheese in the late 1970s, determined to do something with the copious quantities of milk produced by her herd of thoroughly coddled goats. Something she did, indeed.

Chefs and gourmets soon began to spread the word of the remarkable woman in the hills of Indiana who was making world-class cheeses. Five-star restaurants from Picholine to Chicago's Everest Room and Ritz-Carlton to New Orleans's Bayona featured her cheeses. Tony gourmet cheese shops such as Murray's in Greenwich Village sang her praises.

Robert Kaufelt is the owner of Murray's Cheese Shop, a Bleecker Street institution for more than sixty years that the Zagat Survey called "The Big Cheese." A purveyor of 450 different cheeses, Kaufelt said, "Judy's got great cheese. They stand up among the world's best cheeses. Equally important, she is one of the founding mothers of the American Farmstead Movement that is revolutionizing our artisanal cheesemaking." Kaufelt also noted, "She always has time for everybody. She's kind of the Mama Sita, the Den Mother, of American cheese."

Food writers and the popular press across the country trumpeted the tale. In his book, *The Cheese Plate,* McCalman termed her Wabash Cannonball "an American masterpiece." In his groundbreaking compendium, *The Cheese Primer,* cheese expert Steve Jenkins heralded Schad's cheeses as "American Treasures." In time, the *New York Times* and National Public Radio covered her story. *People Magazine* titled its story "Cheese Whiz," featuring a picture of Schad in her old wooden barn amidst her contented goats.

When I arrived one rainy Saturday afternoon, Schad was playing Monopoly with her grandchildren. She is a striking woman with a brilliant smile and eyes that dance with intelligent delight. Larry Schad, her attorney husband (and sometimes goat milker and cheese monger), lounged nearby watching basketball with a grandchild draped across him. Outside the rain poured down on the surrounding green fields and woodlands that are the crucible of Schad's success.

"It all begins and ends in the fields," she said as we settled into her log cabin living room, where a grand piano gleamed in a well-lit corner. Schad is a true farmstead producer, using only milk from her own herd that grazes on her organic farm. Nodding to the limestone-studded hills, she said, "The goats browse out there—sassafras, sumac, honeysuckle, dogwood. The milk and the cheese reflect that forage. Then the manure goes back out to fields to start the cycle again."

She is as Kentuckiana as you get. "I think the place made me," she said. Raised in the midst of New Albany, Indiana, she spent weekends and summers with her beloved grandparents on their small farm at the edge of town. "There was every kind of vegetable and fruit there," she reminisced. "My grandmother was a wonderful German cook. We had *lebkuchen* cookies at Christmas. Persimmon pudding, pies, country hams were always around. I can still remember every Saturday morning cleaning chickens on wet newspapers in the kitchen. I was surrounded by wonderful people growing up."

Luckily for Schad's future vocation, there was a dairy herd across the road where her grandfather got their rich country milk. In the Hoosier farm kitchen at the edge of town, young Judy watched her grandmother make homemade buttermilk and cottage cheese.

After a degree in English from the University of Kentucky, Schad entered the University of Louisville's doctoral program in Renaissance literature. It was years of sonnet cycles and teaching and editorial work in small literary magazines that eventually culminated in the realization that academic life was not her dream future. But the intense intellectual training served her well in her newly chosen position—as a farmwoman in the Indiana Knobs.

In the late 1970s she and Larry sold their comfortable suburban home and purchased an old Indiana hill farm that dated back to the 1830s. Unbeknownst, they had bought the family farm. Later they learned the land had been in Larry's family from the 1830s until the 1950s. On the farm, she discovered her academic skills allowed her to keep their goat herd thriving and to learn to craft her early cheeses. "The love of minutiae, the research that goes with a PhD program, they were incredibly helpful," Schad said.

Inundated with goat milk, Schad began to make cheese in her kitchen. "I didn't have any grandiose plans," she said. "I just wanted to make decent cheese and have people buy it. I've always seen cheese as an extension of my kitchen. It's what my grandmother did."

Their goat herd flourished in the moist woods and pastures of Capriole Farms. Selective breeding of Alpine, Saanens, and Nubian stocks generated hardy high-producing animals. To maintain quality and health, the Schads rarely go outside their herds for new goats, preferring to maintain a "closed herd." The Schads' careful husbandry has yielded calm, tranquil goats, a condition that is vital to top-quality cheese. Stressed-out goats produce milk with broken fat molecules, ultimately leading to *chèvre* with the awful barnyard taste associated with "goatey" cheese. "Judy's cheeses have a delicate zesty flavor," observed Kaufelt. "She obviously lavishes love on those animals. I would deem them happy animals." Referring to the luxury five-star hotels, Kaufelt said, "Obviously, these goats are living in the Four Seasons of Goatdom."

Piper, one of the Schad grandkids, took me out to the barn, where inquisitive goat noses poked out of gates for a rub or treat. Light slanted down from the hayloft where Piper ran to play with a visiting friend. Sleek white-, tan-, and black-coated animals stood serenely in fresh golden hay, a far cry from the concrete floors of most industrial dairy operations. They ambled to the feed bins as though they were regal countesses. The baa-ing kids had the air of cosseted country club children, their every whim satisfied. I wanted to be one of the Schads' goats in my next lifetime.

"We dairy in a very old-fashioned way," Schad said. "I long ago gave up on the volume game. I chose a lifestyle when I came here, not just to make cheese." The Schads have 350 goats, 200 of them milking females, along with about a dozen theoretically happy bucks. Each week, Schad and her crew handle 1,200 to 1,400 gallons of milk in her small, white cheese plant that sits just across the drive from her house.

Capriole Farms makes thirteen different kinds of goat cheese, all hand ladled and shaped to protect the delicate fat globules from breaking. The varieties include fresh *chèvre* that has a subtle lemony flavor.

Wabash Cannonballs are small, vegetable ash-dusted and aged balls, dense with a creamy flavor. The cheese won her the "Best of Show" honors at the 1995 American Cheese Society show. Old Kentucky Tomme is a rustic cheese that is aged four months. Inspired by a French-style cheese, Schad evolved the form into Capriole's Banon, a small disc of *chèvre* that is wrapped in chestnut leaves. Granddaughter Piper, a cherubic red-headed girl, proudly told me her favorite Capriole cheese: Piper's Pyramid, named after her. "I like it's shaped like a pyramid," Piper said. "It tastes good."

Capriole's Mount Saint Francis is a cheese that wins the adulation of cheese experts. It is a unique rind-washed and aged *chèvre*, a technique that is very rarely used with goat cheese. "She's invented a new American goat cheese," said Kaufelt." It's part of Judy's genius." Cheese expert Jenkins exulted, "It is an extremely complicated cheese, with very complex flavors. Ultimately, it's just a brilliant cheese. She's just an alchemist."

With her edgy, university-honed eloquence, voluble nature, and warm regard for her fellow cheese makers, Schad has become somewhat of a designated spokesperson for the farmstead cheese producers. "The biggest thing is that I'm honest and I'm passionate," she said. "I love cheese, and I'm fascinated with the process. It is just magical. I'm just so proud of the American cheese makers and what they've accomplished in the last twenty years."

Tom and Kristi Johnson are two displaced Hoosiers who have made it big in the artisan cheese world with their Bingham Hill Blue Cheese they make in Colorado. They are among the dozens of cheese makers who credit Mama Sita Schad with unstinting advice and encouragement. Tom laughingly noted, "She calls me 'baby.' She calls everyone 'baby.'"

Capriole cheese reflects Schad's omnivorous curiosity about food and life. She travels extensively in the United States and Europe searching for new benchmarks and ideas to commingle with her idiosyncratic American ones. When Schad began to make farmstead cheese, most American cheese makers slavishly attempted to mimic European artisanal offerings. Schad stands out because she also looked to her Ohio Valley roots for inspiration.

Her slightly aged Wabash Cannonball is an evolution of the traditional Provencal fresh goat cheese *boulat* (cannonball). Beyond the witty play on words that clearly anchors the cheese in Indiana, it is unique in its shape and texture. When Schad developed her highly touted Mount Saint Francis cheese, it was a wholly new variety—a commingling of goat milk and washed-rind techniques that were *sui generis.* "That cheese is very American," she said. "I wanted to make a cheese that combined the characteristics of the only true American cheese—the Monterey Jack—with French varieties I love like Epoisses and Liverots. I love that funky stinky thing that happens."

But I think her leaf-wrapped Banon is the most graphic indicator of her Kentuckiana roots. In the Vaucluse region of France, the classic Banons are wrapped in chestnut leaves that are macerated in white wine, brandy, or *eau-de-vie.* Schad wraps her Banons with leaves from her own American Chestnut tree. There in the hills of southern Indiana, she lovingly macerates the leaves in good Kentucky bourbon.

Sofia Solomon in Chicago is Schad's *affineur,* the merchant who buys from the cheese maker and gently coaxes the cheese to perfect ripeness. Solomon sells to a distinguished list of restaurants, such as Danielle in New York and Spago in Beverly Hills. After lauding Capriole cheeses, Solomon mentioned her ethnocentric French colleagues were astounded that an American produced the Wabash Cannonball she served them, insisting it had to be French. But Solomon convinced them that the cheese was a unique marriage of traditional French cheese styles and an iconoclastic American sensibility. Solomon said, "What I love about Judy is she is constantly experimenting. Like any artist, she takes it one step further."

14

STRANGE BREW

AROUND 5:00 AM, THE FIRST OF THE FAITHFUL FORM A LINE
outside Three Floyds Brewing, intent on securing their six-bottle allot-
ment of the legendary Dark Lord imperial stout. By the time the cold,
blustery day dawns, the queue of beer lovers snakes well down the street
of the industrial park in Munster. Hoods up and hunkered against the
wind in blankets, the red-nosed fans await their moment. Beer traders
arrange tables of their bottled wares to pass the time, and a lively swap
meet begins. A gust sends hats flying in the air.

Repeatedly ranked as the world's best beer by ratebeer.com, a leading
indicator of such things, Dark Lord is sold only one day a year—usually
held the last Saturday of April, and the event attracts thousands. "I think
people come for the atmosphere," said Clint Puckett, a Rose-Hulman
Institute of Technology student standing first in line with his parents,
who drove to Indiana from Nevada. "Of course, the beer is fantastic."
And after a pause, he admitted, "Then there's the 'cha-ching.'" While
Dark Lord sells for fifteen dollars a bottle at the event, gray marketers
can make big money reselling their stash—up to $150 a bottle.

By 8:00 AM, the temperature has only climbed to 43 degrees. Traffic around the brewery grinds to a halt. Cars display license plates from
dozens of states—Alabama, California, New York, and Washington
among them. Coveys of cyclists continue to pedal in. Already, hundreds
of locked bikes tangle in vivid kinetic sculptures.

A posse of tent-rental people try to erect a canopy, but the gale
snatches it from their hands. Chilly as it is, the crowd continues to wait.
Many of them are already drinking beer, mostly stouts similar to the

Dark Lord. As the line grows nearly half a mile long, even the most patient check their watches. Just three more hours until the doors open.

Founded by brothers Nick and Simon Floyd, along with their father,
Michael, Three Floyds opened in Hammond in 1996. Located in an old
brick building across the street from the fire department, the brewery
produced its early batches in a rig that was basic to the point of rusticity:
a five-barrel system made of used Swiss-cheese tanks with a wok burner
underneath.

Emboldened by the enthusiastic acceptance of their brews, Three
Floyds purchased a large warehouse building in nearby Munster in 2000.
Their neighbors include a large litho house, wholesale distributors, and
the local school corporation's service building, where yellow school
buses sometimes park. Today, the brewery operates a gleaming, custom-
made, forty-barrel brew rig that produces 11,000 barrels of premium beer
a year—enough to make Three Floyds Indiana's largest brewer, though
well short of those like Sam Adams that do two million barrels annually.
In 2005 the Floyd family established a brewpub nestled against their
now sizable production facility. Like the larger enterprise, it is wildly
successful.

Three Floyds beers have been winning accolades from the very beginning, though the company received perhaps the ultimate honor when
judges at ratebeer.com ranked the brewery the best in the world this year
[2010]. Joe Tucker, president of ratebeer.com, said that beer connoisseurs
have long revered the Hoosiers' work, calling them "a quintessential
American super craft brewer." Tucker notes that judges rated 110,000
beers worldwide for the 2010 ranking, and the results were remarkable:
Three Floyds had three of the world's top ten beers with three different
versions of Dark Lord. Additionally, ratebeer.com reviewers gave Three
Floyds's Alpha King pale ale, Behemoth barley wine, and Dreadnaught
India pale ale perfect 100 scores.

The mastermind behind those recipes is Nick Floyd, a thirty-eight-
year-old linebacker-sized guy with a cue-ball head, tattoos, and a laconic
manner—until you get him talking about beer. "Nothing about our beer
is normal," he said, citing the Bravo hops they sometimes use as an ex-

ample. Tough to access because of the tiny amount of acreage planted in the state of Washington, Bravo hops contain high alpha acids, giving the beer a particularly bitter taste. The Three Floyds' unusual, grapefruity Gumballhead uses the equally scarce Amarillo hops from Texas. The brewery seeks out premium imported malts, such as Simpsons from northern England and Weyermann's from Germany, to impart its brews with rich grain flavors.

Part of Nick's beer education came during his travels in Europe, starting with a trip to visit English relatives in the 1980s. He visited breweries in France, Belgium, and Germany. In the early 1990s, there were brief brewing stints at the Weinkeller, a German-style brewpub in the western suburbs of Chicago, and at the Florida Brewery in Auburndale, Florida, where he brewed on a three-hundred-barrel system for the United States, Caribbean, and Central American markets. In 1991 Nick studied at Chicago's Seibel Institute of Technology, America's oldest brewing school, to accredit his on-the-job experience. But long before he began his formal training, he enjoyed a head start. "Nick started secretly brewing in high school," said Michael, who seems not to have been fooled.

A trim, raffish Englishman with a graying ponytail, "Doc" Floyd— Doctor Michael Floyd—still tinkers in the brewery at age sixty-eight. Always ready with a great story, the retired nephrologist once transplanted a kidney into Philippine dictator Fernando Marcos. His medical work took him to the Pacific Northwest and Houston before he finally joined a large kidney practice in northwestern Indiana, where he settled with his family. Diverse foods abounded in the house when Nick and Simon (now a chef with Gamba Restaurante in Merrillville) were growing up, including complex Indian dishes and other exotic flavors. And there was always good beer.

That love of culinary experimentation and suds made Nick what he is today. After all, Three Floyds did not arrive at the top of the barrel by being conservative. Allying himself with craft brewers against the Evil Forces—bland industrial beers—Nick hopes to further push the envelope this year with Belgian-style, cherry-flavored *kriek* and raspberry-flavored *framboise* beers. He also dreamed up a Berliner *Weisse*, a cloudy, sour wheat beer, though he worries that the new yeast strains could taint the moneymakers at his beloved brewery. "It'll only be available here. We'll never bottle it," he told a trade webzine. "We'd have to napalm the whole bottling line."

Great beer is nothing new to the Hoosier State. In fact, Indiana has been brewing since the pioneer days, beginning in 1814 with German brewers down in the utopian community at New Harmony. When the flood of Germans began to settle throughout Indiana in the 1830s, they created both the Hoosier brewing industry and provided the core market for its consumption. Indiana-German beer, particularly lager, revolutionized drinking in Indiana. Prior to that, Hoosiers were a whiskey-drinking group. Within a few decades, beer drinking became the thing, and has remained part of our culture since.

Prohibition devastated the frothy revolution, and though the industry revived somewhat after repeal, consolidation eventually winnowed the number of state breweries down to just a few faltering behemoths. By the 1990s, these large concerns were brewing fairly anemic, mass-market lagers, and the last of them, the Evansville Brewing Company, closed in 1997. But by then, a different approach to brewing was already coming to a boil here: microbreweries.

Unlike wine or liquor, beer lends itself to small-scale production. A fierce individualist can easily brew a few hundred barrels a year of great beer on a limited budget. With its roots in hippie do-it-yourself culture, American microbrewing began bubbling up on the West Coast in the 1980s. But when the trend reached Indiana a decade later, Hoosier brewers took to craft beer with fervor. Generally defined as those facilities producing 15,000 barrels or less a year, ten microbreweries now span Indianapolis alone: including Sun King, Oaken Barrel, and Barley Island. Around the state, there are twenty-two more—among them Mad Anthony in Fort Wayne, Upland in Bloomington, and The New Albanian in the Falls Cities area. And in a warehouse in Munster, there are the ultimate independents: the Three Floyds brewers, madly fermenting brews that have captured the world's attention.

Nick's creative spark, he said, comes from "traveling and trying other people's beer," not to mention his creative heroes, moviemaker Stanley Kubrick, Dungeons and Dragons creator Gary Gygax, and Genghis Khan. Pick up a six pack of Three Floyds and those influences leap off the bottles. Wrapped with quirky D&D-meets-mad-cartoonist labels, they are visual magnets. "Over the years, they've been among the most creative brewers," said Siebel Institute vice president Keith Lemcke, "Not just with their beer, but also their packaging."

Indeed, tattoos, a shaved head, and a Wild Bunch attitude seem almost obligatory for the Three Floyds brewers. They are a band of merry buccaneers, rampaging the midwestern Main with their flavorful, often idiosyncratic brews. "We do things in a technically sound manner," said Three Floyds brewer and "minister of culture" Barnaby Struve. "But we want to do it our way."

A cerebral South African with shaved head and a Maori-warrior number of tattoos, the thirty-seven-year-old Struve marvels at the rise of Three Floyds into cult status. "None of us got into this to conquer the world," he noted. Instead, the dream of staying small to produce excellent unfiltered, unpasteurized beers sustains him and his craft-beer brethren. While Three Floyds now has worldwide renown, there are only eight brewers on staff.

Three Floyds' flagship is an unusually hoppy pale ale called Alpha King. Robert the Bruce, a Scottish-style ale, sells well, as do the company's inventively named seasonal beers—the spicy Rabbid Rabbit, Moloko milk stout, apricot-hued Broo Doo, Alpha Klaus Christmas porter, Topless Wytch Baltic porter, and Picklehaub Pilsner. Three Floyds also brews an array of small-batch beers that are sold only in the brewpub.

With their imaginative approach, Three Floyds beers often fall outside the rigid style categories that guide brewing competitions. "Usually our stuff is thrown out right away," Nick chuckled. In spite of the Three Floyds independent ways, though, judges at the World Beer Cup in San Diego saw fit to honor the Behemoth with a gold medal, and the Dreadnaught with a bronze. The annual Great American Beer Festival, held in Denver, awarded a silver medal to the Gorch Fock helles in 2007. "The Great American Beer Festival is the Super Bowl of brewing," Nick said. "The World Beer Cup is, well, the World Cup."

But it was Dark Lord that brought Three Floyds into the global spotlight. A Russian Imperial Stout, the beer amounts to a hopped-up version of those originally brewed by nineteenth-century British industrial brewers for the Russian and Baltic markets. The imperial stouts carried extremely high alcohol levels to help them survive the rough Baltic passage. Rich and porridge thick, the imperial stouts became favorites in the frigid northern climates, including among the Russian aristocracy. The famously wanton Catherine the Great was a fan of Russian imperial stouts, adding to its reputation as an aphrodisiac. By modernizing the historic brew and limiting the supply of Dark Lord (about 12,000 twenty-two-ounce bottles) to a single day, the Floyds created a beer festival that now borders on cultural phenomenon.

Just minutes remain before 11:00 AM on Dark Lord Day, and the 5,000 thirsty customers outside the brewery shuffle their feet impatiently. As the Three Floyds' crew steady themselves for the crowd, thumps and electronic screeches from Viper, a heavy-metal band warming up inside, leak out of the brewery warehouse. When the hour finally arrives, a burly bouncer opens the overhead door and Nick stoically welcomes the incoming throng.

With a shriek of guitars, Viper kicks into a scream-heavy, hair-flailing rendition of "Dark Lord." The crowd, for the most part already lubricated by hours of blowsy camaraderie in the parking lot, streams into the utilitarian warehouse that on this day is the epicenter of Beer World. Eager buyers jostle forward with cash clutched in their hands, ready to snatch their precious six bottles from the Three Floyds brewers turned vendors. Whoops of triumph belt out as buyers hold the black, wax-sealed bottles aloft.

Up by the stage, beer geeks throng the merchandise table for Dark Lord t-shirts and hats. By a wall of boxed Dark Lord bottles, queues form for draughts. The viscosity of used forty-weight motor oil, the Russian Imperial Stout fills the air with the pungent scent of roasted malts, coffee, Mexican vanilla, and Indian sugar. Happy folks toast one another, savoring flavors of dried cherries, caramel, and licorice.

With the Dark Lord frenzy still at full tilt, the Floyds seem almost relaxed. Over by the draught line, Doc holds a glass of stout to the light as he extols its virtues to an admirer. Simon takes a break from his chef duties to watch frantic fans pour through the door. And Nick—so often brusque or aloof—finally looks pleased. He holds court with a few fellow brewers who have dropped in for the day. They talk about beer.

15

MARKET DAZE

BLOOMINGTON'S FARMERS MARKET

THROUGH THE PILES OF GLOWING VEGETABLES AND cloudbanks of flowers, a throng of giddy people tote their booty in net bags, rumpled grocery sacks, and canvas carryalls. There is a jostle and a dance as folks lurch for the perfect purple eggplant or clot to chat with friends. Misshapen queues crowd the aisles for celebrated largess—Dunkerly tomatoes or Daviess County melons—and men hauling off a watermelon under each arm.

The smell of deep summer hangs in the air: aphrodisiac flowers mingling with peaches and cut-open melon, basil entwining with the garlic, and scents of exotic vegetables wafting like question marks, punctuating the earthy smell of root crops. "Try a sample?" the maple syrup man in the weathered straw hat offers, and the forethought of autumn wisps through my mind.

It is the Bloomington Farmers Market, a Saturday tradition for twenty-two years. Part market, part club, it is the crossroads of the community, connecting farm and forest to city and campus. "It's just so Bloomington," Mayor John Fernandez said. "It's one of those things you point to and say, 'This is why I live here.'"

There is no such thing as an "average" shopper. Professors scrabble for the best tomatoes with the townsfolk and Asian students' faces alight as they spot oriental produce in their countrymen's stands. Lawyers in their Saturday jeans rub shoulders with aging hippies as they compare vegetables. Local politicians work the aisles and vendors nod to frequent shoppers, plucking their best for them.

From the thin promise of early May till the cold rains of October, the market gathers in a parking lot in downtown Bloomington from 7:00 AM until around noon, or whenever the vendors see fit to fold their tents. Wedged between two libraries at the corner of Fourth and Lincoln Streets, the market's seventy vendors serve more than 50,000 patrons through the season.

The produce follows the season, from the fragile lettuces and starter plants of May through the cornucopia of late summer till the last rutabaga, pumpkin, and mum of late fall. Eggs and herbs and bouquets of each blooming moment fill the market each weekend.

Market Day starts with the vendors sleepy setup about 6:00 AM, accompanied by commiserations over the lack of rain or too much; the blistering heat or toe-numbing cold; the surfeit of produce or lack of it. Soon after, the crafty retirees stride purposefully in, prepared to pluck the best before the layabeds saunter over. About 8:30 AM, the market hits its stride, a swirl of color and sound as the crowds grow till 10:30 AM or so.

Emerging from a sea of sunflowers, David Porter's craggy face is in a wry smile as he holds forth in his weekly sermon on the duplicity of politicians and the silliness of modern life. Lord save the innocent who asks how he gets his garlic to grow in braids. A few stalls down, his old friend Jeff Hartenfeld mans his graphically arranged flowers, a painterly composition of nature and whimsy that is a tipoff to his former life as a design teacher.

Across the way, the Chile Woman, Susan Byers, offers two hundred kinds of chiles, from standards such as jalapeños and habenos to incendiary habaneros to exotica such as Ecuadorian Chocolate peppers and the descriptively named pecker peppers. Her amiable cohort, John, or "Pepper Boy" as he styles himself on market day, compared the market to the Roman forum, where all the classes gathered to discuss the issues of the day.

Down from the syrup man is the Chang family, who have been in Bloomington since arriving from Taiwan in 1988. "Vegetables for people who want Chinese," Mrs. Chang said, smiling before her piles of bok choy, and Chinese melons, garlic shoots, and bundles of slender Chinese green beans as long as garter snakes.

The Edwards family from near Washington, Indiana, farm five acres of red sand to bring some of the best sweet corn and melons to the market. Will Davis, flinty in his gimme cap and jump suit, is the patriach, a remnant of a pre–farm machinery Indiana. "I'd harness the horses and shuck a row of corn before heading to school. Try gettin' 'em to do that now," he said. "They sit around the coffee shop till 10:00 o'clock and then jump on their equipment for a couple of hours and call it quits."

"There won't be none left when we're gone," his buddy Joe, another Daviess County retiree tossed in. "They don't want to work no more. Ain't no air conditioning on that hoe."

Across the aisle, Deryl Dale and Linda Chapman offer bouquets of totemic exuberance, bags of mesclun—greens and edible flowers that change with the seasons. Their children, Anna and Macey, share in the work and the profits. "We're old Back-to-the-Landers," Linda says. "This lets us stay in touch with that. The kids have grown up with the butterflies and the birds."

There is little haggling of the Third World markets. Price guidelines emerge each week, and the vendors basically adhere to them. Naturally, the better growers exact a small premium for their expertise. In general, the extraordinary freshness and sensual joy of the market are purchased at very reasonable rates.

Throughout the season, groups in this music-rich town perform everything from folk music to bluegrass to piano jazz to the rousing airs of the Bloomington Brass Band. At the summer solstice, a group of people who do England's archaic Morris Dancing galloped faux animals through the crowds. The market barely paused. It is Bloomington, after all.

16

PAWPAW REDUX

WHEN I WAS GROWING UP IN SOUTHERN INDIANA, I USED TO hear talk about something called the Hoosier banana, a fruit that grew wild in the nearby hollers and bottoms. I found out what it was one day in late summer when I was five or six. We were visiting some of our country kin, and after dinner they passed around a bowl of greenish yellow, oblong fruit, each about six inches long. Its complex, banana-papaya-pineapple flavor and creamy, custardy texture brought quiet smiles to sun-bussed faces and a surprise to my mouth; its tropical taste was completely unfamiliar to me. Someone down at the end of the table softly sang a snatch of an old children's song: "picking up pawpaws, put-tin' 'em in your pocket."

The pawpaw, I later learned, is the largest edible fruit native to the United States and the only nontropical member of the Annonaceae family, which includes the cherimoya. (Contrary to popular assumption, it is no relation of the papaya.) Native Americans are credited with spreading the pawpaw tree from northern Florida to southern Ontario and west to Nebraska; today it thrives in the moist environs of Appalachia and the Ohio Valley. Daniel Boone ate pawpaws as he traveled, as did Lewis and Clark on their journey west.

Until a wide variety of fruits from temperate and tropical climes started becoming available in the 1950s, rural midwesterners consumed the pawpaw fruit straight off the tree or used it to make pies, breads, custards, and even brandy. Then they seemed to forget about it. Fortunately, as regional cooking has grown in popularity, the pawpaw has enjoyed a revival. Now hill folks are again gathering pawpaws in the late summer and fall, and pickup trucks loaded with the fast-ripening fruit speed to the cities, where the cargo is turning into froufrou fare at prestigious restaurants (I have spotted pawpaw rice pudding, pawpaw soufflé, and pawpaw-stuffed French toast on menus.)

And for two years running, in the rumpled hills of southeastern Ohio, pawpaw fanciers have held a festival to showcase ways of using the fruit. Past stunners have included old-fashioned pawpaw breads and pies, ice cream, and an Appalachian version of lassi, an Indian yogurt traditionally made with banana or mango, but here using America's own "tropical" fruit, the pawpaw.

17

TIBETAN NEW YEAR CELEBRATION

AN ORANGE-YELLOW MOON ROSE GIBBOUS THROUGH THE ganglia of trees, floating beside the spired-white Buddhist stupa as I turned into the Tibetan Cultural Center. Behind me, the western horizon was still burning with the last red embers of the setting sun, silhouetting the people walking towards the Tibetan-style building. It was the Losar celebration, Tibetan New Year, and the Cultural Center was ablaze with light.

To commemorate the Year of the Fire Ox, the Center organized a February 22 dinner and concert by the 1960s avatar Richie Havens. The crowd was a mixture of scholars and renegades, devotees and wannabes, curious town folk and burr-headed monks draped in maroon robes. Smiling Tibetan ladies in traditional dress nodded to aging hipsters in faded jeans, Indian print skirts, and little Chinese slippers. Graying ponytails, grizzled beards, and artistically waxed moustaches gave the gathering the air of an obscure colonial regimental reunion, an amalgam of fiercely held memory and wildly imagined faith.

The line for the buffet dinner snaked through the hall, an architectural memory of the great debating halls of the Himalayan monasteries, where monks endlessly debated the sutras. A frieze painted in the style of Tibetan brocade banners ringed the ceiling above the portrait of the Dalai Lama festooned with katas, silk offering scarves. Large murals painted in jeweled colors of pale turquoise, lapis, coral, and gold decorated the walls, with fearsome and beneficent deities peering down on the hungry crowd. A small altar on the south wall flickered with the tiny lights of two butter lamps.

The food was a far cry from the everyday cuisine of the Tibetan plateau—roasted barley, salted yak butter tea, and rock-hard yak cheese tasting of cask-aged acetone. This was Asian holiday fare of the highest order for carnivores and vegetarians alike: fruit and-vegetable salads, ping, a rice thread noodle and vegetable dish, rogan beef made with peas, spicy Himalayan potatoes, noodles with chicken, and a chickpea stew. Thai, Vietnamese, and Indian flavors mingled with the ubiquitous Tibetan *momos,* boiled and filled dumplings that are the comfort food of Tibetans everywhere, eaten with an incendiary dipping sauce.

"Freedom!" Professor Thubten Norbu called out at the end of his invocation, the deeply held goal of the Tibetan communities. The Center is a locus of constant political activity—boycotts and marches and letter-writing campaigns, incessant lobbying, and speeches—seeking to ameliorate the repressive Chinese rule and return Tibet to a self- governed state. There is hope among the Tibetans that the death of Deng Xiaoping, one of the architects of the Tibetan oppression, will liberalize Peking's policies towards China's minority areas.

The Center also serves as a repository of traditional Tibetan culture and stages periodic concerts and lectures for the larger community. Last July, Norbu's younger brother, the Dalai Lama, visited Bloomington to lay the cornerstone for the Tsong Kha sanctuary, an international Buddhist temple and monastery that will expand the religious teaching and retreats that are the Center's primary focus.

The moon was a smiling white face hovering over the enormous stupa as the sated celebrators emerged from the hall for an amble around the shrine, carrying wands of incense flickering like fireflies in the cold night air. A monk swaddled in his robes murmured guttural Tibetan prayers before a stubbornly smoldering fire with Norbu, who concluded the prayers with a laughing, "Finito," and everyone headed in to hear the evening's entertainment, Havens.

"Come on everyone, pretend it's Woodstock, and scoot up. There's lots of people waiting to get in. Get familiar," the moderator implored. Accordingly, the crowd compressed into a clot of happy campers sitting on the floor waiting for the music.

Havens is a fixture of American music, from the East Coast folk scene through his memorable performance at Woodstock to near-incessant touring. "I've been moving around a lot," he told the audience, "I've been on tour since, oh, December of '67." His stories reflect back on a world of hootenannies and basement coffee shops, big vinyl discs, and people with guitars heading to Greenwich Village from all over the country, coalesces of a culture in change culminating in Woodstock. "Long, Long Road," he sang in a strong voice as familiar as an old blanket, and the crowd was moved to group memory.

He sang the Bob Dylan classic "All Along the Watchtower" in a loping rhythm, a camel canter along the Great Wall. His rendition of the Civil Rights anthem, "The Times They Are a-Changing'" had the calm, patient tempo of an older man who has seen some miles, who knows the inevitability of change, for good and worse. The song left Norbu's face masked in thought.

Billie Holliday's signature tune, "God Save the Child," sounded particularly poignant in this hall of an exiled people, struggling to maintain their remarkable culture. "Been around the world thirty times," Havens said. "Maybe twenty-eight, maybe thirty-one, but around, you know. And not in one country, not one, did the people like their government."

The chords of Havens's classic Woodstock song, "Motherless Child" began to fill the hall, his song of loss and longing, of hope and exultation, a ride from the depths of despair to the aeries of the heavens. "Sometimes I feel like a motherless child/Sometimes I'm an eagle in the air," he sang. "Freedom," he sang, "Freedom." Freedom like a cant, freedom like a promise. Freedom like a possibility, freedom like a certainty. And the crowd sang with him, sang "Freedom" like it was here, sang "Freedom" like it was going to be, sang "Freedom" like they could all see it sailing in the high blue Himalayan sky.

18

LAIR OF THE TURTLE SOUP

A CULINARY TRADITION

I WAS IN THE DEEP SOUTH OF INDIANA, DUBOIS AND SPENCER Counties, on the hunt for authentic turtle soup. For generations, it has been a specialty of the German Catholic communities down there. Packs of men and boys have scoured the stream courses and fields for snapping turtles for a hundred years or more, bringing in the hissing amphibians to fill the giant steaming kettles of the church picnics—three hundred pounds of turtle meat to make four hundred gallons of soup.

The small cafes and bars of the villages and towns take up the slack between the picnics, serving it year round. It is a pungent, dark, thick soup—more a stew, really. Three kinds of meat and a variety of vegetables meld with spices and chilies to form an elixir of gastronomy. No wonder they keep chasing those turtles around.

My trip started in Jasper, the largest town in the area. (Though not necessarily the most important, other towns in the region are quick to point out.) Rivalries are fierce here, some dating back to the warring German principalities that the settlers migrated from in the 1840s. Today, the conflict is mainly restrained to the high school sports arenas and snide comments.

Jasper is a clean, hardworking town, pruned to the Nth degree. The center for the woodworking industry for the state, the town boasts dozens of furniture and cabinet firms that produce work for the international market. Deutsche pride is evident: the town is full of German flags and colors, the streets are strasses, and the fairs are fests. The big restaurant in town is the Schnitzelbank, where there are schooners of beer bigger than your head to wash down the wiener schnitzel.

I headed for a small place, Heichelbech's, reputed to have the best turtle soup in town. It was 8:30 in the morning, and beer-bellied regulars sat at the bar knocking down a few before heading home from the factories with their gimme caps pulled low. Swim-suited lovelies smiled down from the beer banners. A Styrofoam deer head stared fixedly ahead with a broken antler hanging by a thread.

When I inquired about the soup, the bartender warned me. "Now, you know this is mock turtle soup now, don't you? They won't let us serve turtle meat no more."

I was shattered.

He said the Board of Health cracked down in the last few years. No more turtle meat gathered from the wild, so everybody just used chicken and beef. "Even up at Mariah Hill, they used to have a big church supper. They even got them," he said.

I headed south to the more rural areas, where perhaps the long arm of authority had not reached yet. I took the back road through Saint Anthony's to Ferdinand, a meander that swept me into the nineteenth century—rolling hills and fastidious small farms, forested streambeds and hilltops, with each tiny village clustered around an austere church, the steeple piercing the white blue sky. It was scenery that belonged in Bavaria, not Indiana late in the twentieth century.

Ferdinand is a convent town, as restrained and Germanic as you care to find. The trees are as severely cropped as a Junker's flattop. Weeds dare not grow in the immaculate lawns of the tidy brick and blinding-white clapboard houses.

But it was a little looser in Fleig's, the old bar where I hoped to get the real stuff. At 1:30 PM on a Friday, the windowless bar was full of good old boys playing euchre and horse, a local dice game. The players slammed the worn leather dice cup on the table, trying to shake some luck into the ivories. They howled and brayed good-naturedly at one another, their dusty baseball cap bills bobbing like excited ducks. Longneck empties crowded the tables.

I ordered a bowl of soup, red brown, crowded with meat and vegetable. And it tasted good, intense and herby. I asked the bartender, "Turtle meat?" He face fell. "Naw, they don't let us."

I wandered down the road to Saint Meinrad, the archabbey and monastery for this overwhelmingly German-Catholic region. High on a hill above the village, the abbey dominated the landscape. The massive sandstone church and monastery glowed gold in the late afternoon light; verdigrised steeples topped the twin belfries. Cassocked monks quietly trod the forest paths.

But no turtle soup.

The Ohio River at Troy was less than ten miles south, down the small highway that the Germans blazed when they migrated into Indiana in the 1840s. It followed the Anderson River, as pretty a road as you could hope to travel. Forests and fields of young corn and amber-nodding wheat, roadside abloom with day lilies and daisies, clover, and black-eyed Susans. The hay lay in windrows as graphic as a Thomas Hart Benton painting. Where it was gathered, the rolls looked like freshly baked bread.

Down along there, a false-fronted bar appeared, a way station. It was an old, white-clapboard building decorated with an O'Doul's neon sign and a red-and-white beer sign with the bar name in fading letters.

A gray-haired lady in a Mother Hubbard apron bustled from behind the counter and gave me a menu. I asked for turtle soup, although it was not on the menu. When she wrote it down without blinking, I excitedly asked if they still used turtle meat. She glanced up, said, "I just work here," and spun for the kitchen.

I thought I should talk to them before they confused me for an inspector. As I walked to the bar, everyone had their heads down. The owner was a hefty guy with swept-back gray hair that started about an inch and a half from his eyebrows. His pale blue eyes were fixed on his hands that rested on a Lite beer can.

When I told them I was a writer, tracking down real turtle soup, it was as if we switched from a tense black-and-white John Ford bar scene to full color. Everybody smiled, the owner expansively sighed. "Now I don't advertise it, you know. But I sell lots," he said. "People come from all over to buy it, some by the gallon. One guy from Louisville, a salesman, buys ten, fourteen gallons every time he comes."

I asked where he got the turtle meat. "Oh, I buy it from guys around. They want us to use Government inspected turtle meat, but where you gonna find that? Guy from up around Milltown called. He had 500 pounds of snapper in his freezer. So I went up there, said I'd buy it. No, he wanted to keep some, so I bought 222 pounds."

"It's real clean," the owner's buddy offered while he went to get the pickling spice used to flavor the soup. "I help clean them." I asked if the turtles were tough to clean. "No, not really," he said, "We got these big kettles."

I could see my bowl of soup steaming on the table. They shooed me off with an "Eat it while it's hot."

It was like eating a tone bell, the right stuff. A potage of the earth and the creatures that dwelled on it. It was spicy. It was thick. It had what the food writer Bernard Clayton calls "a wild sweetness," the unmistakable addition of Mr. Snapper. It was that ineffable experience of eating real food. I was a happy man.

After a bit, the owner ambled over to see what I thought. I thought I needed to take home a gallon.

Part 4
Artists and Their Craft

A winter vista of Wabash College in Crawfordsville, Indiana, from the 1900s reveals several prominent central-campus structures.

Courtesy of Indiana Historical Society, Indiana Postcard Collection, P 408.

19

THIS RASH ADVENTURE

EZRA POUND AT WABASH COLLEGE

THE WINTER OF 1908 BEGAN WITH STORMS HOWLING ACROSS the Indiana prairie, burying Crawfordsville's stately Wabash College under swales of snow. Not long after yet another blizzard in early February, a distraught twenty-two-year-old professor of Romance languages (and aspiring poet) wrote a jangled letter about losing his job to his father back in Philadelphia:

> Dear Dad
> Have had a bust up. But come out with enough to take me to Europe. Home Saturday or Sunday. Dont let mother get excited.
> Ez.

On the back, he scribbled,

> I guess something that one does not see but something very big & white back of the destinies. Has the turning and the loading of things & this thing & I breath again.lovingly
> E.P.
> In fact you need say nothing to mother till I come.

A few days later he sent another note to his father, this one a touch breezier:

"Have been recalled," he wrote about a reinstatement, but "think I should rather go to ze sunny Italia." And so did the young aesthete. But when the somewhat crestfallen Ezra Pound climbed on board the eastbound train with little more than a few belongings, his Wabash College severance pay, and a severely bruised ego, no one knew he was beginning a journey toward the pantheon of world literature—and an infamous life shadowed by his Indiana scandal.

Pound had arrived at Wabash College barely six months before, in early September 1907, an Eastern dandy just returned from a summer's European tour, his Continental affectations clearly akimbo to the starched sureties of Presbyterian Wabash. He had taken a circuitous route from Philadelphia, traveling the New York Central line through Buffalo, New York; Cleveland, Ohio; and Anderson, Indiana, rather than the direct Pennsylvania Railroad through Indianapolis, almost as though he was putting off his arrival in Indiana as long as possible. En route, he sent a snide note to his parents, "Gee. Talk about 'Rure,' 1 Stone house (i.e. part stone) for the last nine hours . . . corn, corn, corn, or terbakky. . . . And to think we pity the pore ignorant furriner!' Gawrsh, I wont be near as caustic about Yourupeen decadence the next time I see it."

Disembarking at the Big Four Station, Pound headed to Crawfordsville's finest hostelry, the Crawford House, though his meager professorial salary soon had him searching for more affordable lodging. Pound dismissed Crawfordsville as "southish," though the little city of 8,500 billed itself as the "Athens of the Prairie," home to General Lew Wallace, celebrated soldier, diplomat, and author of the best-selling novel, *Ben-Hur: A Tale of the Christ*. Dignified Victorian homes lined the leafy streets and steepled brick churches stood sentinel against the high, domed sky. The *Crawfordsville Journal* crowed about the town's advantages in September 1907 when it published "What Crawfordsville Has," listing among other attributes a country club; stone courthouse; mitten, nail, brick, cigar, and casket factories; four banks; a "modern abbatoir"; twenty-two passenger trains and twenty-four interurban cars daily; telephone, water, and electric light service; a "first class theater"; a Carnegie library with ten thousand volumes; and "Wabash College with nearly three hundred students."

The college was almost seventy-five years old by then—and quite sure of its ethos and values. Founded in 1832 when Crawfordsville had scarcely a hundred houses, the school was staunchly Calvinist in its rectitude, organized by Presbyterian home missionaries to educate young ministers "to furnish the destitute with the preaching of the gospel," as the school's first document read. The school's centennial history, *Wabash College: The First Hundred Years, 1832–1932*, noted, "And through the pulpit and the church press they reiterated the argument for a college where soul and intellect could be trained. They were convinced that only such a measure would save the great Western Country from free-thinkers, atheists, Catholics, and Unitarians."

Wabash College grew into a stolid bastion of mid-nineteenth-century societal norms, educating young men in the established New England college methods. "The traditions of Wabash are, as you are aware, extremely conservative," President George Stockton Burroughs wrote in his 1899 resignation letter, going on to cite the crisis the school faced— enrollment had dropped to 165 men in his last year, the lowest since the Civil War. Things had changed in the dusk of the century. Men now attended high schools rather than the college's "prep" school and burgeoning state universities offered looser entrance requirements, such as foregoing facility in Greek and Latin, as well as offering individualized curricula once the students arrived.

Of course, there was also the issue of coeducation. Beginning with Indiana University in 1868, the state schools had gone co-ed one by one. Even the last midwestern citadels of exclusive male education, such as Beloit, Kenyon, and Illinois Colleges, began admitting women. As the new century dawned, Wabash was a lonely outpost of bachelors, resolutely facing a perilous future.

Athletics pulled Wabash's chestnuts from the fire, so to speak. The new president, Doctor William Patterson Kane, saw college athletics as both an instrument of "moral reformation" and a crackerjack recruiting tool. Soon after his inauguration speech, titled, "The Historic Old Fashioned College: Its Place and Function in the Educational World," Kane evicted the school museum from the old armory and established a gymnasium, replete with basketball hoops, Indian clubs, flying rings, pulley-weight exercisers, and a "German horse." More important to the Wabash legacy, Kane pledged to revivify the college football team that had been moribund since 1896, with a professional coach and a full schedule. In its first game after the four-year hiatus, Wabash beat its nemesis, DePauw, by a 6–0 score. Within a few years, the Wabash Little Giants, as the team came to be known, embarked on a period of extraordinary athletic success, near mythic in the retelling. Beginning in 1904, under the legendary Omaha Indian coach, Francis M. Cayou, Wabash's football team dominated schools their own size, and played the Midwest's strongest teams to a standstill, winning many of the games, barely losing others only after monumental battles. Indiana, Purdue, and Notre Dame fell to the Little Giants. In a series of away games held over eight days, Wabash held the then-mighty teams of Chicago, Illinois, and Northwestern to close scores. On the basketball court, the Wabash team won all of its 1906–07 games, with the 1907–08 team destined to be known as the "Champions of the World" after an unbeaten season that included a national and international tour.

Kane's strategy worked: the athletic successes (along with much-needed curriculum reform) cast a kind of Spartan aura over Wabash, which soon attracted a legion of new students. By early September 1907, when the new Romance Languages professor, Pound, sat down at a desk to register incoming freshman, enrollment had swelled to three hundred men.

Pound cut a foppish figure on campus—a tall, attenuated redhead with his black velvet jacket, soft-collared shirts with flowing bowties, patent-leather pumps, and socks in a jaw-dropping spectrum of purple, orange, lavender, and green. A wide-brimmed panama hat, Malacca cane, and pince-nez that Pound copied from poet W. B. Yeats completed a look that was a sharp departure from the faculty's typical boiled and stiff dignity. Perhaps the contrast contributed to Pound's unease. According to his student, Howard W. Hawk, Pound's initial professorial foray at registration did not go well—after a brief period, he bolted from his desk claiming "severe indigestion" from dealing with "stupid freshmen."

Pound was soon challenging other Wabash mores. In defiance of the college's strict ban on tobacco, smoke from Pound's Bonhommes Rouges cigarillos billowed from under the door of his Central Hall office, located just down the South Wing hall from President George Lewes Mackintosh's office. Student Howard F. Ashby later remembered seeing two or three fellow students smoking in Pound's office with him, "I peeped in and there was Ezra Pound with his feet cocked on his desk and cigarette smoke coming out in clouds." At least once, Mackintosh caught Pound in the act, and threatened dire consequences.

At the compulsory daily chapel, Mackintosh thundered in late September about "drinking and other forms of immorality." Not long after, Mackintosh may have noted the coy reference to his deviant professor in the student paper, *The Wabash:*

> Watch for the faulty end men for stunts!
> Ezra Pounds—Ezra should have been a blacksmith.

The reporter, referencing the blackface "end men" comedians in the vaudeville shows that circuited through Crawfordsville's three theaters, noted the new professor cutting up during chapel, instead of supervising students from his end seat where new faculty sat. The blacksmith comment appeared to have been a clumsy wordplay on Pound's (misspelled) last name.

At Pound's first residence, a Gothic-styled house at 500 Meadow Avenue where he rented a room, he began a cavalier flirtation with the landlord's sister-in-law, Mary Moore Shipman Young, a young widow who was visiting her sister's home. Availing himself of access to the parlor, Pound began entertaining Mary—though he was skating on very thin ice. Mackintosh, a widower in quest of a new wife, also had his eye on her. (Neither ever found favor with Mary—Pound chortled fifty years later that "old Mac" never got the "widdy.") When students began visiting Pound's room until the early hours, it was all too much for the landlord, who suggested in October that Pound find other accommodations.

Pound also proved to be an unconventional teacher, sitting in the class with his rainbow-ankled feet crossed on his desk, reading from his French or Spanish book, now and again dropping it to the floor and issuing "a blasphemous phrase in French" at a flawed student. It was an informal classroom, the students calling their professor, almost their own age, Ezra. There were plenty of laughs. Student Ernest Pegg recalled Pound's formula for pronouncing French: "Wad up a dishrag, stuff it into your mouth and then talk through your nose."

Along with most of the college, Pound took the train to Indianapolis for the climactic football game between the Little Giants and the powerhouse University of Michigan team. Although Wabash lost 22–0, the trip to Indianapolis was a "touch of civilization" for Pound, who felt "stranded in the most Godforsakenest area of the Middle West," as he wrote his friend Bertram Hessler.

Not long after young professor Pound returned from the Wabash-Michigan football game, he moved into a South Washington Street rooming house. Located near the Big Four Station, the place was frequented by students and vaudevillians. Two or three times a week, Pound hosted a "soirée" that began after supper and lasted until the wee hours. There was smoking and more than a modicum of forbidden drinking. Harold Hawk, a student in Pound's French class, recalled beer, "a little vino," and Curaçao, "when we were 'flush.'" Pound read Blake, Donne, and his own poetry, discoursing—often in colorful language—on art, religion and the perfidy of straitlaced attitudes. In an institution that upheld a strict view of theology, Pound told his listeners, "Religion I have defined as 'Another of those numerous failures resulting from an attempt to popularize art.'" Hawk wrote, "All of us were in rebellion, in one way or another, against the stiff Presbyterian conformism and conventional morality of the town."

Rumors began to circulate about Pound. Beyond the drinking and smoking and general rebellion, some said he frequented the "Goose Nibble" girls, who lived across the tracks in the so-named poor section of town and reputedly bestowed favors on Wabash bachelors; others murmured of inappropriate relations with his students. People laughed about Pound's propensity to show up at friends' houses asking to bathe. Even his cooking arrangements were held up to scrutiny: Pound's use of a chafing dish to cook his meals was considered suspect. They talked about his graceful, flowing strides that Pound contended were essential to his philosophy of "Rhythmetics" and the "full circle of living," as he made long cross-country walks to Crawford's Woods and Sugar Creek. Late one night Pound and a student hiked to the graveyard, where they leaned against Wallace's monument and "discussed of Earth and other 'great and ghostly matters.'" James Insley Osborne, a professor who later wrote the Wabash College history, told of Pound pausing on a campus constitutional to tell him, "The most beautiful thing that the mind of man can conceive is a strawberry in the bowl of a spoon—covered in olive oil." Osborne thought Pound insane.

Flaunting bohemian mannerisms better suited to Paris's Latin Quarter than Crawfordsville, Pound seemed nonplussed by the rumors. He wrote Hessler that he had "a crying need ... for mere degenerate civilization as represented by cocktails, chartreuse and kissable girls." Wont to top off his tea with tots of rum while visiting proper Crawfordsville ladies, Pound quickly hid his flask if a faculty wife passed nearly. "The natives would never approve my Continental appetite," he told his friend, Viola Baylis.

Pound's nonconforming ways were soon to cause him grief. He had made friends with a British woman who lived in his rooming house. She was a touring actress who presented a monocled and tuxedoed male impersonator act in vaudeville burlesque shows. She was stranded in Crawfordsville, as the burlesque audiences evidently failed to appreciate her "toff" act—too "subtle" for the Hoosiers, Pound sniffed. He generously shared his coffee and food with the young woman, an act of charity some found unseemly.

In mid-November, Pound wrote a flustered note to Hessler: "Two stewdents found me sharing my meagre repast with the lady-gent impersonator in my privut apartments. Keep it dark and find me a soft immoral place to light in when the she-faculty-wives git ahold of the jewcy morsel. Don't write home to me folks. I can prove an alibi from 8 to 12 p.m. and am at present looking for rooms with a minister or some well established member of the facultate. For this house come all the traveling show folk and must hie me to a nunnery ere I disrupt the college. Already one delegation of about-to-flunks have awaited on the president erbout me orful langwidge and the number of cigarillos I consume." Terming Indiana "the sixth circle of hell," Pound told Hessler he expected the administration would discipline him for entertaining actresses.

Fleeing the scene of the scandal, Pound failed to take to a nunnery, but came pretty close, renting a room across from the campus at 412 South Grant Avenue, an upright two-story clapboard house owned by the Misses Ida and Belle Hall, two of Crawfordsville's most reputable citizens. Tall and prim, the Hall sisters were self-appointed moral guardians, confidents of Mackintosh, and near de facto members of Wabash's board of trustees. Pound was moving into the room previously occupied by Professor Henry Zwingli McLain, a beloved Greek teacher and confirmed bachelor, who devoted his life to classics and the college. The previous January "Dear Zwingli," as he was known, had suffered a fatal hemorrhage while in his church pew—in the view of his admirers, a perfect end to a faultless life. Pound could not have found more respectable lodgings.

But the Hall sisters were in for a change from "dear Zwingli." Pound was, at best, an informal housekeeper. Student John A. Bays recalled, "About the room there were scattered on the floor, piled on chairs or on the bed or in the corners clothing, shoes, shirts, underwear, extra suits, hats, etc. No pictures on the walls, one chair, his bed and sometimes a wooden box. Single-burner stove often on the floor. Student written exercises, exam papers and the like were usually visible in the wastebasket or on the floor near the basket."

Pound continued his soirées. Wabash graduate Fred H. Rhodes recalled, "After the preliminary formalities, Pound seated himself on a chair, while his disciples and satellites disposed themselves gracefully, but somewhat uncomfortably, cross-legged on the floor, at the feet of the master. The leader then began a spirited but disconnected discourse on many topics leaping from subject to subject with the agility of a mountain goat."

Although Pound had made friends of sorts with students, a few locals, and a few select faculty members, he was increasingly hungry to find a community of like-minded aesthetes. The poetry he wrote in Crawfordsville spoke of his yearnings. In his long poem, "Quia Amore Langueo," he begged to be released from his dreams of cosmopolitan Europe, "I bid thee come where the west winds blow ... And forget the world and old world pain." His poem, "Cino," cried out for a wandering life far from small-minded fetters:

> Bah! U have sung women in three cities,
> But it is all the same;
> And I will sing of the sun.

But his Crawfordsville poem, "In Durance," titled after the Middle English word for imprisonment, spoke most poignantly of his longing:

> For I am homesick after mine own kind
> And ordinary people touch me not.

Yea, I am homesick
After mine own kind that know, and feel
And have some breath for beauty and the arts.
Aye, I am wistful for my kin of the spirit
And have none about me save in the shadows.

Ensconced in the Hall sisters' house, Pound made it through the fall term that ended on December 20 without further problems. He spent the Christmas holidays in Crawfordsville, as he did Thanksgiving, when his holiday dinner was some oysters fried in his chafing dish.

By the time the winter term opened on January 7, 1908, the weather began to shift, snowstorms and blizzards commencing on the tenth. With students back in town and the locals done with their holiday gatherings, Crawfordville's three vaudeville theaters booked full bills through mid-month. For the month's lead-off acts, the Majestic offered Alice B. Hamilton, Character Singing Commedienne, and Annette Link, Soubrette, switching to Maudie Minerva's Novelty Act, and Emmett and McNeil, The Singing and Dancing Sisters, for the week of January 13–18. The Grand countered with Burk and Erline, Automobile Girls, while the Music Hall had the Latimore-Leigh Stock Company's High Class Vaudeville. After Pound's long, lonely holiday, the town was perking with vivacious outsiders.

Early in February, the college's student newspaper coyly sprinkled five one-line notices in its "Local" column, amidst reports on the Glee Club, new dogs, Bible Studies, and Wabash students helping quell a Muncie car strike riot:

Ezra was not at chapel on Jan 13.
Ezra was not at chapel on Jan 14.
Ezra was not at chapel on Jan. 15.
Ezra was not at chapel on Jan. 16.
Ezra was not at chapel on Jan. 17.

Coincidence, rebellion, exhaustion, illness—Pound's reasons for missing chapel are lost to history, but the point remains, in a very public way, he was defying one of the college's most adamantine traditions.

Within a few weeks, the college made its final judgment: Pound was gone. A February 15 *Crawfordsville Journal* headline read, "Prof. Ezra Pound Leaves," going on to report, "Prof. Ezra Pound, instructor of Romance Languages in Wabash College, has resigned his position and left yesterday for his home ina [*sic*] Philadelphia."

The retelling of Pound's decisive incident has always been subject to smirks or outrage, depending on the view of the observer, but the denouement seems clear. Late one February night, during yet another blizzard, Pound walked down to the Big Four Station to mail a letter, the night train being the last post available. While trudging back, he encountered the vaudeville actress he befriended at his previous rooming house. She was again down on her luck, stranded in Crawfordsville after her burlesque show had gone bust. It was cold; she was frozen. Pound offered her shelter in the Hall sisters' house, where the actress slept in his bed.

The next morning he had breakfast with the woman, and then left for his 8:00 A M class. And then things got interesting. As the college historians delicately recounted it in *Wabash College: The First Hundred Years,* "The ladies from whom he rented the rooms, the Misses Hall, went upstairs to make the bed and found in it the girl from burlesque. Their only experience with roomers was with Professor McLain. This confrontation bewildered them. They telephoned the President, and a trustee or two."

Not surprisingly, the college authorities called Pound on the carpet for his grave moral lapse. But the complicating factor was that Pound did not sleep with the actress—or even in the same room. He spent the night shivering in his office, with only a coat for a blanket. Afraid of attracting the night watchman, he did not even turn on the light to read. During what the college history termed "a discussion at distinctly cross purposes," Pound stood his ground with the administration. Several of his Crawfordsville friends attempted to intercede with Mackintosh, repeating Pound's "orphan in the storm" story. It bore fruit. Faced with what appeared to be a case of mistaken immorality (though yet another example of Pound's extraordinarily immature judgment), the Wabash elders reversed their decision to fire him. But faced with a recalcitrant firebrand (Pound reportedly told the board "To Go to Hell"), the administration cashiered its controversial faculty member.

Embittered by his experience, Pound never reconciled with academia. Pound wrote William Carlos Williams in October 1908, "Again, if you ever get degraded, branded with infamy, etc., for feeding a person who needs food, you will probably rise up and bless the present and sacred name of Madame Grundy for all her holy hypocrisy. I am not getting bitter. . . . I am amused. The smile is kindly but entirely undiluted with reverence." Pound's poetry just after his dismissal reflected his dismay: "O heart o'me. / Heart o'all that is true in me / Beat again," read "The Rune." Another anguished, "Heart-slain, / Head-tortured, wracked of the endless strain," while another line implored, "Old powers rise and do return to me."

After Wabash fired him, Pound's life got better—or at least more interesting. With his severance pay from Wabash, Pound sailed to Europe in 1908. After a brief period in Venice, he moved to London in hopes of meeting his great literary hero, Yeats. Befriending Yeats, Pound was soon employed as the poet's secretary. Fleeing World War I zeppelin attacks on London, Yeats and Pound rented the famous Stone Cottage in Sussex's Ashdown Forest, where the two of them studied Japanese Noh plays, dabbled with the occult, and, over three winters, revolutionized poetry. It is said that literary Modernism began in the Stone Cottage.

Along with friends such as Yeats, James Joyce, and T. S. Eliot, Pound was a driving force in a number of Modernist movements, including Imagism and Vorticism, which introduced, among others, William Carlos Williams (Pound's college roommate), Marianne Moore, Rabindranath Tagore, and Robert Frost. To his undying credit, Pound edited Eliot's *The Waste Land,* the first Modernist poem to capture a popular audience. In gratitude, Eliot dedicated the poem to Pound, as *il miglior fabbro* (the better craftsman).

In 1915 Pound published *Cathay,* a groundbreaking translation of ancient Chinese poets. Disdaining the strict meter and stanza of earlier translators, Pound cantered off into free verse translations, which still stand as some of the most poetic renderings of the classic texts. Pound eventually translated texts of ten different languages into English.

After World War I, Pound joined the Modernist avant-garde in Paris, where he hobnobbed with Joyce, Marcel Duchamp, and Fernand Leger, while continuing to write his masterwork, *The Cantos.* Married to novelist Olivia Shakespear in 1914, Pound became involved with violinist Olga Rudge seven years later, forming a ménage à trois that persisted to the end of his life.

In 1919 Pound began to compose concertos and operas, and, after moving to Italy in 1924, organized the Rapallo music festival, which revived the forgotten Antonio Vivaldi's music. Pound made important contribution to literary criticism, championing the role of imagination in what he saw as a gray world of academic poetry.

It was also in Italy that Pound achieved his lasting infamy. Enamored with Benito Mussolini's fascism, Pound became a leading Axis propagandist, which climaxed with his arrest for treason in May 1945. After being incarcerated in an open cage in Pisa for twenty-five days, Pound suffered a nervous breakdown. His groundbreaking *Pisan Cantos*, written during his imprisonment about his own desolation amidst Europe's ruin, won the Library of Congress's first Bollingen Prize in 1949.

By then, Pound had been an inmate of Saint Elizabeths Hospital in Washington, D.C., for three years, after pleading insanity at his treason trial—theoretically sparing him the death sentence. The mental institution proved to be a productive venue for Pound—he wrote three books while entertaining a string of visitors, from poets and academicians to the States' Rights Democratic Party chairman, who conferred with Pound about preserving racial segregation. Pound remained sequestered in the mental hospital until 1958, when he was released as "incurably insane, but not dangerous to others." Emerging from Saint Elizabeths, Pound famously decreed, "America is a lunatic asylum."

Pound never reconciled with universities, fulminating to his friend Harriet Monroe, in 1917, "I wish I could get you roused on the meaning of the American university and the menace of it." In 1933 he railed about university teaching, "I don't say Crawfordsville didn't cram on hours of misery, but nowt unbearable. . . . The irritation of fools won't come from stewddents *but* from the 'orthorities.'" But the most telling comment is the note he wrote from Saint Elizabeths to biographer Patricia Hutchins on February 8, 1958: "Must be fifty years to about a day, possibly exact, that I sailed from N.Y. toward Venice, the k-rear as a prof in the corn belt ended in smoak/ and DEEE-spair of the future, etc."

The rise of Pound's star in the years following his dismissal left Wabash College with an awkward situation, as the firing became emblematic of academic priggishness in certain intellectual circles that persists to this day. Pound biographer J. J. Wilhelm wrote, "To some people, the very name 'Wabash College' has become synonymous with provincial prudery." The college history, published in 1932, attempted the best spin. The historians wrote of the school's administrators, "But they were aware

too, from the accumulated evidence of several months, of a gulf too wide
to be bridged between two different philosophies. And they were content to use the occasion to make an arrangement about their contract
that encouraged Mr. Pound to shake the dust of a small middle-western
Presbyterian college forever from his feet and content to rejoice in his
subsequent triumphs in poetry."

By the 1950s, the Pound affair was legendary at Wabash. The poet
would have chortled if he saw the disparaging reference by Byron K.
Trippet (Wabash president from 1955 to 1965) to "the prim Hall sisters
precipitating the firing of Ezra Pound from the faculty." After the Hall
sisters house was demolished, Wabash preserved the gray and white pan-
eled door to Pound's room in the college archives, the record reading,
"As a footnote to literary history, in February of 1908, Ezra Pound entertained one of the performers from a 'stranded burlesque show, penniless
and suffering from the cold.'" But the vagary of history is equally cold:
Not too many years ago a maintenance man, unfamiliar with the old
door's infamy, threw it out.

When Pound was released from Saint Elizabeths in 1958, a gifted
Wabash sophomore, James Rader, decided to write about the Pound
incident for the college literary journal, *The Bachelor*. In the course of
his exhaustive research, Rader contacted Pound, as well as men who
attended Wabash during 1907–08 terms. Pound and sixty ex-students
provided their memories of the event, which Pound called "high comedy
in Indiana." Perhaps former Wabash student John Macy summarized
the affair best: "I think the general feeling of the students was one of
some admiration for his exploit. We knew it was foolish, and that he had
to go, but felt that he deserved our applause, and rather envied this rash
adventure."

20

EROTICA WHOSE PURPOSE
WAS SCHOLARLY

KINSEY INSTITUTE ART EXHIBIT

TWO ELDERLY WOMEN PRESSED THEIR NOSES TO THE DISPLAY case of erect Japanese phallus fetishes while students peered at photographs of copulating couples and glistening musclemen in classical poses. Tattoo art of a naked woman grappling with a cobra and posters from stag movies such as *I Want More* and *Jungle Virgin* shared the gallery walls with a Matisse odalisque and a Rembrandt boudoir scene.

A security guard idly perused the entangled nude figures in Pablo Picasso's *Man and Woman*. A wall label next to the painting read: "When asked to distinguish between art and eroticism near the end of his career, Picasso said, 'But there is no difference.'"

The works are part of *The Art of Desire: The Erotic Treasures from the Kinsey Institute,* an exhibition here that celebrates the fiftieth anniversary of the Kinsey Institute for Research in Sex, Gender and Reproduction. It is the first comprehensive show of the institute's erotic art, a collection that spans 3,200 years as well as the globe, ranging from folk art to Old Masters to the amatory works of amateur photographers.

The collection is composed entirely of donations, many from Doctor Alfred Kinsey's contacts with postal, customs, and prison authorities, who had confiscated some of the materials on display. The 75,000 photographs in the collection include a trove from the nineteenth and early twentieth century, some of them on postcards. Others were taken as part of research; there are pictures of swimming sperm, for example, and copulating elephants. All are catalogued with the scholars' arid code (for example, FIG NUDE XG SIT HND ABV translates as "female figure, nude, genitals covered, sitting, hand above waist").

The 200-plus works on view reflect the range and ubiquity of sexual themes in human culture since ancient Egypt. Academic art commingles with the unschooled—elegant etchings and pristine prints by George Platt Lynes alongside "Tijuana Bibles," comic books depicting characters such as Popeye and Olive Oyl in anatomically unlikely situations. Condoms embellished with motifs such as waving red hands and heads with cowboy hats are preserved in test tubes.

The show is attracting a cross section of the public: students and teachers, women's groups, Hoosiers from the surrounding hills who seldom visit the campus, and older people who knew the Kinseys, revered figures in the community. "They're really packing in here," said Betsy Stirratt, the gallery director and cocurator of the show. "I've never seen people look at a show so intently. They get so close to the cases, it takes a lot of cleaning every day."

In mining the institute's erotica for material, the curators had to be sure it fell within the standards of decency of this university town, tolerant though it is. Given the mass of art, the chore was like "Hercules cleaning out the stables," said Sarah Burns, a cocurator of the show.

The result is decorous. The show depicts beauty, humor, and fantasy that appeal to both sexes and sexual orientations while eschewing the borderlands of violence, pedophilia, or zoophilia. "No animals, no nuns," Stirratt said. "We wanted this to be a positive show, kind of 'up with sex.'"

The exhibit represents a new, more public profile for the Kinsey Institute even as it has come under attack. Last month, a conservative group, the Concerned Women of America, picketed the institute's offices, protesting research findings. And a recent biography, *Alfred C. Kinsey: A Public/Private Life,* presents Kinsey as a pervert, a portrayal that the institute has condemned as a distortion.

"So far we've had no negative responses about the exhibit," said John Bancroft, the director of the Kinsey Institute. "We recognize the need to make the institute more open. We want people to know as much as they can. After all, demystification is very much the name of the game."

21

GARGOYLES AND OTHER CURIOUS CREATURES

A PAGAN CREATURE OVERSEES THE OLD CRESCENT IN THE limestone heart of Indiana University's Bloomington campus, perched on the apex of stately Maxwell Hall, as he has since the hall was built in 1890. Generations of students have scurried under his gaze, spooned in the Well House, wandered the woods, peering up to see a cat-eared, four-legged bat with a somewhat incredulous look, sitting bolt upright with a stone shield that reads "IU."

Up north, in the more ecclesiastic environs of the University of Notre Dame, another winged creature of confused physiognomy sticks out his tongue at the adjoining Law School—perhaps the stone incarnation of a lawsuit-bedeviled doctor. He leans out from the corner of Alumni Hall, leering pop-eyed at the budding barristers. Not too far away, a trio of horned guys put their heads in their hands and await unsuspecting pass-ersby. When an innocent approaches, a cohort in the building is likely to turn on a faucet, and spray the person below, normally to the guffaws of the companions that steered them there.

In the leafy resort town of Monticello, Indiana, the keystone of the old White County Courthouse sits on a pedestal in the midst of the quiet town. A fearsome human face emerges from a thicket of leaves and viands—verily the foliage grows directly from his face, like an eco-horror movie, "Plant Man! Gardener Gone Wild!" In Indianapolis the same visage watches the traffic at the corner of Michigan and Vermont Streets, a bit of anthropomorphic greenery in the most urban of settings.

Dwarves cackle from building fronts, gnomes leer at us, winged lions roar from our roof tops, and furred cat-footed dragons loom over our heads. What are these creatures? Why do they frighten us as children and delight us as adults? What is the resonance between ourselves and the carved creatures that inhabit our stone buildings all over the Western world?

Gargoyles have been around since twelfth-century France. From every medieval cathedral, a lineup of macabre creatures stretched out their long necks to spit and splutter water from the sacred environs out into the profane precincts that surrounded them. Initially, gargoyles were only waterspouts to protect the vulnerable masonry walls. The word gargoyle derives from *gargula,* the Latin word for throat, sliding into French as *gargariser*—to gargle. Rarely were gargoyles found alone. Rather gaggles and clutches of the stone creatures leaned out together, sociable monstrosities ringing the perimeter of the church.

The grotesque carvings' origins reach back into the layered ambiguities of the medieval mind, back even to northern Europe's pre-Christian days, when the old pagan gods sparred with the new monotheism from the Middle East that increasingly dominated the Latin world. Gargoyles (or grotesques as they are known when their waterspout function is replaced by more modern drainage systems) reflect the envelopment of pagan gods into the Christian panoply, a transition that began in northern Europe in the seventh century.

Just as pagan holidays became Christian, and pagan gods metamorphosed into Christian saints of hazy origins, pagan imagery became part of the Christian cathedrals, harnessed to help protect the church, in this case as monstrous waterspouts, glaring down from their heights, channeling pagan evil into Christian uses, and keeping evil at bay. Some say they represented the fate of damned souls—the demons that would devour the transgressors. Frogs grasp the face of loose women as a warning of the dangers of licentiousness. Wolfmen speak of the nearness of our base natures—morality plays in stone. Others speak of the gargoyles and grotesques as symbols of the evil forces that lurk outside the church. In some instances, the gargoyles are seen as benign creatures. The famous gargoyles of Paris's Notre Dame Cathedral, for example, are said to watch out for those drowning in the Seine River.

The initial twelfth-century representations were the most bizarre and frightening. By a century later, the gargoyles are more exaggerated and elongated. By the fifteenth century, gargoyles were less demonic, encompassing human and animal forms in wildly divergent aggregates: winged hippos and duck-headed dragons with lion bodies and lizard tails, snarling winged dogs with lion tails, humans with animal paws, and caricatured stone people retching and defecating rainwater from the church roofs.

These surreal assemblages portrayed the richness of God's diversity, as well as the perversity of the natural order—the potential for ugliness and disorder outside of the authority of the church. Naturally, they also express the fertility of human imagination and creativity, responding to the fascination with the unreal and monstrous.

The image of the man's head emerging from foliage is one of the most potent and enduring of the pre-Christian images. Known as Green Man or Jack-in-the-Green, the effigy is a symbol of nature, fertility, and rebirth—man inextricably part of nature, as intertwined as the branches and vines that emerge for the Green Man's mouth and nose. It speaks of old gods, tree worship, and sacred springs. Celtic in origin, the Green Man is testimony in stone to the severed human heads that hung outside the doorways of Celtic homes from the Black Sea to the Atlantic, the Mediterranean to the Baltic. The Celts were headhunters, and that quirky guy that watches you from the parapets is the memory in stone.

Carved into soft stone with chisel, mallet, file, and calipers, gargoyles and grotesques were deeply undercut for shadowing to highlight features designed to be viewed from far below. Originally they were brightly painted in orange, red, and green, but time has worn away the colors as well as the intensity of their features. So, our modern sensibilities find gargoyles most authentic and appropriate in their unadorned stone state, just the dusty faded remnants of Colonial hues became synonymous with tasteful decorating rather than the garish colors the Colonials actually used.

Stone carvers are still carving grotesques today. Trendy shops in Manhattan sell them, carvers have websites. Dating back to early in the nineteenth century, the Journeyman Stonecutters Association of North America is the oldest, smallest, active union in the United States and an outgrowth of the ancient masons guilds of the Middle Ages. Even at the turn of the century, a skilled stone carver was paid the equivalent of a doctor or lawyer. As late as the 1920s, architectural ornamentation was 4 percent to 5 percent of the building's budget, a far cry from the 1 percent in our spare, stripped-down times. Pneumatic chisels may have replaced hand tools, and customers perusing websites may have replaced clergy in the cathedral stone yards, but the aesthetics remain remarkably constant.

There are more than a dozen active stone carvers in the state, working on a variety of forms, gargoyles among them. Bybee Stone Company in Ellettsville, Indiana, has seven carvers working on grotesques among the other stone work that comes their way. Last year they produced forty grotesques for the law school at Washington University in Saint Louis, including a fox, a justice figure with her eyes veiled, and somewhat incongruously, a woman wielding a clothes iron. Currently they are working on a lion for the Anderson College Fine Arts Building.

Bill Galloway is considered one of the foremost carvers in the country today, working out of Nashville, Indiana. His carvings are scattered all over the country, from the National Cathedral in Washington, D.C., to Evander Holyfield's house. "It is a very tiny clientele," Galloway said, "basically governments, states, churches, and very affluent people." He uses a variety of tools on the Indiana Standard Buff limestone he gets from Bedford and Oolitic, from power rotary and pneumatic chisels to a traditional mallet. "Whatever is needed," he said.

Much of his work goes to the Fertile Crescent, an area from Chicago to New York and Washington, D.C., where the majority of the public buildings are clad in limestone wrested from the twenty- by sixty-mile Stone Belt of southern Indiana. Indiana Standard Buff is specified in government contracts because it is vital for additions and repairs and critical for new buildings that want to blend into the architectural fabric of a place. But one piece of Galloway's has stayed home in Indiana. On the roof of his Brown County house, a compact grotesque clings to his chimney, a piece carved in the style of the thirteenth-century Notre Dame gargoyles.

Gargoyles and grotesques are scattered all over Indiana. A pair of gnomes clutch books alongside the front doors of the Marion County library on East Washington Street. A lion glares from the old Hippodrome Theater in Terre Haute. The stone Wells County courthouse in Bluffton is a veritable gathering of the creatures. Grotesque dwarves howl their disdain from yet another building on the Notre Dame campus. Faces peek from the county courthouse in Princeton. Gargoyles lurk on the NBD Bank in Corydon. On the Monastery of the Immaculate Conception in Ferdinand, four heads emerge from the church wall: an eagle, a man, an ox, and a lion, all four of which sprout eagle wings, representing the four evangelists—Matthew, Mark, Luke, and John, another set of polymorphs ready to lift off.

Just as the medieval church was the collective storehouse of archetypal memory, with elements of the shared subconscious hanging from the roof lines, the grotesques that surround us today tickle our connection to the enchanted environs outside our conventional boxes. They pulse with the ambiguity of a spirit-crowded place, and remind us that there are other gods and other ways of thinking, and that the world is not always what it appears to be.

$\mathscr{22}$

CROSSROADS OF
AMERICAN SCULPTURE

IN THE FALL OF 1954, AN INDIANA-BORN METAL SCULPTOR known for his intensity arrived to teach at Indiana University in Bloomington. The art world had already noticed David Smith. He had mounted several shows of his iconic abstractions and received favorable notices, including a glowing report from Clement Greenberg in *The Nation*. Smith had widely defended the tenets of abstract art in speech and print, taught at the University of Arkansas and Sarah Lawrence, and garnered two Guggenheim Fellowships.

Still, he was low man on the totem pole when he arrived in Bloomington, and the art department assigned him the studio of a professor on sabbatical. Smith remarked: "A few years ago when I taught at Indiana University I had to take another sculptor's studio. . . . It was a hell of a mess when I walked in there, and I didn't know what to do, so I started picking up things that he left behind." In the process, the detritus morphed into another of Smith's abstract sculptures, the oddly anthropomorphic assemblage, *Sitting Printer.*

Smith later deconstructed the sculpture for an art magazine. "This is the top of the broken stool—here's the stool—I had to cast those things—I had to change them a little bit to cast them," he noted. "This is an old type box from a print shop—this is the center part of a chair—a straight-back professor's chair—a classroom chair. The first thing I did was make a sculpture of them, and sent them out and had them cast, and welded up a sculpture. That's all the aesthetics involved in that, outside of personal choice; but it is the first pile of junk I walked in when I came there, before I cleaned the studio."

And that is the way it went for an extraordinary band of post-World War II Indiana-born sculptors—among them Smith, now generally considered America's greatest sculptor; kinetic sculptor George Rickey; pop artists John Chamberlain and Robert Indiana; and post-modern artists William Wiley and Bruce Nauman—who picked up the shards and discards of America's amalgamation culture and forged wholly new traditions out of the bits and pieces.

"It occurred to me there were these six great sculptors who all came from Indiana," Indianapolis Museum of Art senior curator of contemporary art Holliday Day said, "and it struck me those six men gave you an excellent overview of the ideas of sculpture in the last fifty years." The result of Day's inspiration is the Indianapolis Museum of Art's *Crossroads of American Sculpture* exhibit, which will run from October 14, 2000, to January 21, 2001. There will be more than a hundred pieces of groundbreaking art in the twelve thousand square feet that comprise the Allen Whitehill Clowes Special Exhibition Gallery. The exhibit will explore the work of these seminal artists who share an Indiana birthplace and a revolutionary mindset that redefined the interplay between art and culture.

Day writes in the catalogue that the crossroads theme was chosen for several reasons: "First, we felt the name related to the crossroads of ideas that were shared by these artists, representing three generations of sculptors. Second, our research shows that in addition to being born in Indiana, which is known as the Crossroads of America, various artists worked together as friends or had a student-teacher relationship—their paths literally crossed. Third, this major exhibition is occurring as one of the IMA's first exhibitions of the new millennium, a kind of crossroads of time." The *Crossroads of American Sculpture* show provides six mini-retrospectives of the artists' work, while also mapping several diverse confluences of twentieth-century sculptural ideas. The sculptures range in size from Smith's ten-foot-high *Zig II* and *Gubi I*, and Wiley's massive *Nomad is an Island,* to works less than two feet high. The materials run the gamut from caveman to cyberpunk—wood, bronze, iron, steel, neon, video, performance, and beyond.

This exhibit of art from twenty-one museums and a multitude of private collections is a rare opportunity to view the artists' creative processes. "Not only will we present sculptures, but we will also present drawings by the artists," Day said. "We believe this exploration of the creative process will be interesting to both the visitor who is viewing contemporary art for the first time as well as to the more experienced visitors." Her face lights up as she added, "This show captures the essence of America."

DAVID SMITH

America's greatest known sculptor was born in 1906 in the small northeast Indiana town of Decatur to a telephone company worker and a church-obsessed teacher. He was a descendant of Indiana pioneers, a fact he later touted as part of his success: "Smith took solace that he came from tough stock. His pioneer predecessors went without food; he was an artist during the Depression."

Smith was always an independent spirit. He recalled his first art at age three: a roaring mud lion crafted to protest being tethered to a backyard tree to prevent wandering. When Smith was fifteen years old, the family moved across the Ohio border to Pauling, where Smith achieved local fame as a high school cartoonist and amateur thespian before attending Ohio University in Athens for two undistinguished semesters. The following summer he traveled back to the Hoosier State, spending the summer working in South Bend's sprawling Studebaker plant, where he first developed his affinity for a workingman's ethos and the industrial metalworking techniques that were to become his life's work. "I know workmen, their vision, because between college years I have worked on the Studebaker production line," he later told an interviewer.

Through the immensely productive decades that followed, Smith maintained an intense work pace, a ferocious energy, and his metalworkers' union card. A thick-handed man with a brooding face topped by a cloth workman's cap, he was forever laboring on his totems and figures, planes and forms that reached out to embrace the landscape. Painter and close friend Robert Motherwell said Smith was "as delicate as Vivaldi and as strong as a Mack truck."

Critic Clement Greenberg wrote about Smith, "By the early 1950s he had already done enough to make him the best sculptor of his generation anywhere, and had he stopped then and taken to repeating himself, his achievement would still have been enough to ensure him an important place in the art of our time. But far from stopping or falling off, his art renewed itself in those years as if to answer whatever questions about it remained."

Smith's *Forging* series, stark sculptures that celebrated the chance art of an electric trip hammer, and in the process elevated industrial austerity to a raw rare beauty, were primarily done during his sojourn at IU—ten sculptures in four months, plus five or six others. Smith's noted sculpture, *History of Leroy Borton,* now in the Museum of Modern Art's permanent collection, memorializes the Bloomington metal worker who let Smith use his industrial trip hammer.

GEORGE RICKEY

The master of minimalist kinetic sculpture, Rickey was born in 1907 in South Bend, Indiana. While he spent most of his student years in Great Britain, he returned to the United States in the 1930s. While studying at the Chicago School of Design, Rickey was inspired by Moholy-Nagy's radical ideas about kinetic sculpture. Rickey began developing his own ideas of kinetic sculpture while teaching at IU from 1948 to 1954, the beginning of a lifelong quest to explore the elusive principles of the universe that express, in his words, "the morphology of movement."

Rickey was the one most likely responsible for Smith's visiting professor contract, an example of the creative loops and pairings of the six *Crossroads* sculptors. In fact, Smith gave Rickey his one and only welding lesson. While the two shared a mutual friendship and respect, their work took different roads.

Rickey's characteristic sculptures are finely tuned stainless steel expressions of a delicate and subdued aesthetic, often-spindly whirligigs or exquisitely wrought blades riding the ephemera of movement and air current. Rickey writes, "Man loves what lives and moves and renews its being, and loves to make such things if he can—whether with a green thumb or a pair of pliers. If one makes a moving thing one is always surprised, no matter what preconceived the design, at the movement itself. It seems to come from somewhere else—the planting or the pliers have only made the arrival possible."

ROBERT INDIANA

Here's a Hoosier boy who emblazoned his origins on his very identity, changing his name in his twenties from Robert Clark to his celebrated moniker, Robert Indiana. He was born in New Castle, Indiana, in 1928, spending most of his youth in a multitude of residences in his birthplace, Indianapolis, and Mooresville. His early years were one with the American road, a childhood of car trips and road signs and a father who made his living working for oil companies and gas stations. The portrait of his parents, *Mother and Father,* included the family Model-T Ford, "the very keystone of the 'dream'—the chugging chariot carrying them on to greener pastures and redder passions," he once wrote.

Clearly, American popular culture and the ubiquity of commercial art imprinted itself on Indiana. "There was an admiration of American popular culture among the *Crossroads* artists," Day said. "After being told America had no culture for so long, they were looking for a culture. It may not have been European, but it was a culture." Indiana's 66 sculpture is referential to both Indiana's father's job with Phillips 66 oil company and the near-shamanic importance of a common roadside sign.

Indiana also remembered the stark interiors of the Fourth Church of Christ Scientist he attended on the southeast edge of Indianapolis. In a church devoid of statuary or paintings, the only decoration that caught his eye was a small sign, common in most Christian Science churches. As Indiana explained, it was "a small, very tasteful inscription, in gold usually, over the platform where readers conduct the service. And that inscription is God is Love."

JOHN CHAMBERLAIN

Like Smith, Chamberlain also came from Hoosier pioneer stock. Born in 1927 in the northern Indiana town of Rochester, Chamberlain thwarted the family tradition of saloon keeping, being the first in six generations to seek other work. He left Indiana while still a young child, though he returned to Rochester intermittently throughout his childhood to attend grade school. While he dropped out of school in the ninth grade, Chamberlain attended the School of the Art Institute of Chicago during the period when Robert Indiana was also a student there. Chamberlain was later a student at North Carolina's legendary Black Mountain College, where he linked up with poets Robert Creeley and Charles Olsen, later collaborating with them on poetry-sculpture combinations.

Chamberlain is highly respected and collected by notable artists and museums, yet he holds what critic Elizabeth Baker rightly called a "position of enigmatic prominence." Initially, Chamberlain followed Smith's groundbreaking welding assemblage techniques. But soon he, like Robert Indiana, found inspiration in the culture of the American automobile—in Chamberlain's case, the junkyard. There he found the twisted and crushed raw material for his twisted and crushed projective metal sculptures—painted compositional forms that have the strange accidental beauty of high-speed collisions and the stacked, cubed compressions of the scrap yard.

One of Chamberlain's sculptures was once left unattended on a Soho street while in transit between galleries. A city garbage truck wheeled around the corner and the sanitation worker tossed it in. It was never seen again. "Once you get past the materials," Chamberlain wrote, "you see what insanity is."

And insanity is what art is about. It is the sharing of the insanity that has not been suppressed. If you were to play it out in life itself, you would probably get yourself killed or put away. But in art it is looked up to, considered as a genuine piece of information.

WILLIAM WILEY

The influential postmodern artist Wiley was born in Bedford to a family of blacksmiths who worked in the limestone industry. He had an Indiana childhood of picture books and endless hours of drawing. Wiley credited his creative talent to his grandfather, "a multifaceted Hoosier artisan who sketched, played music, and shaped metal."

In the mid-1960s Wiley was a faculty member of University of California, Davis, near San Francisco. It was the ideal time and place to help shape a sea change in American art. Prior to that period, art was considered a discipline with an aesthetic object as the goal. In the heat of the Vietnam War and the growing environmental movement, art became a means of exploring moral issues and affecting social and intellectual change. Wiley's art and his tutelage were instrumental in that shift.

Wiley and others in the 1960s California art scene were influenced by the work of Marcel Duchamp, the surrealist who posed innumerable questions about art with his "readymades" and word play and emphasis on chance. Inspired by an interest in Zen Buddhism, Wiley explored the paradox of two opposing—and true—ideas brought together. Day wrote this about Wiley in the *Crossroads* exhibit catalogue: "Word play, music, and performance were naturally part of his personality. Anything a student wanted to do was basically art. He encouraged artists to think about all manner of subjects that might or might not be art topics."

Art in the Bay Area became more process-driven and less focused on marketability. Art "investigations" by Wiley and his students stirred together visual arts with music, poetry, and performance. Wiley evolved a performance art character, Mr. Unatural, who performed at art events.

Wiley's sculpture *Nomad is an Island* displays his commitment to art as a tool of social change as well as his ability to meld art and language whimsically. The sculpture is an immense assemblage with a verbal pun. A large palette of flat steel represents an island with letters spelling out the island's name, and pop-up silhouettes of figures, boats, and animals populating the place. A fifty-five-gallon drum looms over the island, symbolizing the environmental threat of the nuclear waste dump on the Farallon Islands off of San Francisco Bay. *Martin Luther King,* a sculpture of black friction-tape ball, wooden stool, lead, wax, gold-leaf, feather, and found objects, is a polychrome assemblage with a title that is a vital part of the work.

BRUCE NAUMAN

Nauman, considered the most influential artist of his generation, was born in Fort Wayne in 1941 to a corporate engineer father. Like Wiley, he came from a family tradition of craft—his great-grandfather was a cabinetmaker and his father made furniture in his spare time, teaching his son as he went. In the post-war boom Nauman's family moved often, and Nauman left Indiana when he was five.

The frequent moving left him a solitary child, comfortable with self-absorbed pursuits such as model-airplane construction and making music. Although he graduated from the University of Wisconsin with a degree in mathematics and physics, he had already determined to be an artist. Nauman studied under Wiley at the University of California, Davis. And like Wiley, Nauman was intrigued by the paradoxes of opposing ideas. He approached the conundrums from his study of quantum theory, where two contradictory exclusive events can both be true.

Nauman wields a wide variety of art forms in his quest to investigate his artistic questions, often relating to the relationship between humans and the space they occupy in the world. His graduate work with Wiley involved filming himself moving in a space with a florescent tube. Like the other *Crossroads* artists, Nauman demonstrated a fascination with language. His *Eat My Words* is a close-up of a man eating food in the shape of the letters "WORDS" off of a plate.

Smith wrote about his work, and in the process may have written for all six of the *Crossroads* sculptors, and the viewers of this exhibit as well: "I do not work with a conscious and specific conviction about a piece of sculpture. It is always open to change and new association. It should be a celebration, one of surprise, not one rehearsed. The sculpture work is a statement of my identity. It is part of my work stream, related to my past works, the three or four in process, and the work yet to come. In a sense it is never finished. Only the essence is stated, the key presented to the holder for future travel."

View of the Empire State Building in New York City.

Courtesy of Library of Congress.

23

THE STUFF OF LEGEND

INDIANA AND THE EMPIRE STATE BUILDING

GHOSTLY MEN WALKED THROUGH A HAZE OF WHITE DUST IN the cavernous mill building. Clouds of limestone dust billowed as the stonecutter intently sawed another one for the Empire State Building. The metal saw blades shrieked as they tore through the stone. Men in hard hats looking like the losers of schoolroom chalk fights ambled through the murk with the sweet taste of limestone in their mouths.

The hookers—L-shaped limestone corner pieces that "hook" on the corners of the monumental building—lay all over the workbenches, awaiting the Thursday truck to Manhattan. His eyes danced sideways to telegraph the joke, Indiana Limestone Company General Manager George James said, "We're sending truckloads of hookers to New York City."

More than three quarters of all the stone buildings in the United States are constructed with Indiana limestone, including what was once the planet's tallest building, the Empire State Building. Four years ago, the Empire State Building commenced a $65 million renovation campaign. As part of the project, an engineering firm surveyed the exterior facade of Indiana limestone and found a disheartening picture. More than 50 percent of the building's corner pieces were fractured and cracked; shards of limestone hung precariously in the limestone face, pointed like javelin heads as tens of thousands of people scurried the midtown streets below.

For more than 120 years, Hoosiers have been sawing stone out of the P. M. & B. Quarry, some of the best veins of building-grade limestone

137

in the world. When it came time to replace the weathered stone, there was no question but to return to the original source for new limestone.

So this is the story of limestone—its journey from the rumpled hills of southern Indiana to high on the Empire State Building; the tale of the men who quarry and craft and transport the ancient rock of Indiana, and the New Yorkers who make it the garment of the world's most emblematic building.

About 340 million years ago, this drifting firmament we call Indiana was down by the equator covered by a shallow sea. It was a comparatively calm place where trillions of tiny animals—crinoids and gastropods and other slithery sea creatures—lived out their lives in a placid sea. As they came to their natural ends, their carcasses piled atop one another for eons on end, till shoals of the bodies lay on the ocean floor. Where the sea-bottom and currents coalesced in optimal ways, the shoals rose to great heights.

Time moved on and so did the continent, migrating north to where we are today. The vast shoals, now compressed into rock by the weight of water and earth and endless time, awaited the next great geologic moment. A million years ago, give or take a few millennia, the great glaciers ground down from the North. While the glaciers stopped short of scouring southern Indiana, the meltwater from the mile-high glaciers eroded most of the rock shoals. Only a slender band of the ancient reefs wiggling through southern Indiana escaped erosion, leaving outcrops of pristine limestone—the best in an area only thirty miles long by two miles wide; barely 28,000 acres. And the P. M. & B. Quarry is smack dab in the middle of it.

Not quite seventy years ago, the Empire State Building's elegant exterior was wrenched from the ground not far from the rocky mill yard near Bedford, Indiana, where I stood. "It's not a big deal to match the color," James said. "It's the same quarry. The problem is getting the finish to match seventy years of New York City air."

QUARRYING THE ROCK

George James and I stood with our toes at the edge of an enormous bathtub-shaped hole that yawned beneath us. A light breeze ruffled the water that filled the hole. Trees clung to the rock.

James glanced around at the piles of gargantuan discarded stone blocks that were stacked willy-nilly like the toy box of a giant slovenly child and pointed to the quarry: "The Empire Quarry. The stone for the Empire State Building and a lot of other buildings came out of that hole. Empire State Building called for 220 thousand cubic feet of stone—that's nothing." Limestone was everywhere around us, underfoot and overhead, in mounds as tall as trees and in the bottom of the gaping holes. "There's 900 acres of quarry here," James said. Dozens of quarry holes like the Empire's dotted the P. M. & B. landscape.

QUARRY'S MONUMENTAL TASK

The Empire State Building's stone was being quarried nearby. The limestone was scribed with the sixteen-foot-deep cuts of the diamond-bladed saw, as though the quarry were a block of cheese being cut for a party of behemoths.

After the quarrymen vertically cut the stone, they inflate air bags that were slid into the cuts and "turn" the 50-foot-long, 350-ton slice onto piles of debris and earth. "Breakers" swarm over each slice, drilling and splitting it into manageable blocks. Blockmarkers grade the rock into select, standard, and rustic, and colors of buff, gray, and variegated.

"Silver-buff," James said. "Empire State stone; standard grade. They named the color for them."

Back at the mill, sunlight was slanting though the darkness as the men wire-brushed the stone to mimic the effects of New York's corrosive air. "They thought on it for a long time and then they came up with this wire brush. It puts little pits in the stone," said fourth-generation limestone worker Kerry King. He said he had never been out to New York or Washington, D.C., to see his work. "I went up to Bloomington, though, to see one of those IU buildings. I touched about every piece of stone on that building. Secretly sometimes I put my initials on the inside of some of them stones. Maybe someday they'll take it down and see it."

Roy Woods, who lives near the Lost River and Orangeville in the sinkhole-pocked Mitchell Upland, works for Swift Trucking and spends much of his time hauling Indiana limestone. Many times, Woods has traversed the "Fertile Triangle"—as the stone men call the area between Chicago; Washington, D.C.; and New York, with their wealth of limestone buildings.

He has delivered to Harvard, Cornell, and West Point. He knows the way to the imposing Federal Courthouse in Alabama, which will be crowned with the Corinthian columns being carved in the dusty metal building in Oolitic. "It's been an education," he said. He has taken half a dozen loads into the Empire State Building, leaving on Thursday night to arrive in Manhattan for unloading on Saturday morning.

"I come in through the Lincoln Tunnel, drop down to Thirty-fourth Street and you're right there," he said. "Park right beside the Empire State Building. I go in there of a night and get out in the morning."

STATELY BODY OF ARCHITECTURE

New York City's Manhattan Island is a promenade of limestone; a paean to the Stone Belt. From Wall Street up to Columbia University, hundreds of buildings built over more than a century celebrate the esthetic and mundane virtues of Indiana limestone. With all of its striations and lazy whorls slivered thin and hoisted skyward, the bedrock of Indiana reminded me of home.

Skyscrapers reflect the pale silver light of the quarry, from the grandeur of the Metropolitan Museum with its lofty columns and caryatids peering gravely from the façade, past consulates and churches, tony hotels and grand apartment buildings with liveried doormen and haughty tenants; past Rockefeller Center with the graceful grain of the limestone dancing like sea fronds in the ancient sea. At the New York Public Library on Forty-Second Street, the serene limestone lions looked dapper, sporting top hats and black ties for a hoity-toity fund-raiser.

Herds of tourists, grouped by diverse nationalities, trooped past Cartier's ornate pile and the crazy chaos of carving that decorated the dozens of limestone structures down the boulevard: Greek maidens and hissing snakes, thickets of garlands and viands and acanthus; baroque urns and fanciful dragons. Carvings ranged from Egyptian to art deco. Gothic, Byzantine, Baroque, and French Empire vie with graceful amalgams and wildly eccentric hybrids—all in limestone.

"Limestone is one of those materials that makes New York New York," Bob Furlong said. His company, Furlong and Lee Stone Company, has represented Indiana Limestone Company in New York for four generations, since 1921 when the Bedford company began. When plans for the Empire State Building, the tallest building in the world, were announced in 1928, Furlong and Lee were the stone men chosen for the job.

Initially, it was by no means certain that limestone would be the cladding of the towering structure. Finished brick was a popular veneer in the 1920s. It was also the heyday of terra cotta and marble, and they were possible choices. But the cost of finished masonry brick had rapidly escalated, and in New York's sulfurous atmosphere marble melts and terra cotta crumbles.

Architectural historian John Tauranac wrote, "The logic behind using stone for the facing of the Empire State building seemed irrefutable, the choice of Bedford limestone unarguable."

Furlong sang the praises of Indiana limestone, a great building stone without underlying seams or planes. "It's not going to fall apart if you don't cut it just right," he said. "It's a soft stone; you can plane it, carve it, cut it, without much problem.

"My great-great-grandfather got the company started in the 1880s, bringing brownstone into the city, but the cutters started dying of black lung disease. Brownstone is sandstone—silica. Limestone is calcium carbonate. You can breathe it all day long and it just passes through. So we switched over to limestone."

While Chicago pioneered skyscrapers, New York took them to their logical end. By the 1920s, New York had five times more skyscrapers than Chicago and every other city trailed behind. H. G. Wells proclaimed the Manhattan skyline to be "the strangest crown that a city ever wore."

And in 1931, the Empire State Building was the crown jewel, rising majestically at midtown from a diadem of surrounding skyscrapers.

CONSTRUCTION WAS HURRIED

The Empire State Building was an immense undertaking: 103 floors, 6,400 windows, 10 million bricks, 27 miles of elevator rails; a structure weighing 365,000 tons. It rose faster than any previous building. Built in less than a year, it leapt upward at the rate of four-and-a-half stories a week.

The 220,000 cubic feet of limestone came into the city in blocks to be milled into the panels and corners as needed. Prior to World War II, it was impossible to bring any finished stone into New York City because of the strength of the local stonemason unions. Indiana limestone production was so well organized, all of the stone for the building was quarried in six weeks.

Completed just as the Great Depression took hold, the building suffered at first with only a 20 percent occupancy rate. Wags called it the Empty State Building. But by the 1940s, it was the most profitable building in the world.

New York's 1970s financial woes and the fashion for International Style-glass towers cost the Empire State Building its cachet—and crucial parts of its maintenance budget. Grout began to fall out of the seams between the limestone panels and water seeped into the interior of the structure.

The building had been designed with an air space between the internal masonry brick and the limestone veneer. Limestone acts like a sponge and the dead air space prevents the moisture from wicking into the crucial steel frame and stone anchors. However, in their haste, workers swept their debris into the most convenient place—the air space at the perimeter of the building. "When they started renovation on the veneer, they found everything—old lunch boxes, beer cans, 2×4s, everything," Furlong said.

Without the air space, the stone could not dry out and the moisture attacked the steel, causing rust, which eventually expanded and fractured the limestone facing. "Rust expands like twenty times its size," project manager Steve Holland said. "Every corner from the thirtieth to the seventy-seventh floor had to be replaced."

His twenty-fourth-floor office is a clutter of construction equipment, well-marked blueprints, and limestone-dusted desks, distinguishing it from the neighboring commercial and legal offices. With his Jersey accent and weathered face, Holland was the quintessential New York construction boss. "Yeah, it's command central here," he said as he juggled workers' walkie-talkie and telephone requests while logging the weekly football pool.

"Yeah, most people don't go on a scaffold," he said as I looked down the precipice of the building. "My father did it thirty-eight years. I started as a helper when I was a kid. Had to go get the beer."

A REPAIR SHOP IN THE SKY

Setting the new limestone veneer is the work of waterproofers. They scale the tall buildings, repairing the ravages of time and weather, replacing stone and brick, tuck-pointing, and caulking—handymen on a giant scale. At forty dollars an hour, waterproofers are among the top of New York's construction trades. And there never seems to be a dearth of work.

"You may have heard these buildings keep falling in the street," Holland said. "Long as that keeps happening we got work. At any one time, we had as many as 150 guys on this project. Now we got 15–16 guys and one woman. We're setting limestone."

It was lunchtime, and the inevitable din of construction-grade repartee rattled around the front office. "You want to go up and see?" asked Holland. The waterproofers were working off a platform that angled around the corner of a building, cantilevered out from the side with bolts sunk five inches deep into the concrete floor slab.

Wanda Castro, the lone female in the pack of waterproofers, came in wearing an old striped sweater and a Tommy Hilfiger sock hat. She was a young Dominican woman, with the jaunty give-it-back-to-'em attitude of women in male enclaves. In an island-lilted voice, she told me about the work: "When you're on the seventieth floor and the wind hits you—whoooa!"

She had two partners on her work crew. Jorge Jones was a Panama-
nian with a black pirate scarf, a mustache, and a Nets t-shirt. He'd been
at the trade for twenty years. "In the beginning, I was a little bit scared,"
he said. "But now . . ."

Andy Haughton was a black Brooklynite with wary eyes. He nodded
and stepped out the window of the fifty-sixth floor.

The work platform was about five feet wide with the center taken up
by the elevator mechanism, leaving narrow walkways for scuttling beside
the building and out to the perimeter where the safety rail was lashed
together with fraying nylon rope.

All of the creative tumult and aesthetic chaos of New York stretched
around us: the Hudson River quays, the bustling avenues, the brick and
brownstones of Brooklyn, the sprawl of New Jersey, the tiny Statue of
Liberty. People below were the size of perambulating popcorn and taxis
looked like mobile credit cards.

Wind buffeted the crew as the platform rattled. "Oh, when the wind
pushes the scaffold three to four feet from the building, scare you to
death," Castro said. Haughton topped her. "Once I was on the narrow
scaffold and the wind flipped it around," he recalled. "The railing was
against the building and the other side was open. Had to ride it down
that way. We quit for the day. Said that was it."

The platform barely stopped jiggling when they began troweling
mortar from plastic buckets onto the brick wall that backs the limestone.
As Haughton climbed above with a hoist, Jones danced on a brace to
Latin music from a mud-covered radio. It was a well-practiced construction team moving to a Latin beat.

Soon, limestone clouds poured from Jones' grinder as he adjusted
the anchor slots that secure the limestone to the structure. An enormous
C-clamp was attached to the limestone panel and with a rattle of chains
and some terse directions in Spanish, the limestone levitated to its place
on the wall.

Leveling, adjusting, anchoring, tuck-pointing. Eight pieces—a
floor—go up every day. Limestone dust covered their shoes—just as
the limestone dust covered the mill workers' shoes only a couple of days
before in Indiana.

THE END OF THE JOURNEY

Far below, dozens of immense structures clothed in the stone of the Indiana hills ranged down the avenues like images of the quarries turned upside down. Above the crew, the magnificent manmade cliff face loomed, a gray eminence in the bright sun.

The Indiana truck driver, Woods, sees it all from street level: "It's what I come home to tell my kids. If people don't feel something, they don't like history. You have to have a certain feeling."

Part 5
The Present Past

24

JOHN DILLINGER'S FUNERAL

BANK ROBBER JOHN DILLINGER CAME BACK TO CROWN HILL on Wednesday July 5, 1934, three days after he had died in a rain of bullets outside Chicago's Biograph Theater. His killing ended a nearly yearlong escapade that had captured America's imagination. During his rampage, he and his gang had stolen $300,000 in multiple bank robberies, including $21,000 from Indianapolis's Massachusetts Avenue Bank on September 6, 1933. When casing banks and jails, Dillinger's gang had been wily: posing as Indiana State Police, bank security alarm salesmen, and movie executives scouting for locations. Dillinger had escaped supposedly impregnable jails, once with a carved wooden gun. "See what I locked all of you monkeys up with," he laughed at his disarmed jailers as he turned the key on them. For months Dillinger led hundreds of police officers and federal agents on a wild chase across four states. To some Great Depression-ravaged Americans who had lost farms and homes to voracious banks and felt abandoned by an uncaring government, Dillinger looked like a Hoosier Robin Hood. To the authorities who counted as many as twenty-three people killed by the gang, John Dillinger was Public Enemy Number 1.

The night Dillinger died, people dipped handkerchiefs, newspapers, even dress hems in his drying blood in the alley beside the Biograph.

Famous pose of Indiana outlaw John Dillinger holding a Thompson machine gun in one hand and a pistol in the other, circa 1930s.

Courtesy of Indiana Historical Society, Bass Photo Company Collection, P 130.

The next day thousands of morbid Chicagoans filed through the Cook County morgue to see his bullet-riddled body, while Dillinger's father, stepbrother, and Mooresville mortician E. F. Harvey drove north in an old hearse to retrieve the remains. When his family arrived at the Chicago funeral home then storing Dillinger's body, journalists questioned his father, John Dillinger Sr., who told them, "They shot him down in cold blood." John Sr. asked why federal agents shot his son when they had so many guns trained on him, then conjectured maybe it was better he had not been captured alive. Led in to see his bullet-torn son, John Sr. just said, "My boy!" before being led away.

The Dillinger family arrived back in Mooresville on Tuesday, July 24, when another line of curiosity seekers filed into the funeral home until 2:00 A M. The next day there was a simple family funeral at the home of Dillinger's sister in the southwestern Indianapolis neighborhood of Maywood, where a mob of 2,500 gawkers gathered. A minister gave a short invocation, and the family sang the hymn of spiritual encouragement, "God Will Take Care of You," which began with, "Be not dismayed whate'er betide, God will take care of you." After the service, a cortege of five cars and the hearse slowly drove toward Crown Hill, but had to repeatedly stop for police to clear crowds from the route.

So John Jr. was coming back to Crown Hill. In February 1907, when he was three years old, his mother, Mollie, had died. During the funeral, young Johnnie had stood on a chair by the casket, shaking his mother as if trying to wake her. Dillinger's mother was laid to rest in the sixteen- by twenty-foot family plot that his father had bought in Section 44, Lot 94, located near the Boulevard Street fence. Less than three decades later, as the small cortege accompanying Dillinger's body approached the cemetery, a huge throng of 5,000 surged near the gate and along the fence. The police struggled to maintain order in the glowering 104-degree heat. That morning the newspaper had blared a front-page story about Dillinger's upcoming Crown Hill interment, leading with, "Through the triple gateway of Crown Hill cemetery, with its slender gothic towers of carved Indiana limestone covered with Virginia creeper, the body of John Dillinger, public enemy No. 1, will pass to its last resting place." The family was relieved to learn the crowd would not be allowed to enter the cemetery during the burial ceremony.

The Crown Hill staff began preparing for the hoopla when they learned of Dillinger's death. When some Crown Hill plot owners complained about Dillinger's upcoming interment, superintendent Raymond E. Siebert stated the cemetery had to do its duty. He told reporters, "The cemetery has no legal right to object to the burial of Dillinger in the family lot. John Dillinger, Sr. has owned the lot for several years and his wife is buried there. He is a man who bought property from us, and as owner of that property, has a legal right to bury the body of his son there." In the twenty-seven years since he bought the plot, John Sr. had already buried his parents, two wives, and two grandchildren in Crown Hill. It was the place to bury his boy.

The Dillinger family huddled under the tent erected at the burial site, trying to ignore the crowd pressing against the Boulevard Street fence. As the minister began to give the final invocation, the skies opened, drowning his words in cleansing rain and claps of thunder. Lightning flashed as undertakers lowered John Jr.'s wooden casket into his grave. As the family motored away from Crown Hill, the police unleashed the mob of onlookers, who raced for the gravesite to snatch flowers and even handfuls of mud. When the police at last restored order, the cemetery authorities established a round-the-clock watch over the grave to protect against grave robbers and the ghoulish general public.

But John Sr. was still concerned about his son. According to Crown Hill executive Howard T. Wood, interested parties offered the Dillinger family ten thousand dollars for the body, which they wanted to exhibit in a sideshow. A few days after the funeral, John Sr. returned to Crown Hill to arrange for the casket to be reburied under a protective cap of concrete and scrap iron that was then topped with four immense reinforced-concrete slabs placed in stepped gradations above Dillinger's body. Because of their fears of grave robbery and desecration, the family waited two years before erecting a tombstone.

They were right to be concerned. Almost immediately after the monument company installed the low rectangular marker, people began chipping off pieces. The gravestone was soon reduced to an oval, as the Dillinger grave became a pilgrimage site. Almost a decade after Dillinger's burial, a newspaper story reported, "There has been no grass growing on the plot of ground," because of the thousands of people tromping around the grave. It all took its toll. In 1959 Dillinger's surviving sister, Audrey Hancock, gave her permission to the Blakely Granite Company to replace Dillinger's headstone. The permission stipulated, "The new stone will be exactly like the old one (with the exception of the damage now evident on the old marker)." The original gravestone eventually became a museum piece at the John Dillinger Museum in Lake County, Indiana, where the bank robber made his famous wooden-gun escape. But the new gravestone did not last either. There were thefts. A motorcycle gang stole Dillinger's tombstone in 1980, intending to mount it on the wall of their clubhouse—but authorities got the marker back. In 1990 workers replaced the now battered and chipped Dillinger marker with a third headstone.

A panoramic view of the French Lick Springs Hotel in French Lick, Indiana, circa 1910.

Courtesy of Indiana Historical Society, Bretzman Collection, P 431.

25

TWIST THE TIGER'S TAIL

"LID PUT ON FRENCH LICK," THE BOLD PAGE-ONE *INDIANAPOLIS Star* headline blared on May 7, 1949, Kentucky Derby weekend. Governor Henry Schricker, who campaigned for "clean government" in a trademark white hat, had sent the Indiana State Police to close down the Springs Valley casinos the previous weekend. The owners protested mightily, with Elmer Thacker, the proprietor of the luxurious Brown's Casino, even taking his case to the governor's statehouse office. But Schricker remained firm, indicating "the shut-down order was for keeps."

"It's pretty quiet down there now," Schricker said. "They [the gamblers] have been told to straighten up." It was an economic blow on the valley's busiest weekend, as twenty packed trains per day trundled celebrators sixty miles from Churchill Downs in Louisville, Kentucky, to the valley. At the peak of the railroad era, a hundred private railcars stood on the French Lick sidings during Derby week. On Derby day 1949, the French Lick Springs Hotel was filled to capacity with guests, including Governor and Mrs. Adlai Stevenson of Illinois and Captain Eddie Rickenbacker of Eastern Airlines.

Encompassing the tiny towns of West Baden Springs and French Lick, Indiana, the sulfurous-smelling Springs Valley in Orange County's remote hills was first renowned as a mineral springs spa in the nineteenth century. Well-to-do health seekers, punctiliously taking the waters, filled the luxurious resort hotels. The modest hotels and boardinghouses catered to the middle classes. But the rise of the more fashionable resorts in California and Florida, and the debunking of the therapeutic quality of mineral water, caused the valley's businessmen to rely increasingly on casino gambling to draw crowds.

Following Schricker's Derby-weekend raids, however, the casinos that dotted the valley and anchored the main street stayed closed. The governor cited a "cold war" among the gamblers as the reason for the raids. "There's been some bad blood and even a little shooting," he said. Orange County sheriff Ben Nadell had had little luck in shutting down the establishments seven weeks earlier; it took the Indiana State Police and power of the governor to accomplish the task. Thus ended the era of wide-open gambling in the Springs Valley, an illegal activity that flourished with few interruptions for more than half a century.

While home to the most sumptuous and long-lived of the state's gambling operations, the Springs Valley was not an isolated case in Indiana. Gambling has been a part of the state since the beginning, as have been the attempts to curb it. On July 16, 1795, Northwest Territory governor Arthur St. Clair adopted and published "A Law to Suppress Gaming." In eighteenth-century parlance, lotteries were distinguished from gaming and betting on horse races.

In 1810 the Indiana Territory legislated "AN ACT authorizing a Lottery for the benefit of the Vincennes Library" to raise $1,000. History fails to pass on the results of the lottery, but minutes of the library board remained uncelebratory. The lottery in 1818 to finance a canal around the Falls of the Ohio at New Albany also failed, as did the canal.

The legislators were in a sober mood when they passed the 1851 Indiana State Constitution, legislated after the canal boom and bust that bankrupted the state. Article 15, Section 8, reads, "No lottery shall be authorized; nor shall the sale of lottery tickets be allowed," language that remained unchanged until the 1989 state lottery. In 1852 the legislature also passed laws prohibiting betting, gaming houses, and horse races.

Although the 1851 Indiana State Constitution outlawed gambling, the vagaries of human nature and political realities thereafter conspired to keep gambling establishments prospering in the Springs Valley and throughout the state. Large-scale gambling operations existed in many of the state's larger metropolitan areas. At one time or another, major gaming took place in Indianapolis, Terre Haute, Muncie, and Evansville.

In the spring of 1901 possibly the most highly touted casino in Indiana opened in Long Beach. The Monte Carlo was announced to the

Chicago sporting community with an engraved invitation and brochure that read, "You are invited to the finest equipped and only Monte Carlo in America, delightfully situated in Lake County, Ind., near the Standard Oil Works in Whiting. No 'interference' from county or State officials. Open the year round. The place is delightfully located on the south shore of Lake Michigan, the surroundings being picturesque, the rooms light and airy, having a gallery on the four sides of the building where you can enjoy the cooling breezes off the lake. Ample accommodations for 5,000 people." The blueprints showed a veritable fortress protected by an eighteen-foot stockade, sentry boxes, alarms, bloodhounds described as man eating, and escape tunnels.

Among the state's gambling establishments, however, the casinos of Springs Valley were always the most lavish; some say they were among the most lavish in the world. The West Baden Springs Hotel casino, connected to the hotel by a two-deck promenade that was twenty feet wide and three hundred feet long, was "rivaled only by the Monte Carlo Casino in Monaco for opulence," historian James Philip Fadely wrote. In 1906 one journalist noted the luxurious gaming rooms, the ubiquitous poker games in the private rooms, even the newsboys matching pennies on the sidewalks outside the hotels. "The very atmosphere of these resorts is charged with the gambling spirit, engendered, nurtured, and fostered by the hotel management," noted one minister.

Casino gambling began early in the Springs Valley, when owner Lee Sinclair built a casino at the West Baden Springs Hotel in 1895, prior to the construction of the enormous domed structure. The French Lick Springs Hotel also had a casino by 1901 in a small frame building on the resort grounds. Propriety and fear of political scandal motivated the hotel management to move it across the street a few years later.

From the turn of the century through the Roaring Twenties through the 1940s, the mere mention of West Baden Springs and French Lick conjured up gambling in the nation's mind. Former West Baden Springs Hotel employee Park Flick recalled his army buddies playfully grabbing their wallets and jumping back when he told them he was from French Lick, Indiana.

The larger casinos catered to the high-rolling moneyed classes who flocked to the valley in April, May, and June—"the season"—en route from their Florida winter homes to their northern homes. A lesser fall season lasted from September through the first half of November. "They'd dress up every night in tuxes and had a great dinner at the hotels, then they'd come on down to the clubs to try to twist the tiger's tail, as they used to say back then," dealer Russell Bledsoe remembered.

Bejeweled ladies and prosperous men in evening dress cavorted beneath the chandeliers playing baccarat, chemin de fer, roulette, and the slot machines. "The lower floor of the clubhouse was devoted to slot machines of all kinds and descriptions," a 1906 visitor to Brown's Casino recalled. "I stepped from the colonnade into a sumptuously furnished reception room. Costly rugs covered the floor, velvet covered chairs and divans abounded."

Upstairs she found more luxury: "A long, narrow room, with heavy velvet floor covering, which gave back no sound of footfall. Nine tables, with polished wood dials attached to them, and stacks of white disks piled on them, ranged upon the sides of the room. Men and women crowded around these tables, putting down bills, gold and silver, receiving the disks in return, and then giving up the disks to the men behind the tables, or receiving more from them, as they won or lost."

The two main hotel owners in the valley controlled most of the gambling by the 1920s. Ed Ballard ran the West Baden Springs Hotel as part of a vast casino, real estate, and circus empire. His personal wealth was estimated to be between $20 million and $100 million by his death in 1936. Ballard was a local boy. He started his gambling career as the owner of the Dead Rat Club in West Baden Springs and had a million dollars by the age of thirty. He managed the West Baden Springs Hotel casino for Sinclair and eventually owned the hotel and most of the gambling places in the valley, as well as casinos in Arkansas, Florida, and Havana, Cuba.

The owner of the French Lick Springs Hotel, Thomas Taggart, a Democratic politico and businessman, kept an arm's length between himself and the gaming house, though the Brown casino and the French Lick Springs Hotel even shared the same heating system. Taggart leased the Brown for "billiards and bowling," while taking in $50,000 a year for the concession—a million dollars, tax free, over the course of his ownership.

Al Capone was a regular at the valley clubs, walking through downtown in a knot of five bodyguards, tooling around the valley in his steel-plated Lincoln automobile with combination-lock doors. The natty Hoosier composer Cole Porter tried his luck, as did John Dillinger, Diamond Jim Brady, and the Marx Brothers. French Lick Springs Hotel veteran Auttie Shipman remembered the night a woman with Hopalong Cassidy won $100,000 at the roulette tables, only to lose $200,000 the next night.

Up in the forested hills above French Lick, a crowd of more modest means disembarked under the elaborate porte cochere at the yellow-brick Gorge Inn, as famous for its dance floor and fried chicken as the roulette tables. The gardens and grounds were beautifully landscaped with classic statuary and grand bridges.

Dozens of clubs, such as the Club Chateau, the four-story, mansard-roofed Sutton House with twin mascot dogs that looked half-hyena, the Oxford Hotel, the Ritter House, the three-story Colonial Club with a wraparound porch, the Kentucky Club, the Indiana Club, the Green Acres casino, the clapboard Roundtop Inn, and the Homestead, were scattered through the valley towns. They serviced customers of different races and classes. The Babylon Club, for instance, catered to the resorts' black bellhops and waiters, whose service was renowned. Other locals could gamble in the basement of the Ballard building that stood at the corner of the highway and the entry boulevard to the West Baden Springs Hotel or in the basement of the Oxford.

The Hoosier Club, formerly the Colonial, boomed on Sundays, when many of the other clubs were closed. Located across from the West Baden Sprudel arches, the Homestead Hotel, built about 1912 by Ballard, featured a casino in the basement and a beautiful fountain in the courtyard.

The top roulette operators in the country were from French Lick, migrating seasonally from Cuba and Florida to Springs Valley to Mackinac Island. As many as forty dealers at a time worked the tables at the Brown alone. The Ballard organization dispatched four-man "wheel crews" all over the country. From French Lick to Hot Springs to Havana to Saratoga Springs, they traveled the railroads with their wheels. "I knew very few in French Lick at one time who were not croupiers or dealers," former French Lick Springs Hotel manager Charlie Bennett said. "Gambling and those hotels was the lifeblood of the valley," Martinsville attorney and Democratic gubernatorial adviser John Hurt said.

The Springs Valley gambling scene operated with impunity, even with the tacit approval of the authorities. The town marshals were hired at the behest of the casino operators. Footsie Hendricks, named for his immense feet, ran the trolley between the two hotels before he became the marshal.

Prior to the establishment of the Indiana State Police in 1933, enforcement of state law fell to the local sheriffs, who were subject to the community standards of the ballot box in a county with hundreds of casino workers, as well as the lure of the casino owners' largesse.

The owners of the two main resorts provided the major part of the political protection. Between Ballard, a Republican, and Taggart, a Democrat, both sides of the political aisle were covered. Taggart was particularly well connected, being the Democratic National Committee Chairman and the leader of the state party. Many a state Democratic convention was held in French Lick, within sight of the Brown and the brothels attached to it.

Reportedly, the governor's office was in on the take for decades. Shipman, who worked for both Taggart and his son, Thomas D., tells of driving the son's car with a Star Number Seven license plate to Indianapolis monthly for years with money from Ballard and Taggart. His destination was the governor's office. "One guy," he said, "he just couldn't believe the Governor would take money. I said, 'Mister, when the Governor grabbed it, if you didn't let go of the envelope, he'd take your arm off.'"

Schricker's 1949 raids were not the first gambling raids in the valley. In 1906 William Randolph Hearst, stung by Taggart's opposition to his presidential candidacy, assigned muckraking journalist Evelyn Campbell to write an expose of the wide-open gambling in the valley. The Hearst newspaper chain soon trumpeted a tale of vice and social horror to the nation giving the views of Campbell as well as of a minister who had visited.

"West Baden and French Lick Springs is a foul stream, the banks of which are lined with suicides, murders, divorces, feuds, broken and blasted homes and lost and ruined souls. It has become the mecca of corrupt and vicious politicians who flack [sic] there to gamble," reported Reverend R. Keene Ryan.

In 1905 strict moralist Governor J. Frank Hanly, later the Prohibition Party's presidential candidate, halted gambling in connection with horse racing at the Indiana State Fair. On July 3, 1906, spurred by the Hearst articles, Hanly ordered the state militia, assisted by the Orange County Sheriff, to raid the Springs Valley clubs. The state sued for receivership and revocation of the hotel charters.

One of the writers in the Hearst articles presciently said, "There is no fear of the law in Orange County," and he was right. The state case was assigned to Orange County judge Thomas B. Buskirk, a political crony of Taggart, who allegedly enjoyed the gaming tables himself. Not surprisingly, he ruled in favor of the defendants. The appellate court case drifted into the fogs of political convenience after a shift in governorships.

In 1933 Governor Paul McNutt, himself no stranger to French Lick, having been driven there many times by Shipman for political conventions and consultations as well as relaxation, recommended to the legislature that the Indiana State Police be formed. Al Feeney, formerly captain of the Notre Dame football team, was the first head of the state police. One of Feeney's first acts with his newly constituted troopers was to close down the gambling operations in French Lick and West Baden Springs—the first sustained interruption in the illegal activities in more than twenty-five years. McNutt, though opposed to gambling, responded by sacking Feeney.

State authorities tolerated the Springs Valley gambling partly because it was in a remote location and partly because it was generally patronized by the classes that had disposable income to lose. There is, however, evidence of community resistance to the gambling. A 1934 flyer from the Citizens' Committee said the gamblers came to the valley "like lecherous parasites to prey on the people." It went on to say: "When gambling is allowed unfettered as it always has been in West Baden and French Lick, the right to exist cannot be denied to all other forms of evil and debauchery. The example is paved to admittance for [the] underworld's licentiousness in all its sordid ramifications. Numerous times the decent citizens of both towns, who after all are in the great majority, having endeavored to stamp out the activities of the unwholesome element, have met with defiance and rebuff of this element, and efforts to do away with it have been hopelessly futile."

But the valley retained its immunity because of the politically well-placed local control, without outside gang influence. Though mobsters Capone and Dutch Schultz frequented the valley, they came to play, not to work. At worst, the valley was a junket destination for corrupt Chicago policemen, brought down by the Chicago syndicate for a holiday. There were exceptions. In 1906 gangsters out of Chicago demanded protection payments from the resort owners. When rebuffed, they dynamited the veranda at the French Lick Monte Carlo and blasted the gaming room at the West Baden Springs Hotel.

In 1946 Thomas D. Taggart sold the hotel to John Cabot. Although there were slot machines in the French Lick hotel lobby during Taggart's ownership, gambling became increasingly flagrant under Cabot's ownership. Slots were even in the upstairs hotel corridors, lest guests miss one last opportunity before retiring.

The younger Taggart died in January 1949, and with him died the last of the political protection that the valley enjoyed. The final raids that closed down Springs Valley gambling happened the next spring. In the decades that followed, most of the casinos and smaller hotels either burned or closed, standing empty as silent reminders of a lost past. The French Lick Springs Hotel survived by focusing on the convention trade and golfing. The West Baden Springs Hotel was already a memory, closing soon after Black Tuesday 1929. The remarkable building, termed "the eighth wonder of the world" in its day, remained, but its glory faded. The Jesuits took over the property in 1934 and used the vast rococo structure as an austere seminary for decades before selling it to a private college, Northwood Institute.

In 1983 even Northwood Institute was gone, and the biggest hotel in the valley stood empty for the first time since its 1903 grand opening. By 1991 the formal gardens and classical structures were lost in a thicket of weeds and trees. The grand 700-room structure was boarded up. In January 1991 six floors at the back of the hotel crashed to the ground.

The West Baden Springs Hotel saw hope for new life in 1996 when a remarkable partnership acquired the property: the Historic Landmarks Foundation of Indiana, a premier architectural preservation organization, and the Bloomington-based Cook Group, an international medical technology company with a deep interest in historic preservation. The partners unveiled a $15-million plan to restore the structure and grounds, with the final use undetermined. As the structure echoed with the cacophony of construction in late 1997, a number of uses were consid-

Interior view of the French Lick Springs Hotel. The lobby had a mosaic floor and extensive seating for guests.

Courtesy of Indiana Historical Society, Jay Small Postcard Collection, P 391.

ered, including as a high-end resort hotel, retirement home, or corporate headquarters. But the final chapter is as yet unwritten. There is even a possibility that the hotel may again be used as a deluxe casino.

For more than fifty years, gambling was a major part of the Springs Valley's prosperity, locally controlled and reasonably benign. After the dice stopped rolling in 1949, the valley was never the same—the dandies and swells moved on to other locales. A few months after the 1949 Kentucky Derby weekend raids, Shipman recalled, a big car pulled up to the long steps in front of the French Lick Springs Hotel, and the liveried doorman came over to help. "Gambling going yet?" the people called out the window. When the doorman told them it was not, they were off, calling out, "We're heading to Saint Louis, then."

An October 23, 1923, group photograph of the Indiana State Police, created just two years before by the Indiana legislature. By 1927 the State Police had become a full service, statewide police agency.

Courtesy of Indiana Historical Society, Bretzman Collection, P 431.

26

THAT'S IT

PROHIBITION IN INDIANA, 1918–1933

PROHIBITION COMMENCED IN INDIANA AT MIDNIGHT ON April, 2, 1918, when thirty-one breweries and 3,520 saloons (547 in Indianapolis alone) closed their doors. A driving rainstorm swept across Indiana the night before prohibition, but it failed to stop revelers from enjoying their last legal drinks.

In Indianapolis the manager of the posh Severin Hotel had to ask the police to clear the elegant barroom at midnight, as the dancing celebrators refused to go home. The manager needed to close the cabaret, as it was being transformed into a coffee shop the next day. In the slightly more downscale Brevort Café, a young buck sprayed the crowd with beer a few minutes before midnight, sparking a melee that brought out knives.

A thousand people lost their jobs in Terre Haute, as both the town's breweries and 263 bars closed. In spite of the bad news, the city's bars and dives were clamorous until closing time. In Evansville the cabarets and cafés were busy until midnight with "general celebration." Quite a few of Evansville's citizens staged their own festivities: "The number of parties in private homes, where the basis of the merriment was a keg or two of beer, was astounding," a correspondent reported. With eighty-three bars and both breweries closing in Lafayette, hordes of people turned out for a last fling. The sixty-five saloons in Vincennes did "a land-office business" right up to closing time. Anderson's twenty-eight bars did not last that long—the patrons drank up the remaining stock long before midnight. In South Bend, Muessel's brewery was dark, but the city's 215 saloons only shut down after "the busiest day in their history." In more sanguine—or perhaps depressed—Fort Wayne, the city was fairly quiet, although 157 bars and the state's two biggest breweries were closing.

Passage of state prohibition was the culmination of an enormous offensive the year prior by the "drys," led by the Indiana Anti-Saloon League. In the days leading up to the January 1917 vote on the bill, Indianapolis was swamped with 25,000 prohibition supporters waving banners and pigeonholing legislators in Statehouse halls. Petitions arrived so heavy that aides had to hoist them on their shoulders. When the vote passed the Indiana House, 70 to 28, wild temperance-style celebrations broke out, the Statehouse halls reverberating with "Onward Christian Soldiers."

As the Indiana Senate debated the bill, the IASL cried for 300,000 advocates to descend on Indianapolis; petitions with more than 175,000 names were delivered to the legislators; hymn-singing temperance supporters waving signs paraded through the Senate chambers. Buckling under to the overwhelming dry support, the Senate unexpectedly passed the bill in a landslide 38 to 11 vote, uncorking "wild jubilation" in the galleries and around the state. The brewers had until April 1918 to put their affairs in order.

In the interim, the Indiana Brewers Association warned that Indiana would forfeit a trove of taxes, and more than 13,600 workers would lose their jobs. Some German brewers in Evansville told the local paper they would return to Germany; saloonkeepers just thought they would move to Kentucky. But soon after April 3, 1918, there was little hullabaloo—with Indiana soldiers already on the frontlines in France, media attention shifted to Liberty Bonds and crushing the Hun. But Kin Hubbard, the pithy cartoonist who created Abe Martin of Brown County fame, caught the internal dialogue with his cartoon that fateful week: "Sometimes a woman'll get so hard up fer somethin' t' boast of that she'll say her husband is goin' t' buy a car when the state goes dry."

Arrests began soon enough, though Doc Vanderhook, who ran an Indianapolis chili parlor on Massachusetts Avenue, managed on April 4 to get out of the charge of running a speakeasy. On April 13, police busted Indianapolis saloonkeeper H. C. Bloomberg for having nine barrels of whiskey and a substantial supply of beer and wine in the cellar of his "soft-drink parlor" at English and State Streets. It was the first of thousands of arrests for prohibition violations. Blind tigers and speakeasies began to spring up all over Indiana, selling now-forbidden booze and beer. While most imbibing households still had substantial (though illegal) stores, enterprising Hoosiers were already making homebrew beer and distilling corn whiskey. In some parts of the state—particularly those with large German and Italian populations—brewing, winemaking, and distilling were destined to become substantial cottage industries.

The passage of Indiana's state prohibition law put additional pressure on Congress to institute national Prohibition through a constitutional amendment. In December 1917 the House of Representatives passed the Eighteenth Amendment, which Indiana legislators voted to ratify on January 14, 1919. Three days later, Nebraska became the thirty-sixth state to ratify, making the Eighteenth Amendment part of the Constitution. America went dry on January 17, 1920, one year after ratification. Billy Sunday, the volcanic evangelist from Winona Lake, Indiana, thundered, "The reign of tears is over. The slums will soon only be a memory. We will turn our prisons into factories and our jails into storehouses and corn-cribs. Men will walk upright now; women will smile, and the children will laugh. Hell will be forever for rent."

A LONG TIME COMING

The temperance and prohibition movements had a long history in Indiana. In the years prior to the Civil War, there was widespread pressure in various states for prohibition. Primarily led by women, local temperance groups coalesced across Indiana, determined to rid the state of evil liquor. In one case in the 1850s, a number of Centerville Methodist and Presbyterian women roused themselves to action. Armed with hatchets and hammers, the good sisters invaded John Vonderwight's saloon—known locally as "Dutch Jake's." Stove-in whiskey barrels and smashed hogsheads of beer soon gushed onto the floor. Cigars and tobacco flew through the air. A torrent of intoxicants ran down the gutters from broken barrels the women had rolled into the street. Their wilding complete, the ladies marched triumphant from the shattered saloon, brandishing

Vonderwight's commandeered account books. But an account book held a surprise. Unbeknownst to one of the temperance warriors, her son was one of Dutch Jake's best customers.

Fourteen states eventually passed pre–Civil War prohibition laws, including Indiana, which in 1855 passed a law that prohibited the manufacture or sale of any intoxicating liquor, save cider and wine made from domestic fruits. But Indiana's first prohibition proved to be short-lived, as the state supreme court declared the law to be unconstitutional within a few months of its ratification.

In the years following Appomattox, the temperance movement continued to pick up steam, spearheaded by evangelical church people and politicians virulently opposed to "Rum, Romanism, and Rebellion"— the Romanism referring to the terror that the foreign-born Papists represented, particularly the Irish with their propensity for whiskey and the German Catholics and their love of beer. Pushed by temperance advocates, an 1883 prohibition bill came within four votes of being passed by the Indiana General Assembly. The prohibitionists marched on after the 1883 vote. Each Sunday, the walls of evangelical churches trembled with temperance songs, such as:

> Oh, the Brewer's Big Horses coming down the road
>   Toting all around old Lucifer's load,
> They step so high, and step so free,
>   But the Brewer's Big Horses can't run over me.

Temperance lobbyists made sure prohibition bills were introduced in every session of the Indiana General Assembly after 1883, though the vote was never as close until 1918. But the 1883 prohibition vote must have been the last straw for many Hoosier brewers: an extraordinary number closed in 1884, when more than three dozen breweries changed hands or drained their vats for the last time. Beyond the growing prohibition movement, Indiana brewers had been suffering from wild economic panics, tight credit, and erratic crops for ten years. Many of the closings were small breweries that were now competing with larger brewers equipped with newer and more productive equipment. When it all came to a head in 1884, when Bremen, Bowling Green, Cannelton, Huntington, Jasper,

Kendallville, Lawrenceville, New Albany, Richmond, Saint Peter's, Seymour, and Tell City all lost their breweries, as did Troy and Valparaiso.

In 1895 the prohibitionists pushed through a law governing taverns, which legislated the establishment had to be on the first or basement floor, as well as banning food, music, partitions, and booths. The strictures helped form the iconography of the turn-of-the-century saloon: free (albeit salty) lunches to accompany libations, which were downed behind the swinging doors and gauzy curtains that shielded the patrons from busybody eyes. With booths prohibited, the brass foot-rail at the bar served as a convivial substitute.

The continued growth of the Women's Christian Temperance League and the founding of the IASL in 1898 brought together impassioned foot soldiers and highly skilled organizers, embodied in the IASL's firebrand executive Reverend Edward S. Schumaker. The IASL soon began using the Nicholson remonstrance law to its fullest extent. Named after the Quaker minister who wrote the law, the measure permitted communities to vote on the establishment and continuation of individual saloons. Through the statute, petitions could be circulated, and if there were enough signatures, a special election could be called to determine the saloon's destiny. It was a contentious system, as towns wrangled over the petitions. In the southeastern Indiana town of Waldron, there was even a pitched battle between gunslinging wets and drys.

As the twentieth century dawned, prohibitionists turned to a deadlier weapon: local and county options, which allowed localities to vote on prohibition. The drys got a boost when J. Frank Hanly took office in 1905. Hanly championed prohibition (as well as Indiana's infamous Compulsory Sterilization Law, a eugenics statute that mandated sterilization of individuals in state custody). In his last year in office, Hanly waged "bitter and relentless war" against the brewers and spirits industry—that "unholy traffic," as he called it. By the time he left office in 1909, seventy of Indiana's ninety-two counties were dry. But counties with large German populations stayed wet, including Allen, Vigo, Wayne, Tippecanoe, Marion, Floyd, Knox, Franklin, Dubois, Lake and La Porte. (Rendered dry by local option, Broad Ripple tipplers made an effort to merge their village with wet Indianapolis, so they could drink again.)

In a period when breweries owned 70 percent of Indiana's saloons, the statewide impact was major: 10 percent of the state's 3,681 saloons in 1908 went out of business within a year. In the face of local and county options, some taverns adapted. The telltale swinging doors came down, and "hop ale" replaced beer. Patrons got their whiskey in genteel china cups and saucers. "Literary" and "Educational" Clubs abounded, as did fraternal orders. But as county options took their toll, breweries closed across the state.

There was some reprieve in 1911, when Indiana governor Thomas Marshall told legislators that local and county options enforcement "breeds perjury, discontent, bitterness of feeling and local anarchy." Marshall's law, called the Proctor bill, ended county options, instead controlling saloons through county commissioners and high license fees and bonds. But the new law offered brewers only a short respite before the dry forces, deciding that statewide prohibition was their best alternative, attacked again. By 1917 the Hoosier drys had accomplished their great mission—prohibition in Indiana.

After former governor Hanly's term had ended in 1909, he took up the cudgel of temperance full time: He was the keynote speaker of the Anti-Saloon League's Jubilee Convention in Columbus, Ohio, on December 10, 1913, rousing the crowd into "a roar as wild as the storm outside," as they frenzied for the Eighteenth Amendment. Hanly then formed the "Flying Squadron" of prohibition speakers, who barnstormed the forty-eight states lecturing more than a million people in less than a year. Emboldened by the response, Hanly ran for president on the Prohibition Party ticket in 1916, but only garnered 221,030 votes, about 1.2 percent of the total. In January 1918 Hanly wrote in the conservative *Literary Digest* that Hoosier brewers had "the arrogance of a Hun." Hanly railed, "In all the history of the political and civic life of the American people there has been no combination or organization of power so brutal, so domineering, so corrupt, or so dead to every sense of civic interest or concern as the brewers of America." In his final jeremiad, Hanly screeched, "The legislatures of the States will be organized into firing squads, and the beer trade will be compelled to meet its fate."

BREWERIES DURING PROHIBITION

The thirty-one Indiana breweries that survived up to prohibition included two each in Evansville, Fort Wayne, Lafayette, Terre Haute, South Bend, and New Albany, as well as six in Indianapolis. The smallest of the group was the Tell City Brewing Company. After April 2, 1918, several, such as Thieme and Wagner in Lafayette, Muessel in South Bend, Terre Haute Brewing Company, Madison Brewing Company, Peru Brewery, and Tell City Brewing, just closed their doors—if they had not already done so in the months prior.

The breweries that remained open struggled along with a variety of strategies. Most brewed near-beer, which had to have an alcohol content of less than half of 1 percent. The Indianapolis Brewing Company manufactured soft drinks and cereal until 1930; C. F. Schmidt made Ozotonic and malt extract until closing in 1920. Hack and Simon stumbled along for a while brewing near-beer they called Elite, after their best-selling pre-Prohibition brew. The Evansville Brewing Company, under the name, Sterling Products Company, started selling soft drinks and a near-beer called Sterling Beverage—"that 'foody' drink with all of the golden grains of which it is made." Like many breweries, Sterling also sold a malt extract that could be used to homebrew and boost near-beer up to normal potency. Of course, drugstore alcohol could do the same thing. Zorn in Michigan City made soda pop. In South Bend, Kamm and Schellinger sold soft drinks and distilled water under the name of Arrow Beverages Inc. South Bend Brewing sold near-beer, root beer, and Hoosier Cream Soda. The Huntington Brewery converted to making caffeine, soap, tannin, and other chemicals. Fort Wayne's Berghoff Products Company, as it was renamed, produced Bergo near-beer, soda pop, and Berghoff Malt Tonic. Advertisements running in major Indiana papers around the start of prohibition pitched their near-beer to saloonkeepers, soon to become soda jerks: "Bergo, The Quality Drink. Keep your place open by using Bergo." Another ad aimed at patrons showed a winsome Dutch lass bringing Bergo to a happy American family sitting in a soda fountain, while another offered that Bergo was "a snappy drink" that was ideal to drink before retiring. Centlivre Brewing survived by leasing cold storage and selling ice and their near-beer, called That's It.

BOOTLEGGING

"Prohibition is better than no liquor at all," humorist Will Rogers quipped, which seemed to sum up the Volstead era. During Prohibition an ocean of bootleg hooch flowed through the porous U.S. borders. Bootleggers hid moonshine stills in haystacks, concocted gin in bathtubs, and fermented Dago Red in closets and cellars. Crippling Jamaican-ginger Jake ravaged the lower classes. Basement-brewed beer was ubiquitous. One thing was clear, America sure was not going beerless: The Prohibition Bureau estimated that each year Americans consumed several hundred million gallons of homebrew.

Bootlegging was rampant in Indiana from Dubois County farms to the Calumet Region's slick mob-run operations. From the illegal casinos of French Lick all the way up to the speakeasies of Chicago, tipplers particularly respected "Dubois Dew," renowned as a relatively safe and palatable moonshine. Indeed, Al Capone himself repeatedly junketed to rural Dubois County to sample the output of stills concealed on Ferdinand, Dubois, and Haysville farms. Chicago gangsters in their big Chryslers and Packards were a common sight on the county back roads—one folktale of the region tells of a shoot-out with tommy guns on a remote farm, with the local moonshiner-farmers burying the loser in the woodlot. Folks from all over the state came to buy, along with policemen from Evansville and other large cities.

The moonshine was not all that was exported. In Ferdinand, Wilfred Olinger remembered the homebrew arrangement that the persnickety owner of the Covered Bridge establishment had: "This family, they were all making beer for him. And he knew which was capped, and aged, you know, to be served. And we went and got the batches that he send us to and brought them up there. And he had the home brew and like horse troughs with ice, you know, we had no refrigeration, not yet. Oh ja, and moonshine, the Dubois Dew, you know, whisky, that was made out in the county, with stills, you know." In overwhelmingly German Dubois

County, moonshiners were not only culturally acceptable, but economically critical. During the Great Depression, Ferdinand Township had the least people on welfare in the entire state.

During Prohibition, northwest Indiana was also a hotbed of illegal brewing under the Capone and Johnny Torrio organizations. In June 1923 Prohibition officers seized the West Hammond Brewing Company for brewing real beer. Near to the state line and Chicago, the brewery had started in 1909. By 1923 it was sold and disappeared from view. In La Porte police raided Guenther's Brewery, where workers were brewing real beer for "known gangsters" from Chicago, as well as their Atlasta near-beer. A local history reported, "In a flourish of righteous indignation, Police Chief Alfred Norris led a posse into the brewery and smashed the kegs with axes, thus saving the citizens from the evils of drink."

The Southern Indiana Brewing Company in New Albany brewed Hop-O, its near-beer—and quite a bit that was not. Federal Prohibition officers busted the company for bottling beer at 6 to 7 percent alcohol level to send to southern states. Michael Schrick, president of the brewery, was arrested and the brewery license was revoked.

During Prohibition, Virgil Hosier was the bottle shop foreman for Ackerman Brewery, part of Southern Indiana Brewing Company. In 1993 the eighty-three-year-old Hosier reminisced with the Fermenters of Special Southern Indiana Libations Society: "And at one time, when they got to making beer up to 5, 6, and 7 percent, we had trucks coming from Louisiana and Alabama. We didn't have a bit of trouble selling beer—we just didn't have enough of it." Hosier remembered a friend of his, Fred LaDuke, was operating a bottling machine when a man walked to it and told him to shut it down. "He [LaDuke] said, 'who the hell are you to tell me to shut it down. I'm not shutting it down.' The man just pulled his coat open. 'I says shut it down,' and they shut it down. Internal Revenue."

The Anderson papers began headlining the T. M. Norton brewery on June 17, 1923, the day after Prohibition officers searched the plant. "Two Truck Loads of Beer Is Seized," the *Anderson Herald* ungrammatically blared, also noting that "Bert Morgan Also Here." Morgan was Indiana's Prohibition director, a rare "Untouchable" in the midst of raging corruption. At one point, Morgan reportedly declined a $250,000 offer to turn a blind eye. At Norton's the officers arrested the two Ohio truck drivers, incarcerating them at the county jail along with the forty-nine kegs of 5 percent beer found in the trucks. Morgan also found another ninety barrels of beer in the brewery vats. Police had raided the brewery two years prior, when they confiscated a large quantity of bottled beer. On June 19, 1923, authorities charged brewery executive William J. Norton with conspiracy to violate federal Prohibition laws and padlocked the plant. Norton was at the plant when the raid began but ran as the police descended, leaving the hapless drivers to take the heat. By the end of the month, a deal had been struck: authorities closed the Norton brewery for a year, but did not confiscate the property, as they could have under the Volstead Act. After his conviction for liquor-law violations, Norton served time at the federal prison in Atlanta.

REPEAL!

As the 1920s wore on, Hoosier prohibitionists attracted some unsavory allies—the Ku Klux Klan. At the peak of their power in Indiana, the KKK shared many of the drys' conservative views and took to Prohibition enforcement with zeal. Using the previously existing Horse Thief Detective Association, the Klan formed an unfettered civilian legion to uphold the dry laws, sometimes abusing their power to harass wet proponents.

In the mid-1920s, the Prohibition laws got even more draconian. Indiana's Wright Bone Dry law that the legislature passed in 1925 tightened enforcement. Considered one of the most repressive laws ever passed in Indiana, the statute offered financial inducements for successful prosecutions, which, not surprisingly, fueled an arrest and prosecution binge. By 1927, however, the tide was turning. Concerned with enforcement excesses, Indiana attorney general Arthur Gilliom softened the Wright law. Much to the chagrin of the prohibitionists, Gilliom instructed the state's prosecutors to no longer prosecute for possession of "medicinal" whisky prescribed by doctors, as it did not violate the "spirit" of the law.

With a growing revulsion against mob-controlled bootlegging and widespread corruption, public opinion began to lean toward repeal. The board of directors of the Indiana chapter of the Association Against the Prohibition Amendment included Hoosier literary luminaries George Ade and Meredith Nicholson, as well as a pantheon of executives, bankers, attorneys, and politicians.

But it was the 1929 stock market crash and the Great Depression that followed it that ultimately did in Prohibition. In the austere new era, beer meant jobs and tax revenues. And perhaps there was a biblical element: As the Book of Proverbs rejoined, "Give strong drink to unto him that is ready to perish, and wine unto those that be of heavy heart. Let him drink, and forget his poverty, and remember his misery no more." As public and political sentiment shifted, visions of beer kegs began to dance in brewers' heads. In April 1932 the *Evansville Courier* reported, "Evansville brewers are ready to begin manufacture practically on short notice," though they were not "especially optimistic about the legalization of beer in the near future." By November of that year, the paper trilled, "Evansville sees brighter prospect of Brewing Jobs," anticipating two hundred men would be hired at Evansville Brewing, whose executives promised to start brewing within thirty days of repeal.

By 1932 both national parties added repeal planks to their platforms, as did Indiana's Democratic and Republican Parties. After Franklin D. Roosevelt's inauguration in March 1933, Congress permitted the sale of 3.2 beer. The Twenty-first Amendment repealing prohibition was right behind it. Governor Paul V. McNutt used the momentum to call for the end of the Wright Bone Dry law and pushed through the Alcohol Beverage Act. On April 7, 1933, legal beer returned to Indiana.

At the beginning of April 1933, Indiana newspapers made the imminent arrival of beer their front-page story. "Beer Trucks Will Race Beer to City Friday," the *Indianapolis Star* headlined on Monday, April 3. With only a few Indiana breweries up and going, most of Indy's beer was coming from Cincinnati, Saint Louis, and Milwaukee. Kamm & Schellinger in Mishawaka and Berghoff Brewing in Fort Wayne were going to have beer ready for the first day, but Evansville Brewing could only promise June at the earliest. Centlivre and Cook both applied for licenses. The city was in a tizzy, with speculation about availability, price, and quality. Seven hundred applicants flooded the state office for retail beer licenses. It seemed like Friday was never going to come.

On December 9, 1920, three officers from the Indianapolis Police conducted a raid on a farm near New Bethel (today Wanamaker) and confiscated a large still, thirty-eight gallons of "white mule" whiskey, a gallon of malt, fifteen pounds of flour, a hundred pounds of corn sugar, and two hundred gallons of mash.

Courtesy of Indiana Historical Society, Bass Photo Company Collection, P 130.

The White House got the nation's first shipment of 3.2 beer at 12:05 AM on April 7, trucked in under Marine guard. Roosevelt sagely sent it to the press corps. Around mid-morning on April 7, beer trucks began to trickle into Indianapolis, just in time for the promised lunch-hour debut. But it was far too little, a drop in a beer-thirsty desert. Some trucks had gotten trapped in Milwaukee and Saint Louis traffic jams that were "miles long." There were rumors of truck hijackings in Lake County. In spite of the Indiana State Police reporting that thirty-five of the forty-six trucks checking in at the Seymour weighing station were loaded with beer, Indianapolis still did not get all the beer it wanted. "Early Rush Exhausts Beer Supply," the *Star* headline read. Cheery crowds had jammed the cafés that had beer—"packed after the manner of a delegation of sardines in a can." Anderson drank up its allocation of Berghoff beer in two hours. Evansville and New Albany got some Falls City from Louisville. Poor Teutonic Batesville did not get any at all. By Sunday, April 9, the *Star* ominously headlined, "Beer Famine Threatens, as Demand for Brewery Supply Exceeds Supply." The paper figured that locals had consumed 600,000 pints in the first few days that beer was legal.

There were some changes in the fifteen beerless years: There were no more "saloons"—bars, taverns, and cafés were now the preferred monikers. And women were right there, drinking out of bottles and slender little glasses, a long way from their older sisters' homebound growlers. But in terms of the beer, the *Star* said it best, "Those who knew the real article in preprohibition days pronounced the 3.2 as 'genuine.'"

27

BLACK-GOLD ERA'S
LUXURIOUS PERCH

EVANSVILLE PETROLEUM CLUB

THERE IS AN EXPANSIVE VIEW FROM THE EVANSVILLE
Petroleum Club, perched atop this city's tallest skyscraper. As they nibble their lunches, club members can look far upriver past Evansville's suburbs to the rolling hills of Warrick and Spencer Counties and across the Ohio River to flooded Kentucky.

It is a luxurious aerie. Enormous brass chandeliers light the oak-paneled walls, the English antiques and ancient ceramics, the old stained glass and new oriental rugs, the gilt-framed minor Old Masters and flamboyant bronzes. An original Toulouse-Lautrec graces the bar. Trumpet music flares in the background as dark-suited men and polished women with slender, expensive noses share the buffet line, hailing one another with gusto. The linen is crisp, the service soft and solicitous.

Once, 99 percent of the members were engaged in some part of the petroleum industry, said club manager Mark Krug. Cowboy hats and dusty boots, blue jeans and large diamond pinkie rings were dining room attire for many years; drawls of east Texas and Oklahoma as common as southern Indiana twangs. But those days have passed. "Our membership is primarily professional," Krug said. "Lawyers, doctors, CPAs, owners and VPs of companies—the region's movers and shakers, you might say. But only about 2 percent of the membership are part of the petroleum industry. I don't know if it is sophisticated or just more toned down."

The Petroleum Club began in 1948 at the height of the Illinois Basin oil boom. Then it was in the McCurdy Hotel, the residence of choice for the hundreds of oil men—geologists, engineers, oil scouts, and independent promoters—drawn to the wealth of the new patch. The Illinois

Oil Basin stretched for 100 miles through Indiana, Illinois, and western Kentucky, and Evansville was its unofficial capital.

The first major discovery was in 1938, near Griffith, Indiana, and other wells paid off in the years that followed. More than 300,000 barrels a day were coming out of the patch, pumping a million dollars a day into Great Depression-era Evansville. The basin soon was a hive of drill-rig roustabouts and pipeline workers, smooth-talking promoters, and hundreds of money-men who wanted to gamble on a gusher. "They called the investors 'et als.,'" said Indiana Geologic Survey research scientist Dan Sullivan. "The Petroleum Club is where the promoters took them to wine and dine." Sullivan continued, "The way the oil business is set up, the landowner gets one-eighth royalty on any oil, and the rest is split up between the investors. Shares as small as $\frac{1}{132}$ were sold on some deals."

The Illinois Basin reserves were modest by Texas standards and the major oil companies could not gain large acreage positions. So, within a dozen years, the oil patch became the bailiwick of hundreds of independent operators, brokering deals in coffee shops and barbeque stands and out in the fields and swamps of the region. "There were tens of thousands of deals put together by individuals," Sullivan said. "That is the romance of the Illinois Basin."

The boom lasted through most of the 1950s, and the basin seemed to breed characters—men with names such as Top George and Titanic Thomas. Many were gamblers who knew little about oil, but knew a good chance when they saw one, learning as they went. When they made it they lived high. "Tom Lange, he had thirty-some racehorses," Sullivan recalled. "Dick Beeson went through three or four fortunes and numerous marriages."

Ray Ryan might have been the most unforgettable of all. He drifted up from the oil fields around Midland, Texas, early in the Illinois Basin boom, and began putting together deals almost immediately. Within a decade he had become almost mythic, a freckled Irishman made good, sporting monogrammed shirts and gold-link bracelets.

Ryan owned oil wells in more than a dozen states, a canal and resorts in Montego Bay, and the prestigious Mount Kenya Safari Club with actor William Holden that was frequented by such famous guests as Clark Gable and Winston Churchill. He owned seventy-three miles of

Yugoslavian seacoast and was called "Mr. Palm Springs" because of his extensive holdings there.

Ryan was best remembered for being a gambler though, both in the oil patch and at the gaming tables and tracks. Among the most-recounted game was a high-stakes pool game with another oil-man/gambler, Hubert Cokes. Since Cokes was a better player, Ryan demanded a handicap. So Cokes used a mop handle for his cue, while Ryan played with a standard one. The outcome is unrecorded.

A reputation for underworld connections followed Ryan through most of his career. When several sticks of dynamite blew up his blue Lincoln Continental on October 18, 1977, after he lunched at the Petroleum Club, Evansville mourned his passing. "The new breed of oilmen gave the city a gamy charm," the *Evansville Press* wrote in a page-one obituary the next day, "that has since been 'redeveloped' by various programs."

John Coombs is one of the club's last oilmen, a white-haired petroleum engineer who spent much of his career developing fields for both major companies, independents, and now himself. He talked about oil as he ate his soup (a Friday special named Coomb's Clam Chowder in his honor). A waitress in a black mess jacket hovered nearby.

"The first well drilled for oil was in Titusville, Pennsylvania in 1859 because of a whale oil shortage," Coombs reminisced. "Snake oil salesmen used to bottle crude oil and sell it for fifty cents a bottle back then. It was 40 percent gasoline. It'd clean you out."

After booming through the 1940s, production in the Illinois Basin peaked in the mid-1950s. Fortunes were made overnight. One well in western Kentucky made $8 million in two months. While more than 4.5 billion barrels have been extracted from the Illinois Basin, geologists believe hundreds of millions of barrels remain. But the price of oil, currently below $10 a barrel, has severely depressed the oil business. Drilling is at its lowest point since records were kept, industry publications note. "There were 40,000 independent operators across the country after World War II," Coombs said. "Now there are less than 10,000. It takes oil at twelves to thirteen dollars a barrel to break even with Illinois Basin oil. Everyone pretty much has to hang it on a hook."

Out at the edge of Evansville, the army-green Ohio River surges through the flats and lowlands. Forlorn trailers sit perched on stilts, and a sky the color of dryer lint hangs low over the "buy here—pay here" car lots and remnant carpet outlets, and the old cafes where ten thousand deals were done.

Encircled with a large empty parking lot, the House of Como is a white, masonry-block bunker that sits back from the road near the river. A worn Las Vegas-style sign that has seen better days announces the club to the passing traffic. "It looks closed," someone at the Petroleum Club said, "but it's not."

Nearby, the Old Kentucky Bar-B-Q's faded sign promised mixed drinks, package liquor, and country ham. Inside, a lineup of afternoon drinkers surrounded the horseshoe bar. When someone asked for a bar-b-que mutton sandwich, everything stopped, shot glasses and beer cans pausing in mid-sip. "Oh, honey," the waitress answered with a gravelly voice, "the kitchen is closed. There's been an emergency."

In its heyday, there were thousands of men employed in the petroleum business in the Illinois Basin. Now the little oil towns are full of rusting petroleum equipment still tagged with "For Sale" signs. Some wells, in the richer fields still, pump away, wells, like so many giant insects endless foraging. But more sit idle.

At the Petroleum Club, dining room captain Tommie Wilson, an employee of thirty-three years, recalled the earlier days. "Mr. Ryan, he the kind of guy, he take two martinis, three cigars for lunch," Wilson remarked as the dining room began to fill with members in tweeds and pinstripes. "Mr. Ryan, he was charismatic, he walk in that door, everyone turn around. 'Give me that check,' he'd say. I used to have people fight for those checks.

"The men played their role. There was so much money. They spent it on drinking, clothes—one guy that owned horses, he had a diamond stickpin in the shape of a horseshoe—and having a good time. The wives, they was always trying to fashion out." Wilson summed it up, "When you came here you were at the top of your game."

A herd of elephants parade through downtown Peru, Indiana, March 1906.

Courtesy of Indiana Historical Society, Jay Small Postcard Collection, P 391.

28

LIONS, TIGERS, HIGH WIRES

AT ONE POINT NOT SO LONG AGO, INDIANA WAS A CIRCUS. IN the old railroad town of Peru and down in the rugged green hills of West Baden, townspeople learned to keep time by the roar of the lions' feeding hour. The towns were the winter headquarters for several of America's largest circuses, their annual retreat to prepare for the next season under the big top.

Hundreds of parade horses clopped down small-town streets. Elephants tugged the tableaux wagons along the cobblestones. Wild animal trainers put the big cats through their paces as trick horses cantered around the practice rings. Aerialists swept through the air and teetered across abysses as trained dogs leapt through rings. Clowns sharpened their satire while jugglers added ever more balls and spinning plates. Painters spruced up the gaily painted wagons and sideshow banners, and managers ordered the circus posters that were vital to the shows—art that meant "Circus!" to hundreds of towns across the country. The posters depicted a lurid, transgressing world, where men and animals coexisted in exotic interplay. Seemingly sexually charged women performed prodigious athletic feats. Freaks were attractions and clowns mocked the rules of a prim society. The posters promised generations of Hoosiers that a trainload of Jungian dreams and tenors was trundling down the tracks toward them, and things were never going to be the same.

The Indiana Historical Society is celebrating the heyday of the Indiana circuses with the publication of *Life in a Three-Ring Circus,* a book of thirty-two posters and interviews with circus veterans, as well as an exhibition of twenty-five original posters at the IHS headquarters. Fierce lions stalk the posters, barely mastered by fearless trainers. Scantily clad equestriennes balance on elegant white horses. Clowns grotesque with face paint leer from the sheets, joined by stolid hippos, capering monkeys, and horses outfitted for the ring with boxing gloves and trunks— "Direct from England; first Time in America," the poster promises. It is art that conjures the smell of sawdust, caramel corn, and greasepaint, the call of the ringmaster and shill of the barker, the tootle and squeal of the calliope mingling with the roar of the big cats.

The enormous growth of railroads in the post–Civil War era fueled the golden age of circuses. In the 1870s Hoosier native William C. Coup designed the equipment and techniques that allowed circuses to quickly stow wagons and cages aboard trains. (Equally important, he was the first to learn to paper the countryside with garish circus posters to advertise the show.) Instead of plodding through the mud at ten miles a day from small town to small town, circuses hitched their railcars to trains and clattered to cities hundreds of miles apart overnight. By the end of the 1870s, twelve large circuses crisscrossed the continent, a traveling aggregate of wild animal acts, performers, clowns, grifters, and con men, leaving a path of delighted locals and disgruntled city fathers in their wake. Indiana's central location and excellent rail connections soon made it a natural haven for the traveling shows.

Peru ("PEE-ru" in the local argot) on the upper Wabash River stood at a handy rail intersection with trains leaving in all directions. The city became the winter home of several major circuses such as Hagenbeck-Wallace, Sells-Floto, and the American Circus Corporation. Each winter as many as seven troupes returned to roost in the small Indiana town, with many famous performers such as Emmett Kelly and Clyde Beatty using Peru as their permanent address. As their performing careers ended, many of the veterans of the big top returned to Peru as a retirement home. There has been more circus activity in Peru in the last century than anywhere else in the country. Today the town is known as the "Circus Capital of the World."

It all began in the 1880s when local livery owner Ben Wallace acquired a blind lion, a trained baboon, a cage each of birds and monkeys, and a host of colorful circus trappings and clothing in lieu of a defunct circus's feeding bill. Wallace's 1884 circus played in front of five thousand people in Peru, the horses head-tossing nervous because they had never performed with music or before people.

The circus wagons headed out bearing the grandiose name of Wallace and Company's Great World Menagerie, Grand International Mardi Gras, Highway Holiday Hidalgo, and Alliance of Novelties," later shortened to "The Great Wallace Shows." By 1892 the Wallace Shows had made such a name for itself for grifting that it traveled the West under the name of Coo and Whitby. Homeward bound at the Mississippi River, the circus stopped and repainted the wagons, proudly returning to Peru with the Great Wallace Shows again emblazoned on the wagons.

Peru's tradition as a circus winter quarters began in 1891 when Wallace bought the farm of Miami chief Francis Godfroy who received the land as a government grant in 1820. Godfroy, one of the enterprising Miami chiefs who prospered in northern Indiana, was said to be the second-wealthiest Native American in the country. When he died, New York fur merchants owed him $15,000.

The winter quarters, the largest in the world, were located at the confluence of the Wabash and Mississinewa Rivers. In its heyday, the 3,000-acre farm had more than forty buildings and barns sheltering the animals and wagons of several circuses. At its peak, when the American Circus Corporation and Buffalo Bill's Wild West Show also were wintered there, one pasture held the herd of one hundred zebras and another held a thousand giant circus horses. Sixty elephants walked the grounds. Lions roared from the Hoosier barns. Today, an old sign that reads "Elephants—Big Cats" still hangs over the entrance to a looming yellow barn.

When Wallace purchased the Hagenbeck Circus to form the renowned Hagenbeck-Wallace Circus, the German wild-animal show was stranded in Mexico. One cold and icy January day, fifty-six railcars from Mexico arrived in Peru. Sixteen Indian elephants walked two and a half miles to winter quarters with their feet wrapped in gunny sacks, steeled against the subzero cold with a gallon of whiskey-soaked bran apiece. Up on their backs, their blue-lipped Hindu trainers shivered in breechcloths and cotton sarongs.

In 1913 the Wabash and Mississinewa Rivers rose in a fearsome flood. The workers released the horses, and they raced to the high ground nearby. The workers were unable to free the wild circus cats, and they perished in their cages in the barn. The roustabouts and trainers found refuge on the roof of the old Godfroy house as the water rapidly rose. Around and around them, the elephants swam, wanting to stay next to their turners. As each hour passed, one less elephant swam trumpeting around the house, until finally there were none. Some of the enormous bodies floated downstream to Peru, where they lodged under the Wabash River bridge.

For a number of years, the Hagenbeck-Wallace Circus wintered in the spa town of West Baden in southern Indiana. Ed Ballard was an extraordinarily successful casino-and-resort owner who had a hankering for circuses. Involved with the Hagenbeck-Wallace Circus since 1915, Ballard knew the commercial potential of the circus wintering in West Baden during the slow resort season.

Each spring after the winter of practice, the circus held a final dress rehearsal for the locals in a field near one of the spas. On occasion Ballard held circuses in the West Baden Springs Hotel's immense atrium. Lions prowled from the columned entries as five very large elephants danced their ungainly mazurkas on the priceless mosaic floors. "Considerable trouble was experienced in getting the elephants in and out of the dome," the local newspaper noted.

A tragic train crash in 1918 killed eighty-six Hagenbeck-Wallace circus people, causing Ballard to reorganize financially. But the following spring, the circus was again on the road, joined as the years went on with other shows Ballard combined into the American Circus Company, which also called the valley home. In 1929 Ballard lost a flip of the coin to John Ringling and sold his circus holdings, and West Baden no longer reverberated to the roars of the wintering big cats.

The Great Depression hit the entire circus world hard, and by the 1940s Peru's days as a winter home were also over. Peru's circus memories almost faded until 1956, when the National Convention of the Circus History Society met in Peru. The resultant to-do revived the circus in Peru. Circus City Festival Inc., a nonprofit organization celebrating

An aerial view of the winter quarters for the Hagenbeck-Wallace Circus in Peru, Indiana, 1928.

Courtesy of Indiana Historical Society.

Peru's circus past, was formed in 1960 and the annual circus festival began. By 1974 scouts from Shriners' and Barnum and Bailey joined the 20,000 spectators to watch the fifteenth year of performances. More than 250 Miami County youths flew through the air and teetered across the high wire, juggled and clowned, and paraded with zest. Today, the circus exhibits its prowess in the circus arts more than a dozen times annually, both at the festival and on the road from Indiana to Monaco. The town's high-wire act recently joined with Guinness Book of World Records with an eight-person pyramid crossing a twenty-foot-high wire, one more person than the famous Flying Wallendas.

The old winter quarters near Peru are now the site of the International Circus Hall of Fame, a national historic landmark. The gargantuan circus wagon building houses the Hall of Fame Collection, honoring the luminaries of the big top from the eighteenth-century beginnings to the 1920s' golden days to modern performers such as Gunther Gabel-

Williams. The museum has more than forty wagons and calliopes, arti-facts, props, costumes, posters, handbills, and lithographs from circuses around the world. The Hall of Fame gives daily circus performances under the big top throughout the summer. As the steam calliope bur-bles and whistles and the local animal trainer gives "tiger talks" to the gathered crowd, it's clear the tradition of the circus is alive and well in Indiana.

29

CONFLICT AND CONCILIATION

THE MORNING OF MAY 6, 1970, DAWNED COOL AND CLEAR ON the Indiana University, Bloomington campus, perfumed with the scent of flowering trees. All across the university, people were up early, getting ready for a momentous, quite possibly terrible day. Police helicopters whickered over Dunn Meadow, troopers checked out their riot gear. In dormitories and town apartments, students began the recommended preparation for the massive antiwar rally: taking off their earrings and braiding their hair, putting on long pants and good running shoes, and remembering to bring their Vaseline for Mace and vinegar-soaked cloths for tear gas. By noon clots and rivulets of students were making their way across campus toward Dunn Meadow, where the rally was scheduled for 1:00 PM. In spite of the gamboling dogs, Frisbees, and rock 'n' roll, there was an air of foreboding.

IUB student body president and Black Panther Keith Parker had warned student demonstrators a few days earlier, "All who turn out must be fully aware that there is a very real possibility of violence." Already the red Viet Cong flags of the hardcore student radicals were fluttering in the light breeze. Across the street, an elderly Hoosier lady in a winter coat watched the gathering crowd with her hand over her mouth. "The Communists are here," she whispered. "The Communists are here."

"I was lean and mean back then," says Parker (Class of 1971) of his term as a confrontational student leader. Afro-haired with a moustache and fulsome muttonchops, Parker served during the turbulent 1970–71 school year.

When President Richard Nixon announced the American invasion of Cambodia and Laos on April 30, 1970, a thousand IU students boiled out onto Kirkwood Avenue, with broken windows and edgy police in their wake.

Four days later, Ohio National Guardsmen gunned down four Kent State University students during an antiwar demonstration. Parker spoke the following afternoon at a large protest rally in Dunn Meadow and then led a march on Bryan Hall to present a list of five demands to university administrators. Parker had earlier written, "Education must be taken out of the hands of the pig administrators and put back in the hands of the people." While Parker and David Derge, IU vice president, challenged one another, forty police officers in riot gear nervously guarded the halls, and the university chimes played "We Shall Overcome."

Plans for a moratorium on classes and other "revolutionary actions" were to climax at the mass May 6 Dunn Meadow rally. The very future of the university seemed to be at stake as students filled the meadow to overflowing, and zealots shouted rebellion through their bullhorns.

But at a moment when tensions were at their height, both the activists and the university administration pulled back from the brink. A hybrid of both the Black Power movement and the Methodism of his minister father, Parker decried any calls for violence by protestors as "rampant mad dog adventurism." Ignoring the calls for the National Guard by some of the more reactionary state officials, the university administrators opted for a strategy of accommodation and conciliation.

Rather than the rampage and reaction that scarred other universities, ten thousand IU students marched fifteen abreast across the campus to peacefully protest against the war.

"We are disciplined people who are not fools," Parker told the crowd as they dispersed. The university canceled the next day's classes in memorial to the Kent State students. As teach-ins about the war in Southeast Asia abounded across campus, many students continued to boycott classes. The semester entropied to a close with the faculty council voting liberal grading options so student boycotters were not penalized. The next spring, as U.S. bombs continued to drop, Parker traveled to Hanoi to witness the devastation of the American war on North Vietnam.

TIME AND TIDES

With today's students more focused on résumés than revolution, many activists of the 1960s and 1970s still ponder those spring days of rage, when the ideas of alternative lifestyles, participatory democracy, anti-imperialism, and racial, gender, sexual orientation, and class equality blossomed. What does a generation of IU activists have to tell us about the importance and legacy of that era? How have those ideals informed their own lives and careers?

In his current position as assistant vice chancellor of government and community relations at the University of California, Los Angeles, Parker now sits on the other side of the desk listening to student demands. "Sometimes I do have to laugh at myself—sometimes I hear myself saying the same things I heard thirty years ago," he said. Revising his original trajectory of becoming a medical doctor, Parker taught African-American studies in Minnesota before joining the UCLA administration in 1981 in the Affirmative Action office.

"I believed in empowerment of people who were not empowered," said Parker, proudly noting that his IU student administration spearheaded student legal aid and day care. He credits his era of student activism with the growth of ethnic and women studies and the "engaged university" of today.

His activism continues as UCLA's assistant vice chancellor, laboring to keep college education available for the broadest range of the society. "I'm not as lean," he said. "I've got a beard now. I'm fifty-six years old. I'm older, wiser, have more maturity. But I still have the same spark of idealism and passion. I'm still antiwar, still believe in empowerment. Education is still critically important to me—access, affordability, diversity—all those things are still important to me."

IN LOCO PARENTIS AND THE SDS

Guy Loftman recounts, "I never imagined that people would be calling me up about this forty years later. I just thought it was a wild and crazy thing I did."

Now a Bloomington, Indiana attorney, Loftman was a Students for a Democratic Society firebrand, who won the 1967–68 IUB student body presidency on a platform of student rights. In the process, he began a tradition of student government activism that continues to resonate.

For many decades, the university regulated students with *in loco parentis* policies, without any substantive student input. Among the rules that seem almost incomprehensible today, the university dictated dress codes at dorm dinners (no blue jeans), where students lived, and when they could have cars. But the most hated regulations related to women's hours—a Byzantine set of rules that mandated women return to their dorm or sorority by 11:00 PM on weeknights and 1:00 AM on weekends. Male students were free to roam, the administrators assuming if they sequestered the fairer sex, the men would meander on home.

Students wanted change, and the time was right. The fight for civil rights had engendered activists with a fervent belief in grassroots democracy and the training to organize mass movements. The Baby Boomer generation began hitting the nation's campuses in the mid-1960s, creating a seismic cultural shift.

As the youth culture began to flex its power, the small military advisory mission in Southeast Asia escalated into the juggernaut of the American war in Vietnam. Fed by the relentless Selective Service military draft, 537,000 soldiers were in Vietnam in 1968. By the end of the year, 24,486 young Americans had died in the war—a thousand deaths a month in 1968. More than 58,000 American soldiers eventually lost their lives in Vietnam.

Using tactics from the Civil Rights movement, radical student groups such as the SDS called for antiwar actions, as well as participatory democracy on campuses. The activists included Loftman (Class of 1967), who helped organize an IU chapter of the SDS. In Loftman's first campaign in 1964, he argued for the abolishment of the mandatory Reserve Officers' Training Corps training requirement, commingling antiwar activism with a very real grassroots student issue.

Loftman had arrived at IU in 1963 as a conservative fraternity boy, but the tenor of the day moved him rapidly to the left. With the help of his wife, Connie Keisling Loftman (Class of 1979), who acted as his campaign manager, Loftman won the 1967 election for student body president on a platform of student rights. His party, the Progressive Reform Party, announced it would engage in "open confrontation" with the administration about such issues as women's hours, sprawling survey courses that were often devoid of faculty involvement, free bus service, twenty-four-hour library access, and student control over nonacademic policies. With the political pressure of the Loftman-led student government and other engaged groups that included the Association of Women Students, the university rescinded many of the onerous parental regulations over the next few years.

"Connie still tells me where to go, and I still figure out what to say," Loftman said with a laugh in his sunny Walnut Street law office, where he has a sole general practice in a restored Victorian house. As she has for twenty years, his wife and former campaign manager acts as Loftman's office manager.

After his term as student body president, Loftman had to deal with the Selective Service and a culture in crisis. He spent two years serving as a conscientious objector in the Bloomington Hospital before joining the legendary Needmore Commune in Brown County. He and his wife then worked as juvenile prison guards for more than two years. In 1972 Loftman entered the IU School of Law at Bloomington, graduating in 1974.

Loftman has remained an activist. He's one of those stalwart folks protesting the war in Iraq each Wednesday on the Monroe County Courthouse steps. He counsels young people about military recruiters and the potential for a draft.

"I remain highly committed to ending this awful, awful war," he said. Loftman has long been involved in the local Democratic Party. He is also a perennial member of community boards and a soft touch for needy nonprofits seeking *pro bono* work. He has been part of the ongoing fight for racial equality since his college days, serving on the local National Association for the Advancement of Colored People executive committee and as a leader of an intensive six-year study of race and criminal justice in Monroe County that the American Bar Association recognized as a national model of community relations.

"The fact is," Loftman said, "the values I formed then are still my values. Patterns of activism are still my patterns."

STUDENT STRIKERS AND THE COUNTERCULTURE

The tempo of conflict increased in the late 1960s. With student deferments increasingly curtailed, the Selective Service scoured the campuses
for fresh soldiers. Equally determined antiwar activists fought the military machine with mass demonstrations and threats of armed resistance.
With Vietnam casualties soaring, protests expanded exponentially. Facing almost certain electoral defeat, incumbent Lyndon B. Johnson withdrew from the presidential race in February 1968. The assassinations
of Martin Luther King Jr. in April and Robert F. Kennedy in June of
that year convinced many that nonviolent protests were futile, and the
Chicago police riots against student demonstrators at the Democratic
National Convention in August further illustrated that young protestors
were now fair game. There was continuing violent upheaval at Berkeley
and Columbia, and in Paris the Mai '68 student riots toppled the French
government.

In the spring of 1969, IU was a bubbling cauldron of discontent. A
host of activist groups were on campus, including the SDS, the W. E. B.
Dubois Club, the Young Socialist Alliance, and the Committee to End
the War. Emboldened by their fellow activists' success, IU radicals
pressed for further student rights and for the university to sever itself
from the American war enterprise.

The youth culture was increasingly codified with long hair, anti-au-
thoritarian music, and more than a modicum of drugs, which promised,
if not consciousness raising, at least a very good time. It was the year students arrived as khaki- and kilt-clad preppies, morphing by Thanksgiving break into bellbottomed bohemians. Shaven-headed Hari Krishna
devotees dressed in orange panhandled the campus verge. Gaily painted
Volkswagen buses with large dogs named "Moon" and "Toke" parked on
side streets. Shops emblematic of the nascent counterculture, such as the
Other Side and the Black Market, marked Kirkwood Avenue with the
scent of Patchouli oil and the throb of aggressive rock 'n' roll.

Inside, students could buy essentials such as incense, Jimmy Hen-
drix posters, bongs of various sizes and complexities, and Indian water-
buffalo sandals that were sure to stain suburban feet, all the while con-
spiring to overthrow the state with other new hipsters. On the Friday

before spring break began, March 28, 1969, the IU trustees voted, without any warning or student input, to raise tuition 68 percent. With the broad array of financial assistance available today, the increase seems laughable: the tuition for in-state undergraduate students went from $195 per semester to $325 per semester. But for the less prosperous students of the late 1960s, it was another seemingly insurmountable barrier to higher education.

The students returned from spring break abuzz with angry talk—as much against the increase as the high-handed manner with which it was handed down. Over the next few weeks thousands of students protested, including an April 28 rally in the new fieldhouse, where eight thousand students and faculty demanded the administration rescind the fee increase, establish a student budget committee with real power, and reduce tuition to zero within three years. They insisted on a response within two days.

A few days later, Bloomington's underground paper, the *Spectator*, published a "Special Pre-Barricades Issue." In a series of rallies, IU students voted to boycott classes. "All strike; shut it down," was the cry as thousands participated in the student strike. On Sunday, May 4, as an enormous throng of students debated tactics in Dunn Meadow, smoke from the burning Graduate Library in Franklin Hall billowed into the warm spring sky. Though a disgruntled library employee was later charged with the arson, anarchy seemed to be in the air.

A young dissident, Michael Shoemaker (Class of 1970) was among those in the meadow that day. A former fraternity member, business major, and editor of the right-wing alternative newspaper, Shoemaker had drifted steadily left. In 1968 he had been elected to the Student Senate, and joined other activists demonstrating against the university administration's decisions. "I was an action-oriented person, pushing us to strike," he remembered from his Portland, Oregon, ashram, the Nityananda Institute.

Shoemaker took a different route out of the 1960s. "People mostly call me Swami," he said. He is now Swami Chetanananda, leader of a spiritual group with centers in New York City; Boston; Santa Monica, California; Oslo, Norway; and Kathmandu, Nepal. He tells of a fellow IU student government officer, Kerry Kaplan (BS 1970, MS 1972), "dragging me to a yoga class and introducing me to yoga." In the chaotic summer of 1970, Shoemaker and other IU students founded a commune in a bankrupt fraternity house, where twenty-eight people eventually lived and practiced various Eastern spiritual disciplines.

"It was so stressful and intense," Shoemaker said of the times, "we turned to spiritualism as a way to anchor ourselves." The group eventually became the Rudrananda Ashram, which was instrumental in a number of successful Bloomington ventures, including the Tao restaurant, the Vienna Dog House, and Graphic Glass.

Today, Swami Chetanananda is a recognized religious teacher in both Hindu and Tibetan Buddhist practices. Speaking of his status as a recognized reincarnate teacher, he said, "I'm probably the only person in the world who has received linage transit in the Hindu Shaivist and Tibetan Buddhist traditions."

Since 1996 his spiritual practice has included Chöd, the esoteric Tibetan Buddhist tantric technique that involves midnight meditations in charnel grounds. He spends six months a year at his center in Kathmandu, where he focuses on the Chöd practice. "As you can imagine, I spend a lot of time in some pretty weird places," he said.

"IU was a beacon of hope for young people in Indiana," Swami Chetanananda said of Bloomington activism in the 1960s and 1970s. "It was exciting to be there, and I look back on that time with some gratitude and some regrets. On the one hand, there was a sense of new possibilities. But the question remains, there were thousands of us there. Where are they now?"

Though he says, "IU taught me a lot about what I didn't want to be," Swami Chetanananda counts himself among those who live out their youthful ideals. "I'm at the center of a community of a few hundred people. We're living our political values every day. Our community exists in contrast to the greed of the entire culture."

TIME FOR A WOMAN

A Young Democrat from the small town of Zionsville, Indiana, was also in Dunn Meadow during the student strike.

"I came from a sheltered high school," Mary Scifres Grabianowski remembered. "There were eighty kids in my class. I tried to take part in everything at IU—speakers, music, organizations, everything. It was just so neat to be part of all of this." Grabianowski (BA 1979, MS 1992) says she was a do-gooder in high school, thanks to a "political gene" inherited from her family's long political involvement.

"I got involved with Young Democrats from the giddy-up," she said. She recalled the huge changes as she and her classmates spun off into new, uncharted orbits in the 1960s; singing church hymns with Black Panthers one winter day at a radical camp on Lake Webster; Yippie Jerry Rubin vainly attempting to foment revolution at IU; and Woodstock poster-boy Louie Zantashi eternally whirling in Dunn Meadow in his signature loincloth and black cape.

Grabianowski's political gene stood her in good stead at IU, where she was a political science major and a stalwart Young Democrat. After the tuition strike in the spring of 1969, she marched on Washington, D.C., in the Vietnam Moratorium demonstration, as well as the campus protests after Cambodia and Kent State. She became a student lobbyist at the Indiana legislature, arguing for more dollars for higher education, for the eighteen-year-old vote, as well as for an eighteen-year-old drinking law that she now is happy to have seen fail.

In the spring of 1971, Mary Scifres ran for IUB student body president. "Clarine Nardi Riddle (BA 1971, JD 1974), who was the president of the YWCA, said, 'You ought to run. It's time we had a woman. You'd be good.'" Scifres defeated a slate of thirteen male candidates, and then immediately faced a funding crisis: In the aftermath of Parker's trip to Hanoi, the university trustees revoked all funding for student government. But the trustees soon relaxed when they realized they now had a moderate, if highly mobilized, leader at the helm. With the war winding down in the spring of 1972, Dunn Meadow was quiet for the first time in many years.

And then—"after I finally put a bra back on"—she began working on larger campaigns. After the voting age was lowered to eighteen, she helped register twelve thousand IU students to vote, and then campaigned to elect a young law graduate, Frank McCloskey (BA 1968, JD

1971) as Bloomington mayor. For many years, she worked for U.S. Senator, Birch Bayh (JD 1960, LLD 1995) and Common Cause.

In 1987 Grabianowski returned to Zionsville High School as a teacher, a highly involved, highly motivated one. Her many awards are testimony to her dedication, including one in 2003 for outstanding teaching from the IU Center on Congress, headed by Lee Hamilton (JD 1956, LLD 1991) and the 2005 Olin Davis Economics Award for outstanding teaching of economics.

"My years in Bloomington as a student activist and an observer helped me to be open to change, to other people, to other ideas," Grabianowski said. "It was such a crossroads of politics, the arts. I encourage my kids to be active. That's what makes good citizens."

MAGICAL BLOOMINGTON

Jeff Richardson (BA 1973, JD 1977, MPA 1981) was there, too, when the edifice of monolithic university education cracked, and a whole generation of students poured into the gap. He arrived at IU in 1968, staying until the early 1980s. "My family says I zipped through school in twelve years," he said. "I fell in love with Bloomington. It was just magical. Robert Kennedy spoke. Eugene McCarthy. I swam in the quarry. I saw people—myself—transforming themselves and how they saw 'the establishment' to use a term from back then."

In Richardson's case, he transformed himself into an activist, marching against the war, campaigning for antiwar U.S. Senator Vance Hartke (JD 1948), and serving as IUB student vice president in 1971–72 and president in 1973–74. He served on Bloomington's Common Council from 1976 to 1980, with a focus on protecting student rights through legislation such as the landlord-tenant laws.

Under Governor Evan Bayh (BS 1978, LLD 1996), Richardson headed two state agencies, including the thirteen-thousand-person Indiana Family and Social Services Administration. After serving as the executive director of the Gay Men's Health Crisis, America's largest AIDS service, education, and advocacy group, Richardson became the executive director of Step Forward, an international relief organization dedicated to the growing number of children impacted by AIDS. Both the School of Law at Bloomington and the School of Public and Environmental Affairs have honored Richardson with distinguished alumni awards. "I can't imagine being in college in a more interesting, more dynamic, more energizing school," he said. "I am so grateful to have been there in that period of time. It's not just the energy and the activists. It's the unlimited possibility. Bloomington represents the good things that can happen when you get good people together."

DADA ACTIVISM

While IU's political storms abated after the early 1970s, Bloomington continued to swirl with creative energy. A number of former activists settled in the town to start small businesses and families. And yet another group of engaged and engaging characters arrived on campus to continue the high jinks. Leon Varjian was one.

Varjian (MA 1975), arrived as a graduate student in 1972 from New Jersey's Montclair State. A math whiz with a puckish sense of humor, Varjian sported a luxuriant Groucho Marx moustache and Veronica Lake hair, dressing in ensembles of plaids and patterns that can only be described as inspired. "Coming to Bloomington was like 'anything goes,'" Varjian recalled. "The administration had their hands full with students burning the ROTC building. We did kind of a hit-and-run, somewhat ethereal, ephemeral. It was there; it's gone. And we always cleaned everything up."

So after years of doctrinarian seriousness, Bloomington soon came to savor the surreal antics of too-bright Leon: rubber-band assaults on Bryan Hall, free campus transportation (via grocery carts), and his annual Banana Olympics, where entrants competed in events such as banana tosses, belly-to-belly banana races, and banana-peel slipping contests. Varjian's frenetic ringing of an old school bell outside of Ballantine Hall often heralded his madcap announcements, such as President Richard Nixon's resignation because of an ingrown toenail or IU's reorganization as an amusement park, "IU-Land." There was the hard-fought "Name that Tuna" contest for the Monroe County Courthouse weathervane, and the proposal that the Courthouse square be turned into a giant Monopoly board. "It would have fit perfectly," Varjian insisted. He would know: Varjian chalked up the sidewalk with game squares as business owners warily watched.

Politics naturally called. Varjian ran for IUB student body vice president as part of the Birthday Party slate, each campaign event beginning with the party's anthem, "Happy Birthday." "Everybody knew the words," Varjian said. Emboldened by his lack of electoral success, Varjian ran for Bloomington mayor in 1975, finishing third in the Democratic primary with 776 votes.

It was a sad day when Varjian left town. Armed with his master's degree, he headed to Washington, D.C., for an unlikely job in the bowels of the Bureau of Labor Statistics—"I was a bureaucrat!" he insisted. But after a year, academia again whistled, and Varjian headed north to Madison, Wisconsin, for what he calls "post-graduate-level prankdom."

He is still fondly remembered in Madison for delivering on a promise made during his successful campaign for vice president of the student body. Varjian pledged to airlift the Statue of Liberty to Madison's centerpiece, Lake Mendota. One frigid winter morning, Madison was stunned to see the Statue of Liberty indeed out in the lake, surrounded by ice. Well, people actually could not see the entire Miss Liberty, only her head from the nose up and the tip of her torch. According to Varjian, when the helicopter dropped her off the night before, the statue broke through the ice and plunged to the bottom of the lake. Madisonians still talk about trudging across the ice to inspect Varjian's plywood and papier-mâché ruse.

"I always thought I was doing a public service," Varjian said of his college-days tomfoolery. But twenty years ago, he did another unlikely thing: he became a New Jersey high-school math teacher—and not surprisingly, a superlative one. In 1996 he was honored with the Presidential Award for Excellence in Science and Mathematics Teaching, the most prestigious award a math teacher can receive.

"I think my pranks prepared me for going into the classroom," Varjian said. "I've called on every element of those pranks in the classroom. You get their attention, you do your spiel, you get out. It's the same. But you try to reach beyond that and get to the mathematician within."

MAKE A DIFFERENCE

Black Panther, university chancellor, SDS community attorney, fraternity-hippie Swami, feminist civics teacher, student activist AIDS executive, and campus-clown math teacher. Stories and paths that became interwoven in a few tumultuous years on a leafy campus in Indiana—a few years when youthful activism became a habit and shaped lifetimes.

As Richardson said, "If you get that spark when you are in school that hopefulness can change the world, it will stay with you your whole life. The great revelation I got in Bloomington is that one person can make a difference."

30

JIHADIS IN INDIANA

OSAMA BIN LADEN SAT IN INDIANAPOLIS WITH HIS PREGNANT wife and two sons, waiting for their flight at Weir Cook Airport. It was 1979, and the bin Ladens had been in Indiana for weeks, visiting a friend, getting medical care for their son, and meeting with his mentor, a radical Islamic scholar and cleric named Abdullah Azzam, the father of global jihadism.[1]

Sitting in the terminal, the bin Ladens were an arresting sight for American midwesterners: the tall, wealthy, twenty-two-year-old Saudi with his patchy beard and diffident manner; his wife, Najwa, swathed in black from head to toe in her Arabian attire of long, flowing abaya, head scarf and thin veil that obscured her face. Hoosiers stared at the couple and their two quiet sons. A few people snapped photographs.

It was Najwa bin Laden's first visit outside the Arab world. As a traditional Saudi wife, Najwa had been in *purdah,* primarily restricted to home. She had been surprised when her husband announced the family was going to travel "to a place I had never heard of, a state in America called Indiana." While in Indianapolis, she stayed with a girlfriend, who took her on outings unimaginable for a woman in Arabia. "We even went into a big shopping mall in Indianapolis," she recalled. When the bin Laden babe in arms, Abdul Rahman, became ill, Osama bin Laden arranged for an Indianapolis doctor to examine the child. "I relaxed after that kindly physician assured us that Abdul Rahman would soon be fine," she stated. "I came to believe that Americans were gentle and nice, people easy to deal with."

Bin Laden and Azzam were not the first fundamentalist Muslim radicals to visit Indiana to discuss jihad, holy war. Nor were they the last jihadists to make their way to the Hoosier State. Indeed, as America became increasing engaged in the roiled Islamic lands, Indiana became a destination for a generation of jihadis.

The tumultuous year of 1979 proved pivotal for the Islamic world and the Indiana Muslim community. In January 1979 Iranian Shiites under their leader, Ayatollah Ruhollah Khomeini, overthrew U.S.-backed Shah Mohammad Reza Pahlavi and established a Muslim theocracy. Egypt and Israel signed a controversial peace accord. In Afghanistan fundamentalist Islamic tribesmen revolted against the Soviet Union–supported Afghan Communist government. The Central Intelligence Agency was soon clandestinely supporting the mujahideen as proxies against the Soviet Union.

In 1979 the Indiana Islamic community was also in flux, perhaps the reason bin Laden and Azzam met in Indianapolis. Indiana was already home to growing numbers of Muslim immigrants. Prior to World War II, the number of Middle Eastern immigrants settling in Indiana had been small in comparison to Europeans. In 1920 there were only 3,600 Hoosiers of Middle Eastern extraction; only 5,619 by 1960. But after the Immigration and Nationality Act of 1965 gave preference to immigrant professionals, more Muslim medical doctors, engineers, and academics began to arrive in Indiana.

Organized in 1963 by Islamic scholars studying at midwestern universities, the influential Muslim Students Association had opened its first headquarters in 1973 at the Masjid al-Amin mosque in Gary, Indiana. One of the MSA's first three chapters was at Indiana University. Arab and Pakistani students established a small Indiana University–Purdue University at Indianapolis chapter in the early 1960s.

While the MSA had a diverse membership representing the entire Islamic spectrum, many of its leaders were part of the Muslim Brotherhood. Founded in Egypt in 1928, the Brotherhood promulgated a philosophic strain of jihadism that glorified war and martyrdom. Over the next decades, the Brotherhood spread through the Islamic world, and then Europe. In the 1960s, Brotherhood members began organizing in the United States through organizations such as the MSA. Through the

1970s, Saudi Arabia and other oil-rich Arab countries funded fundamentalist Islamic missionary activities. Supported by Saudi money, the MSA journal, *Al-Ittihad (The Unity)*, consistently published anti-American articles by prominent jihadists.

MSA chapters also sponsored many speeches by traveling jihadists, including firebrand imam Azzam. As part of its Cold War anti-Communist strategy, the CIA had recruited jihadists such as Azzam, who became one of the agency's most trusted Middle Eastern assets. By 1979 when Azzam repeatedly met bin Laden in Indianapolis, he had already been using CIA funding and visas to preach jihad in America, eventually speaking in more than fifty U.S. cities. "I traveled to acquaint people with jihad," Azzam stated. "We were trying to satisfy the thirst for martyrdom."

A Palestinian from Jordan, Azzam fought against the Israelis before embracing the militant teachings of Muslim Brotherhood theorist Sayyid Qutb. After getting his PhD in the Principals of Islamic Jurisprudence from Cairo's celebrated Al-Azhar University, Azzam became an activist for a pan-Islamic revolution. In the early 1970s Azzam began teaching in Jedda, Saudi Arabia, at King Abdul Aziz University, the school that Osama bin Laden attended.

Bin Laden was the son of one of Saudi Arabia's most influential men; a scion to great wealth from his father's powerful construction group. He was an important jihadist connection to the Arabian Gulf's vast trove of petro dollars. Introduced to the Muslim Brotherhood at his elite Saudi high school, bin Laden became increasingly involved with radical Islam in college. In time, bin Laden became the chief private financier of the jihadi movement. So the reported Indianapolis meeting of the two men who later cofounded al Qaeda was momentous.

And bin Laden and Azzam had friends and colleagues in Indianapolis. In 1979, four other members of the Muslim Brotherhood were living in Indianapolis. Yusuf Mustafa Nada was a wealthy Egyptian banker who led a major cement company in Saudi Arabia, where he may have had linkages with the bin Ladens' construction empire. Jamal Barzinji and Ahmad Totonji were Iraqi Muslim Brotherhood members who were founders and officials of the MSA. A third Iraqi Muslim Brotherhood member living in Indianapolis, Purdue University graduate Hisham Altalib, worked for Nada. Beginning in 1975 the four men collaborated on the development of Muslim Brotherhood-associated institutions in Indiana. After the 9/11 attacks, federal authorities charged that all four men were involved with financing al Qaeda operations.

In 1976 the MSA bought a 123-acre farm in Plainfield, Indiana, with the intent of building a North American Islamic Center. Meeting in Plainfield in early 1977, MSA officials conceived of an umbrella organization called the Islamic Society of North America that would encompass the MSA and the North American Islamic Trust, which would finance mosque construction. Other Muslim organizations became founding ISNA constituents, including the Muslim Community Association of the U.S. and Canada, the Islamic Medical Association, the Association of Muslim Scientists and Engineers, the Association of Muslim Social Scientists, and other Islamic societies.

Though the MSA and ISNA moderated through time, the originators conceived of the organization as being part of earlier Islamic jihadist efforts. Naming the Pakistani and Egyptian jihadist movements, Ihsan Bagby, director of ISNA's Islamic Teaching Center wrote, "In actuality, ISNA is a successor and inheritor of the other Islamic movements, especially Jamaati Islami and the Ihkwan."

In January 1978 the center's officials announced plans for a new ISNA headquarters in Plainfield. The ISNA compound would include office space, a mosque, library, publications facility, and a camp retreat. To finance the center, the ISNA leaders anticipated tapping resources in oil-rich Saudi Arabia and other Arabian Gulf states.

The ISNA proposal was controversial. A Plainfield group called the Concerned Citizens of Hendricks County formed to fight the proposed center, arguing that the ancillary facilities violated church zoning ordinances. The Hendricks County Board of Zoning Appeals voted 3–2 to permit the development, but the contretemps continued. In 1979 the Islamic Center's secretary-general, Doctor Mahmoud Rashdan, a Jordanian education professor, told a reporter that the Muslims chose Plainfield for their headquarters because 60 percent of the Muslims in the United States live within two hundred miles of Indianapolis. He said the Muslim leaders had posited that Indiana's traditional religiosity would encourage tolerance, "even if the religion is different."

While the court eventually denied the remonstrators' appeal and construction began in 1980, it was a challenging time for the leaders of Plainfield's Muslim center. "We're not really sorry we've chosen Indiana," Rashdan told the reporter. "But we are discovering some problems."

The Soviet Union invaded Afghanistan on Christmas Day, 1979. Intent on crushing the growing Afghan rebellion, the Soviet Politburo pitted one of the world's greatest military powers against a rag-tag collection of Islamic tribesmen—the mujahideen. The invasion galvanized Muslim fundamentalists across the globe, including bin Laden. "The more he learned, the more anxious he became," Najwa wrote, "my husband's heart had been burned to a crisp." By the spring of 1979, bin Laden and Azzam were helping the mujahideen in the Afghan borderlands, where they later established al Qaeda. And the next chapter of jihadis in Indiana began.

The U.S. support to the mujahideen ramped up every year the Soviet forces were in Afghanistan. The United States eventually funneled more than $20 billion into mujahideen military support. In 1985 President Ronald Reagan met in the Oval Office with a group of bearded and turbaned Afghan jihadis, calling them "freedom fighters." The American media trumpeted the jihadi cause. As the Afghan-Soviet war grew ever bloodier and millions of Afghan refugees fled their country, the mujahideen were transfigured into American cultural heroes, valiant holy warriors fighting the godless Communists. An entire network of Afghan support developed across the country, including Indiana.

The Soviet attack helicopter wounded the young Afghan fighter in 1983. Despite the horrific wounds to his arm and chest, the Afghan man was determined to continue his jihad—and three years later an Indiana doctor helped him do that. Doctor Richard Idler was a hand surgeon who volunteered to treat the warrior, who had been a farmer before the Soviet invasion.

With the help of the Intergovernmental Committee for Migration and U.S. military transport, the wounded Afghan arrived in Indianapolis for rehabilitation in 1986. While undergoing treatment, he stayed in Plainfield at the newly constructed $21 million ISNA complex that donors from Saudi Arabia, Qatar, and other Arabian Gulf states had funded. After undergoing extensive hand surgery at Saint Vincent Hospital, the jihadi began therapy. Anxious to return to the fight against the infidels as soon as his therapy was complete, the Afghan was a highly motivated patient. "This is the first one, to my knowledge, that came to this area," Idler said. "Hopefully there will be more."

There were. Many hardened Afghan jihadists eventually underwent medical treatment in Indiana. To select wounded men most likely to benefit from treatment in Indiana, Idler had traveled to the sprawling Afghan refugee camps in Pakistan's tribal regions with a U.S. Agency for International Development grant administered through the International Medical Corps. Most jihadis were treated at Saint Vincent and Methodist hospitals, but at least one fighter had surgery and rehab in Anderson at Saint John's Health Care facility.

Nur Muhammad Bada was an Afghan fighter who had been hit in the right knee during a firefight. Hauled by his comrades across the mountains in a litter, he had been chosen for treatment at Saint John's to free up his frozen knee. Orthopedic surgeon Doctor Paul Ramsey rebuilt Bada's knee in a two-hour surgery. After his long, painful recovery under the care of a physical therapist Laurie Julian, Bada said, "People are but instruments of God. I fought for the pleasure of Almighty God. My being healed is also Allah's doing."

"We always had seven or eight mujahideen staying at ISNA," Bagby told me. Bagby was the director of ISNA's Islamic Teaching Center from 1985 to 1991 and is now a University of Kentucky professor. An African-American Muslim who converted to Islam as a young man at Oberlin College, Bagby came to ISNA after receiving his University of Michigan doctorate. During the time Bagby worked at the ISNA headquarters, Plainfield was on the jihadist circuit. Many touring jihadis stayed in the little Mujahideen House on the property.

In 1987 three Afghan mujahideen, Muhammad Agha, Ismail Muhammad, and Nabi Muhammad, were waiting for their surgeries at the ISNA compound, where they met with an *Indianapolis Star* reporter. Sponsored by Congressman Dan Burton, the men arrived in Indianapolis on a U.S. Air Force medical evacuation flight. Through an Afghan interpreter, the jihadis told the reporter they had fought the Soviet gunships and attack jets with cheap Chinese machine guns and captured Russian rifles. They had been blown up by rockets; wounded by mortars. Blind and crippled, the men were determined to fight the infidels again. The mujahideen said that "their fight is more than just a battle for ownership of political control of their land—it is a holy war. To die for their god is to go to paradise."

While deeply rooted in Indiana, the MSA and ISNA were also deeply engaged in the international jihadist movement during the Afghan-Soviet War. While many of the first generation of post–World War II Muslim immigrants espoused the Muslim Brotherhood's nuanced jihadist beliefs, most of these new Americans did not advocate violence toward the United States. Instead these Muslim Americans used the fire of rekindled twentieth-century Islamic fundamentalism to influence their community's intellectual and ethical positions, which included American Islamic support for mujahideen fighting infidels elsewhere.

A 1986 article by Mohammad Fadel in *Islamic Horizons* issued a call to arms. Titled "Jihad is Imperative to Muslims," Fadel deftly illuminated the many shades of jihad (struggle) in Muslim thought, from the internal struggles to overcome sin to violent jihad against transgressors. Fadel reiterated that "jihad is a duty for all able Muslims," essential for the "self-interest of our community's survival." The rewards were great: "A believer who participates in jihad is superior to a believer who does not." And: "Anyone killed in jihad is rewarded with Paradise"

The 1980s were turbulent for the Indiana-based ISNA, though the decade did begin on a positive note. On Labor Day weekend 1982, MSA leader Doctor Sayyid M. Syeed announced to the Muslim Students Association convention being held in Bloomington that the ISNA organization was now official. The newly constituted ISNA had continuity:

according to Muslim Alliance of Indiana executive director Shariq Siddiqui, the organization "continued the missionary work of the MSA," with educational outreach programs for Americans converting to Islam, as wells as espousing MSA's fundamentalist internationalism. Through the 1980s, the majority of ISNA's contributions still came from Muslim countries, and about half the speakers at the annual convention were from outside the United States, including leaders from jihadist groups such as Jamaat-i Islami. In 1986 the ISNA international convention was in Indianapolis, the same year ISNA leaders reaffirmed their goal to help Muslims in North America "adopt Islam as a complete way of life." According to Siddiqui, the phrase echoed "the oft-repeated words of various participants of the global Islamic religious revival of the era."

By 1988 the Federal Bureau of Investigation field office in Indianapolis was investigating leaders of both the both NAIT and ISNA for ties to the Muslim Brotherhood. An FBI report noted the NAIT and ISNA leaders were "in a position to direct the activities and support of Muslims in the U.S. for the Islamic Revolution." And a December 15, 1987, FBI report on NAIT stated that there was evidence that the leaders and members of NAIT were in "support of JIHAD (a holy war) in the U.S." The FBI agents were particularly concerned with NAIT support to Black Muslim separatists for travel to Iran, where they were ostensibly trained for violent Islamic Revolution.

But even during the great turmoil of the Soviet-Afghan War, American Muslims were adapting to their new home, and the ISNA was moderating. In 1986 Ishan Bagby wrote an *Islamic Horizons* article. While acknowledging the association's roots in the Islamic jihadist movement, Bagby argued that the ISNA should not be a "clandestine" political group like the Muslim Brotherhood, but instead should evolve into an open organization that reflected "our particular situation here in North America." And that is what happened.

As the 1980s progressed, there was growing tension between the MSA and the ISNA. Moderate ISNA leaders began to move the younger organization away from the MSA's internationalist positions. "Some of the old MSA types fell away," Bagby said, "and some were pushed away." ISNA was also coping with Muslim-bashing media and hostile Americans. In the fall of 1986 ISNA Secretary General Iqbal Unus convened a press conference to protest Western media coverage that demonized Muslims as terrorists.

The multiple struggles ravaged the organization's finances. The IS-NA's ongoing operating deficits climaxed in 1989, when the board failed to approve an operating budget and the North American Islamic Trust had to assume ISNA financial operations. Things got worse in 1990, when donations from wealthy Islamic countries plummeted after ISNA opposition to the Gulf War angered Saudi Arabia, a key U.S. ally against Iraq.

After the decade of tumult, ISNA went through a metamorphosis in the 1990s. ISNA reorganized under Syeed, who brought long-term leadership after a series of "acting" directors. The organization retrenched with job cuts and reduced programming, and then proceeded to evolve into a strong institution serving a thriving Muslim American population. In the twenty-five years following the liberalized immigration law, the Islamic population in the United States had increased substantially—to between three million and seven million Muslims, depending on the estimate. By 1990 there were almost nine thousand Middle Easterners living in Indiana.

Under Syeed, the ISNA hired professional staff to manage the annual convention, publications, and fund-raising, some trained at IU's Center for Philanthropy. "While previous employees tended to be religious missionaries," Siddiqui wrote, "this new generation was pious Muslims not previously part of any religious revival movements." Siddiqui stated that the ISNA was "not an organization of 'Muslims in America' but one of Muslim Americans." ISNA now "emphasized the idea that Muslims and Islam could flourish in a pluralistic and democratic environment."

It took a civil war, oil, and Texas determination to get the next bunch of jihadists to Indiana. The last of the defeated Soviet Army withdrew from Afghanistan on February 15, 1989. After a decade of war, the Islamic jihadis had won. The Soviet Union splintered apart soon after, ending the Cold War. And soon after that, U.S. attention shifted from the mujahideen.

But war waged on in Afghanistan. With rival tribesmen enculturated to battle and armed to the teeth by the United States and its allies, a civil war soon erupted. By the mid-1990s the country was divided into fiefdoms, some were marginally stable; others nearly anarchic. Out of this brutal reality, the Taliban emerged. Beginning near Kandahar, the Taliban jihadis quickly established a draconian order in much of Afghanistan. By September 1996 the militant, staunchly fundamentalist Taliban were the de facto rulers of Afghanistan.

President Bill Clinton's administration played it both ways with the Taliban government. A 1997 State Department memo bluntly stated that the U.S. policy "will inevitably be messy and the policy we follow will be ridden with inner tensions, as we simultaneously engage with the Taliban and criticize their abuses." Criticizing was good politics. Lambasting the Taliban's hyperconservative Islamic gender policies polled well with American feminists, a key element of the Democratic base. American officials reproached the Taliban for opium-poppy production and for harboring bin Laden, who had been implicated in the 1993 World Trade Center attack.

But on the other hand, there was gas and oil. That was the "engagement" part of the U.S. policy. The U.S. energy company Unocal had been maneuvering to build trans-Afghanistan gas and oil pipelines to link Turkmenistan natural gas and Caspian oil with burgeoning South Asian markets. But Afghanistan was wild and wooly—until the Taliban enforced its rough justice. Unocal wanted to do business with the Taliban, and had major State Department support. "We found a real sweet spot for the State Department," former Unocal president John Imle told me. So with the backing of the U.S. government, Unocal launched a charm offensive. And that is how the Taliban came to be in Indiana.

Unocal began a major push in 1997 to sign agreements with the still-warring mujahideen. Company executives, including vice president Marty Miller, traveled across the restive country in little white pick-up trucks, signing cooperation agreements with warlords of every ethnic stripe. But the Taliban controlled much of the pipeline routes across Afghanistan, so their agreement was essential.

To facilitate the U.S. side of the campaign, the company engaged well-connected American diplomats, including future ambassador to

Afghanistan and Iraq Zalmay Khalilzad and former ambassador to Pakistan Robert Oakley, whose wife was chief of the State Department's intelligence wing. Unocal's other State Department supporters included Assistant Secretary of State for South Asia Robin Raphel and her successor, Karl Inderfurth. Both made numerous trips to Kabul to push the pipeline proposal with the Taliban leaders.

Unocal also signed on an influential Afghanistan expert. Director of the Center for Afghanistan Studies at the University of Nebraska at Omaha, Thomas Gouttierre had been a Peace Corps volunteer in Afghanistan before earning an Indiana University masters degree in Islamic Studies in 1969. Through the 1970s, his Nebraska center was one of the few U.S. institutions studying the then-obscure nation, and Gouttierre had considerable success securing government and private money for his Afghanistan programs. During the Soviet War, the center had famously used $60 million of CIA money to produce jihadi-glorying textbooks for Afghan boys.

With their U.S. supporters in place, the Unocal officials decided to impress the deal-cautious Taliban leaders with a road trip. In February 1997 senior Afghan officials traveled to the United States: Mawlawi Wakil Ahmed, senior adviser to one-eyed Taliban leader Mullah Omar; United Nations ambassador-designate Abdel Hakim Mujahed; diplomat Mawlawi Abdel Wahab, and Mawlawi Abdel Raqib, the Taliban's refugee minister. Bouncing between New York and Washington, D.C., for two weeks, the jihadists dialogued at the State Department and lobbied at the UN, all the while spinning a positive picture for the media. "There is a lot of propaganda," Wakil Ahmed said. "We wanted to explain ourselves, who we are."

Later that year another delegation of Taliban junketeers hit the states for an even more upscale outing. The group included former Foreign Minister Mullah Muhammad Ghaus, incoming Foreign Minister Wakil Ahmed Muttawakil, the Minister of Education and Minister of Information and Culture, Mullah Amir Khan Muttaqi, an extreme fundamentalist even by Taliban standards, as well as Minister for Mines and Industry Ahmed Jan, Planning Minister Din Muhammad, and Taliban permanent representative designate to the UN, Abdul Hakim Mujahid.

Arriving in December 1997, the Taliban VIPs stayed at a five-star Houston hotel, visited the zoo, hit the National Aeronautics and Space Administration's Space Center, and went tire kicking at the local Toyota dealership for SUVs and pick-ups, conjecturally for their trademark bed-mounted machine guns. "We wanted to get them out of their own environment," Imle told me. "Let them see what the civilized world looked like. What was possible."

As the negotiations wound down, the oil men treated the jihadis to a lavish dinner at Unocal vice president Marty Miller's mansion. "We wanted to establish credibility; to develop a relationship," Miller told me. "The Taliban didn't have a commercial bone in their bodies. They were religious fanatics." So Miller made sure his house was Taliban-appropriate. "I had a Muslim come over before the dinner to be sure there wasn't anything in the house that would offend the Afghans," Miller said. The seven Christmas trees in the Millers' house intrigued the Taliban. "They were interested in what it was for and what the star represented," Miller said. "The first day they were stiff and cautious. But before long they were totally relaxed and happy."

The next stop was Gouttierre's center in Omaha, where the Taliban went to the Super Target store to stock up on stockings, toothpaste, combs, and soap. The bearded and black-turbaned Taliban went to Mount Rushmore to stare down the stone presidents, which Gouttierre said "they liked very much." In Washington, D.C., Taliban envoys met with Assistant Secretary of State for South Asia Karl Inderfurth, who lobbied for women's rights, elimination of poppy production, and the expulsion of bin Laden. The Afghans deflected the demands for bin Laden and opium reduction, and retorted that the treatment of Afghan women conformed to their traditional culture. But oil was foremost on everyone's minds.

Like so many mujahideen before them, the Taliban envoys traveled to Indiana. December 1997 was an inflection point for Hoosier Muslims. Only five months before, ISNA had hosted the first "Islam in America" conference at the University of Indianapolis. The conference reflected a generation of Muslim acculturation. During the three previous decades, the American Muslim community had evolved ways to participate in the pluralistic American society. Though the immigrant generation's jihad-ist-inspired internationalism still influenced Muslim-American thought, mainstream moderation was increasingly the dominant philosophy.

So when the militant fundamentalist Taliban visited ISNA head-quarters, they did not encounter a receptive crowd. "Their visit to Plain-field was not pleasant," said Doctor Nazif Shahrani, an Afghan anthro-pologist who has been a professor at IU since 1990. Shahrani was among the hundred Muslim Americans who gathered to confront the Taliban and ask why they were giving Islam a bad name. "Most people were there as protestors," Shahrani said.

Over the next few years, there were more jihadi junkets to America, including some more side trips to Mount Rushmore. In May 1998 two Taliban ministers visited Omaha for talks. A few days later, women's rights groups disrupted the Unocal shareholders meeting to protest the Unocal-Taliban "consortium," prompting the oil company to end Gout-tierre's contract. The Unocal pipeline deal itself was under increasing pressure. On August 7, 1998, it all blew up when al Qaeda bombers hit the American embassies in Kenya and Tanzania. The FBI placed bin Laden on its Ten Most Wanted list and seventy-five American cruise missiles descended on terrorist training camps in Afghanistan. Unocal called it quits. Though the pipeline project made sense in boardrooms, it collided with the ground reality in the Hindu Kush. Three years later, on September 11, 2001, a silver plane tilted out of a resplendent blue sky, and nothing was ever the same again.

NOTE

1. Najwa bin Laden recounted her husband and Abdullah Azzam's visit to Indiana in *Growing Up bin Laden* (New York: St. Martin's Press, 2009), 26, which was referenced by Steve Coll, "Osama in America: The Final Answer," *New Yorker*, 30 June 2009. Coll also references bin Laden's early travels in "Young Osama," *New Yorker*, 12 December 2005, as does Michael Scheuer, *Osama bin Laden* (New York: Oxford University Press, 2011), 206 n23, and A. J. Caschetta, "Writing the bin Laden Story," *Middle East Quarterly*, Summer

2013, 79. Abdullah Azzam's CIA and Muslim Student Association connections and his US travels are noted in Lee H. Hamilton, Daniel K. Inouye, *Report of the Congressional Committees Investigating the Iran/Contra Affair* (Washington, D.C.: Government Printing Office, 1987), 361, 363, 370; Lawrence Wright, *The Looming Tower* (New York: Knopf, 2006), 125; Thomas Hagghammer, "Abdullah Azzam, Imam of the Jihad," in *Al Qaeda in Its Own Words*, (Belknap Press of Harvard University Press, 2008), 89; Deborah Scroggins, "The Most Wanted Woman in the World," *Vogue*, March 2005, http://www.vogue.com/873623/read-it-now-wanted-women-faith-lies-and-the-war-on-terror-the-lives-of-ayaan-hirsi-ali-and-aafia-siddiqui/; Andrew McGregor, "Jihad and the Rifle Alone," *Journal of Conflict Studies*, Vol 23, No 2, 2003. *https://journals.lib.unb.ca/index.php/JCS/article/view/219*; Chris Suellentrop, "Abdullah Azzam, the Godfather of Jihad," Slate, 16 April 2002, *http://web.archive.org/web/20020504150857/http://slate.msn.com/?id =2064385;*

The US travels of fundamentalist Islamic jihadis such as Azzam and bin Laden needs further investigation. Vital information is currently veiled by government security classifications and the not-unreasonable reluctance of American Muslims to speak candidly about an era a few decades ago when the US government, media, and a broad spectrum of citizens enthusiastically supported Islamic jihadism.

An Indiana National Guard Agribusiness Development Team
security soldier on alert in Khost Province, Afghanistan.

Courtesy of Douglas A. Wissing.

31

WAR FARE

AFTER THE SECOND BOMB BLOCKS THE ROAD, WE DETOUR UP a wadi, our convoy of five massive armored MRAPs (Mine-Resistant-and-Ambush-Protected vehicle) trundling along the dry, rocky riverbed like a parade of pachyderms. Naked dun-colored mountains stretch off in the distance. Village boys come running to the edge of eroded riverbanks to silently watch us pass. We are headed to the Bak District Center, a fortified government outpost in eastern Afghanistan's insurgency-plagued Khost Province. A restive Pashtun tribal district on the Pakistan border, Bak is on a Taliban infiltration route and home to its own popular insurrection. The Hoosier soldiers are to meet with District Governor Latifullah about some agricultural aid projects. Though the distance to Bak is about the same as from downtown Indianapolis to Noblesville, it can take, depending on the roads and bombs and restive tribesmen, from a few hours to a few days to get there. If things go very wrong, we may not arrive at all.

It's a typical mission for the Indiana National Guard 1-19th Agribusiness Development Team, an elite group of sixty-four volunteer citizen-soldiers. The ADT soldiers are using their military skills and civilian expertise—especially agricultural expertise—to win over Afghan farmers vacillating between the Taliban and the American-backed government of Afghanistan. Commanded by a former southern Indiana farm boy, Colonel Brian Copes, the team includes some of the Indiana Guard's best and brightest—and toughest—soldiers.

After a jostling ride up the riverbed, we climb a precipitous bank and wind our way through blast walls into the relative safety of the Bak

District Center. It's *Fort Apache* and *Apoclypse Now* combined, little more than a few hardened structures surrounded by watchtowers and tall HESCO barriers festooned with tangles of razor wire. Burned and ravaged buildings are testimony to rocket and mortar attacks. The Afghan National Army and Afghan National Police, organizations the U.S. government touts as the saviors of the fledgling democracy, defend the flyblown place. We locate the apparent latrine: a scat-encrusted stretch of dirt around the corner from our bivouac. The ADT security platoon quickly tells the ANA they can have the night off; Hoosiers will man the watchtowers. A Guardsman later confides the ANA likes to start hitting the hash pipes about 5:00 PM, and have a strong propensity to accidentally shoot themselves. (At another compound, I see an ANA soldier twirling his handgun like a Western gunslinger. "Try to keep something solid between you and those guys," a grunt recommended.)

It is a chilly night, the team sleeping on truck hoods and the trailers' canvas canopies; some cramming into the MRAPs like so many armed sardines. The next morning District Governor Latifullah sweeps into the compound in a beaten-up red Toyota crew-cab pickup perforated with two enormous ballistics holes. He leaps out in a flush of oily indignation. A rich landowner, he's a plump, perfumed Afghan with a silver watch and an elaborate black-and-silver turban that sports a rooster crest of pleated flared fabric. A long fabric tail drapes over his shoulder and falls to his waist. The terp (Afghan interpreter) translates Latifullah's fulmination, "The Taliban try to kill him—see," pointing to two-inch holes in the truck, one precisely in the center of the tailgate, the other deftly piercing the structural column behind the driver's door. Colonel Copes glances over. I wonder what kind of weapon makes that kind of hole. Later Copes tells me the U.S. Army had given a new truck to another district governor whose truck had been destroyed by insurgents. He thought someone might have punched the holes in Latifullah's truck with a power tool.

In eastern Afghanistan's Pashtun regions, a shade tree at the village edge often serves as the place for *shuras* (meetings). Here Hoosier farmer-soldiers of the Indiana National Guard 1–19th Agricultural Development Team (ADT) meet with Afghan villagers in insurgency-wracked Khost Province as ADT security soldiers guard against attack.

Courtesy of Douglas A. Wissing.

Later Latifullah sits with a smug smile, fingering his amber prayer beads. One of the terps translates for him: "He says the village where the ADT hit the IEDs is his village. He lives there. Yesterday, I try to talk to you, to lead you here. Your soldiers frightens me." I think, "This guy's Taliban."

Despite the bomb detour and Latifullah's dramatic entrance, the agribusiness development meeting with the Bak officials, *khans* and *mashharaans* (village elders), is anticlimactic. It is a typical KLE (Key Leader Engagement), as the ADT calls their dog-and-pony shows. Throughout the meeting, one gray-bearded *mashharaan* holds his Kalashnikov with a worn wooden grip and tommy-gun canister at the ready. Another sports a Pancho Villa-style bandolier. The ADT agricultural specialists lay out their plans, ask for support, and turn down the inevitable demands for free seed and fertilizer. Determined as they are to establish sustainable projects, not handouts, the ADT resolutely refuses to provide free seed and fertilizer. (While demanding free fertilizer, the villagers complain about the adulterated Pakistani fertilizer they use. Most buried bombs, or IEDs, improvised incendiary devices, are homemade with fertilizer and fuel. IEDs are currently the insurgents' weapon of choice. I imagine the villagers thinking, "Yeah, we can't make decent bombs with that lousy Pakistani stuff.")

One elder says he hears on Radio America the Americans have spent billions in Afghanistan, but his village has gotten nothing. Copes said quietly, "I don't know where the money went, either." Since 2001 the United States has provided about $32 billion in development money to Afghanistan, augmented by an additional $25.3 billion donated by the international community. The Fiscal Year 2009 supplemental appropriations bill will raise the U.S. commitment to $38 billion, with the 2010 budget projected to send it to $50 billion. In June 2008 Congress created the office of the Special Inspector for Afghanistan Reconstruction, SIGAR, to investigate the use of these funds. The investigation is ongoing. Copes again tells the elders about the ADT's focus on small-scale, long-term, Afghan-appropriate projects.

Latifullah is purse-lipped when he learns they cannot get free seed and fertilizer, as poppy-growing provinces can. (Semiarid Khost has virtually no poppy production.) Latifullah insinuates they might need to

A Shobo Khel elder ponders the Americans' proposal as a younger tribesman sits in his shadow.

Courtesy of Douglas A. Wissing.

start some poppy fields. But he gets particularly agitated when he realizes there will be relatively little largess from the ADT. The district governor's sidelong glances becomes a glare, his pursed lips harden into a pout.

PEACE CORPS WITH GUNS

War is one of those short, powerful words—like art and mom and God—that connote things so big we can only grasp in shards. The Indiana National Guard 1-19th ADT is one of those shards, a small accessible element that nonetheless refracts a war too vast to comprehend in total.

Think of the ADT as a Peace Corps with guns. Part of the U.S. government's counterinsurgency efforts, the ADT is endeavoring to partner with Afghan farmers to raise their standard of living and bind them closer to the central government. With more than 70 percent of Afghans working in agriculture, it is a crucial demographic. But as our experience with Latifullah illustrates, it is a frustrating—and often dangerous—mission.

The 1-19th is the first of five Indiana ADTs to be posted to eastern Afghanistan on yearlong deployments, so there will be Hoosiers in Khost for a long time. Sixteen farmer-soldier ag experts, thirty-five security soldiers, and an exceptional number of officers make up the first Indiana ADT. The brass-heavy command team is an indication of the importance the National Guard is placing on this mission. Two colonels with farm backgrounds command the 1-19th: Copes and Cindra Chastain. While rooted in Indiana's farm culture, the handpicked team's credentials show a lot of cultivation. "You can't swing a cat in here without hitting someone with advanced degrees," laughed Captain Bob Cline, a Heltonville farmer with an Indiana University accounting masters and law degree.

Besides months of counterinsurgency training at Camp Atterbury, the ADT's men and women received extensive Afghan-specific agricultural training from Purdue University, and drew on IU's world-renowned expertise in central Asia for concentrated courses on Afghan culture and politics. The university's Center for the Languages of the Central Asian Region taught a crash course in Pashto, the language of the Pashtun tribe that dominates Afghanistan—and the insurgency. The training primed the ADT to develop low-tech, sustainable projects, such as small, villager-constructed check dams and animal husbandry

Khost Province is a semiarid plain ringed by rugged Hindu Kush mountains. With scant rainfall and seasonal streams, the tribesmen rely on irrigation to water their small grain fields and orchards. Taken during a Blackhawk reconnaissance flight, this photo of a village's irrigated fields graphically shows the critical role of water in a parched mountain land.

Courtesy of Douglas A. Wissing.

training. The team hopes to plant trees and seed miles of sere rangeland with a perennial forage grass, perhaps by helicopter. The plan includes ag-related microbusinesses—including some for Afghan women. But the ADT emphasis is on training. One day Copes sits waiting at the airfield for a Blackhawk to arrive. Smoking a Pattonesqe cigar, he ruminates on the value of education: "Knowledge is something the Taliban cannot blow up or burn down. They can't take it away. It'll last long after the Coalition forces have left. When I say that to the Afghans, they get it."

FARM BOY WARRIOR

Copes grew up on a two-hundred-acre family farm near the white clapboard hamlet of Blooming Grove, in the lush hills of southeastern Indiana's Franklin County. The cherished old family farmhouse resonates America, bedecked with flags and a red, white, and blue Uncle Sam yard ornament. Even the front-yard pansies are red, white, and blue.

He was a boy of nature, but his high school rock band and his sweetheart, Donna, soon supplanted frogs and fossils. Marrying young, Copes turned to the National Guard for a career, which turned out to be a long and illustrious one. Beginning as an aircraft mechanic, Copes eventually climbed into the cockpit as a pilot. Officer school at Fort Benning led in time to serving as Indiana National Guard Adjutant General's Chief of Staff. Copes's marriage also turned out to be long and illustrious. He and Donna are now in their thirty-second year together, comfortably ensconced in their suburban Shelbyville home, hub for both kids and grandkids. As the commander's wife, Donna serves as her husband's sounding board and helps ADT families cope with challenges.

The ADT command fits Copes like an old work glove. He can draw on his long experience with small-scale hill farming. He likes the Afghans and wants to help. He is a tough guy, who knows what to do in a fight. He knows how folks accomplish things with little money. "It ain't about big dollars," he says about the ADT projects. "It's about impacting big numbers of people. Little money, lot of people." Copes is not even fazed by rustic Afghan sanitation—his own family did not have an indoor toilet until 1967.

TO INDIAN COUNTRY

The ADT missions most often begin at Forward Operating Base Salerno, the ADT post near Khost City, the provincial capital. It is a familiar routine. Thick-armed security grunts swarm over the MRAP vehicles idling in the dusty compound, checking out equipment, washing wind-

Colonel Cindra Chastain, the ADT deputy commander, leads a discussion about a proposed dam project with tribal leaders of Shobo Khel village.

Courtesy of Douglas A. Wissing.

shields, loading the ammo and water. Tattooed gunners fiddle with their machine guns and automatic grenade launchers. A Comm guy wanders the yard with a radio in each hand. Terps are in a huddle. Over by the plywood B-huts, a clot of officers chew on the overnight security report. Already kitted out with more than seventy-five pounds of body armor, weapons, and ag equipment, the Hoosier farm specialists wait for the final briefing.

Though still early morning, the chalky central Asian air is already a sauna. The soldiers gather under a shade canopy, where convoy leader Sergeant Joe Carter, a nuclear power plant security consultant in civilian life, tells them to drink lots of water—two bottles an hour—it is going to be over 100 degrees. Keep your eyes peeled for a white van that has a suicide bomber; watch out for an oil tanker packed with explosives; keep people back from the MRAPS—they throw in grenades. As with every mission, the convoy leader reads from a laminated Escalation of Force form that codifies the use of firepower. A young soldier calls from the back, "Is it true warning shots are no longer necessary?" Carter glances up, "Let's not spread that around till we hear for sure." Former U.S. Army Ranger and team chaplain Major Shawn Gardner reads a bible selection; the Hoosiers recite a heartfelt "Our Father" and it is time to mount up.

Just inside the base gates, the soldiers clamber down from the tall vehicles. Surrounded by high bastions, this enclosure is the place to "go red"—load the weapons for war. "Yea, bullets," calls one gunner as he clicks a cartridge belt into his machine gun. Locked and loaded, the soldiers climb in and combat-seal the vault-like doors with a hiss of compressed air. If the brutish MRAPs were dinosaurs, they would be triceratops. Developed after IEDs devastated troops in Iraq, the heavily armored 37,000-pound MRAPs have V-shaped hulls to deflect bomb blasts. For ambush protection, gunners in the open-topped turrets man M240- and.50-caliber machine guns and MK-19 grenade launchers. Because of the high risk of attack, there is a minimum of four MRAPs per convoy. Powered by Cummins diesels, the trucks rumble past the last security barriers and into central Asia.

It is a circumscribed view. Clad in their full body armor, Kevlar helmets, Nomex fireproof gloves, and blast goggles, cinched tightly into the hard seats with lap and shoulder harnesses so they do not go flying in IED blasts, the soldiers in the armored cabin are constricted at best, damned close to immobile if the truth be known. With small, bulletproof windows, a Sceni-cruiser it is not. All communications are over headsets crammed up under helmets. So rolling along in an MRAP is somewhat akin to traveling through Afghanistan in a submarine with portholes.

The intercom distributes unending truck banter, the sacred and profane merrily commingled. Fast-food yearnings, till all of our mouths are watering. Critiques of war movies; reminiscences of Barney, Power Rangers, Mary Poppins. Scatology of near-poetic levels. A little country-music singing; a Christian pop song about "voices calling out to me," led by Copes, who then swaps favorite heavy-metal bands with the young guys. The colonel and a truck commander exchange youth minister wisdom: "Youth want real-life answers." A flyer about a Saturday night dance generates conversation: "The Ladies of Salerno present . . . Shake Things up on the Da' Dance Floor," promising "R&B, Hip Hop, Salsa, Merenge, Bachata and much more!" There being few actual "Ladies of Salerno," the men make alternate arrangements. One guy asks his buddy, "So who gets to lead?" Rejoiner: "I do." "No, I do." Some bass-voiced bickering, concluding with "Who's the girl?" After some negotiation, they resolve the temporary dance gender, but the "girl" makes one last requirement: "No dirty dancing."

Golden wheat fields reach off to the rugged Hindu Kush mountains. Turbaned farmers bend to scythe the grain, straightening to watch the convoy. Mud-brick villages hunker on the landscape. A flock of fat-tailed sheep waggle by; a bedraggled camel lounges in a dirt lot. There is talk about insurgents' animal-borne IEDs—sheep, camels, even dogs. "That's pretty nasty," a grunt says. The few cars we encounter dive for the shoulder of the road, knowing the penalty for appearing to be a threat to an American convoy. The MRAP Street Thunder siren whoops as we pass an auto accident. "Just letting them know we're here," the driver reports.

The trip takes us through Khost City, the provincial capital of well over 100,000, mainly Pashtun, people. It in the midst of a building boom, five-story office buildings and maxi-mansions rising here and there—financed in general by opium, corruption, and aid dollars gone astray. A tall government building stands windowless and scorched, a casualty of a complex Taliban attack on the governor's office a few weeks earlier. Bullet holes pockmark mud walls along the road. Packs of children boil from the alleyways to hurl rocks; clunks and thunks announcing hits. "You little shit," the turret gunner calls as a rock flies close to his head. Scowling tribesmen with crossed arms watch the trucks pass. A henna-bearded man with a black turban and gray *salwar kameez*, the Afghan tunic and pants the soldiers call man-jammies, glares at the convoy with fiery eyes. "I wonder if it pisses people off, us rolling through with these big trucks," the driver wonders. "Might," a grunt says. "We got to do, what we got to do." The convoy slows as the MRAPs approach a deep, dry riverbed. The metal bridge is a perfect place to plant bombs. "I *hate* this bridge," the driver growls as we crawl forward. Copes warbles a lachrymose tune, something about "I'm a flower quickly fading." He looks up smiling, "My wife and I sing that in church."

IEDs, cheap to make and easy to place, are a stunningly effective tactical weapon. They are so prevalent on some main hardball (paved routes) that the top brass declared them Black, basically closed to military traffic. But the bombs are also tragically indiscriminate. Civilian casualties from bombs far exceed the military's. Just a few weeks before, another ADT convoy hit an IED in the Bak borderlands. "The bad guys are getting frisky," Copes said.

The ADT is facing a multifaceted insurgency that operates in an intricate tribal society. Sometimes called the neo-Taliban to differentiate them from the Islamic militants who ruled Afghanistan until the United States invasion in 2001, the insurgents include some old Soviet-era jihadists and a smattering of al Qaeda foreigners. But the proud Pashtuns along the Afghan-Pakistan border are the heart and soul of the insurgency. Long celebrated as warriors, the ultraconservative Islamic Pashtuns have thwarted empires from Alexander the Great to the Soviet colossus. In the information war being waged, the insurgents say the American-led forces are just the latest Crusaders trying to crush Muslim culture. The rebels insist resistance is the patriotic thing to do. Adding to the rebellion, the Taliban are masters at exploiting the tribal conflicts that constantly flare up among Khost's hundreds of tribes and subtribes.

Recent elections notwithstanding, there are the millions of fence-sitting Afghans, waiting to see who wins this war—the Taliban or the U.S.-led coalition. In the meantime, they keep their options open. Most families have relatives in the insurgency. Most organizations—mosques, criminal gangs, aid groups, government agencies—have open lines of communication with the Taliban. For many Afghans, they feel trapped between the Americans' death-dealing firepower and the Taliban's brutal oppression. Coalition-caused civilian deaths are a major issue among Afghans, as is rampant government corruption related to American aid money.

THEY GOT HIT

The ADT convoy's route through open countryside gives way to narrow lanes bracketed by willows, slender poplars, and deep ditches. Along the road, high mud walls of farm compounds called *qalats* create potential canyons of ambush. Approaching Latifullah's village where the ADT team previously hit an IED, the team tenses. That explosion blew the lead MRAP six feet in the air and knocked the passengers cold. The blast totaled the $1.5-million MRAP. The soldiers all suffered concussions. While most often survivable, the tens of thousands of concussions suffered from IEDs in Iraq and Afghanistan have created a tidal wave of mild traumatic brain injuries, which are associated with post-traumatic stress disorder and other physical disorders. Army sources have indicated that as many as 18 percent of troops deployed to Iraq and Afghanistan have suffered mild brain traumas.

But the ADT soldiers who were in the blown-up MRAP felt fortunate, believing that the casualties could have been worse. Sergeant Major Robert Goodin, a Greenfield postman, was in the MRAP: "I'm thankful for the equipment we have, because if we didn't have it, right now there'd be about nine of us dead—just another body count for the AAF [anti-Afghan Forces]." When the security grunts dismounted to form a defensive perimeter, they barely escaped a second IED. A couple of men were already down the road before "Doc"—Sergeant Phillip Jacks, a medic from Fishers—spotted a glimmer on the fishing-line tripwire and barked a warning. It was the next day before the rescue team could extricate the convoy, a long night in what the soldiers call Indian Country.

The team again creeps down the same claustrophobic lane through the same silent village. The truck bluster is gone—it is all business. Asspucker time, the soldiers say. "Insurgents have planted six or seven IEDs within 600 meters of this spot," Copes said as he watches an Afghan on a rooftop. Probably an inside deal here: the army arrested Latifullah's brother when they found him parked near an IED. Staccato reports begin to crackle over the intercom. "The village seems deserted," a driver said. No traffic, said another. Over in a wheat field, a Pashtun in a wool *muja-heddin* cap stares at the convoy. The velocity of radio reports speeds up, sometimes overlapping. A metal teapot by the road—a bomb? An abandoned yellow shovel seems odd. A donkey blocks the road. Animal IED? A car stops ahead and quickly backs up. Why? A softball-sized gourd hanging from a tree causes a truck commander to yelp "Get Down!" to his gunner. A wheelbarrow with a suspicious bucket. "Someone get eyes on it." Turns out to be holding ice. An Afghan standing by a *qalat* suddenly makes a cell phone call and disappears. "Hey, that guy in brown man-jammies just took off," a soldier yells. A moment later, a concussive blast rolls through the convoy, rocking our MRAP. "IED! IED!" echoes on the intercom, followed by a somber "They got hit."

Squirming, I'm wondering what is next. The ding of Kalashnikov fire? The whoosh and flash of rocket-propelled grenades? But there is quiet as we await news. A terp gets out his pocket Koran and begins reading, his lips moving in silent prayer. Like the soldiers reverting to their training, I jot notes, record sounds, and prepare for the worst. Comfort in routines. The damage report comes in: The IED exploded ahead of the first MRAP. No damage; no injuries. Before the team can move, another report: "Hey, I got a second IED up here." A voice comes over the radio, "These Yakubi tribesmen here in Bak, they don't want American people, they don't want the Afghan government either. These fuckers."

SHOW SOME LOVE

"We're going to show them some love," Colonel Chastain says about the village of Ali Daya, where we are going on an aid mission. The ADT has excellent reasons to try to help U.S.-led forces make amends. About six weeks earlier, on the night of April 8, 2009, a team of American-led special ops crept into Ali Daya on a clandestine raid. Located in the relatively quiescent Gorbuz District, the village's three hundred families were fairly progressive and government friendly. There was even secondary school for girls. Supported by the international aid organization, CARE, the girls' school was notable in fundamentalist Khost. Even rarer, there was a teacher for the girls, the wife of an Afghan army colonel named Awal Khan. (It's not uncommon for NGO- and government-built schools for girls to be standing in a village, but they are often empty because there are no teachers.)

The raiders were in Ali Daya to capture a suspected insurgent. Surrounding the suspect's *qalat*, the Americans climbed on adjacent houses, moving across the flat roofs to take up positions. But they neglected one important detail: to notify the inhabitants of the houses where they crouched. One of the houses was Khan's. He was away on a mission, but his brother was there, guarding Khan's wife, two children and Khan's

Pashtuns, like this Khost Province tribesman, are proud of their thousand-year-old warrior culture, undergirded by the tribal tenets of *Pashtunwali*, which includes *nang* (honor), *tora*, (courage) and *badal* (revenge). There is a Pashtun saying, "It took a hundred years to avenge my grandfather's death—and I am only sorry I was so quick." Equally important is *melmastia* (hospitality) and *nanawati* (sanctuary to a defeated foe).

Courtesy of Douglas A. Wissing.

cousin, a young mother with a newborn. Hearing footsteps on the roof, the Khans thought the Taliban was about to attack them for their work with the government and the Westerners. So they shot through the ceiling at the people above. The shots unleashed America's attack dogs. Thinking the insurgents were below, the Coalition forces responded with a firestorm. When the shooting stopped, Khan's wife, two children, and brother were dead. The four-day-old baby was also shot and killed.

The military initially contended that four "armed combatants" had been shot dead. Only when the international media amplified the uproar from the outraged Khostis, CARE, and the Karzai government did the military take responsibility and begin damage control. The big brass flew in, proffering generous financial settlements and promising an investigation and new procedures. (Some were actually instituted, such as having Pashto-speaking ANA or ANP lead future raids to explain things in a language the inhabitants can actually understand.) Ali Daya got a new generator with lines to all the houses. Eager young U.S. officers are now common in the village, wanting to make nice.

But Ali Daya illustrates part of the terrible difficulty of prosecuting a war in Afghanistan, where the enemy is often ensconced among civilians. Trying to win Pashtun "hearts-and-minds," as the military unfortunately persists in phrasing it, is problematic at best. The more than 22 million Pashtuns are famously independent, primed to exchange their hoes for weapons at the first sign of an affront or invader. The cornerstones of *Pashtunwali*, the thousand-year-old tribal code, include *nang* (honor) as well as *tora* (the word for sword, signifying courage). But *badal* (revenge)—they have very, very long memories—is a crucial tenet. There is a Pashtun saying, "It took a hundred years to avenge my grandfather's death—and I am only sorry I was so quick." When the Coalition drops an errant bomb, or attacks the wrong house, critics say it just lost that village for three generations. In many cases, a vigorous use of Coalition "kinetics"—firepower—fails to dampen the insurgency, but instead fuels it.

Chastain goes over her mission to Ali Daya with subgovernor Mohammed Akber, a respected administrator who oversees Ali Daya. They meet at the Gorbuz District Center, another fortified node of the embattled Afghan national government. Nine-inch-high cartridges sit on the governor's desk beside an arrangement of artificial flowers; a flystrip hangs from a large portrait of President Hamid Karzai. Chastain and Akber talk about check dams and the vet clinic. Akber pulls out a threatening Taliban "night letter" he received. A terp translated: "It says people should not to work with the infidels. The people need to quit." Chastain asks, "By when?" "June—this month," the terp replies. "It says, 'If somebody do not quit, we will kill you guys.'"

After the meeting, Chastain and an earnest young sapper captain working on security confer about Ali Daya. They discuss the ongoing fury about civilian deaths in *shuras* (meetings) across the province. In 2008 there were 2,100 civilian casualties in Afghanistan, a 30 percent in crease from the year prior. Though the insurgents were responsible for 55 percent of the deaths, Afghan public opinion often is more critical of the foreigners. Civilian deaths caused by coalition air strikes dramatically increased in 2008, spiking to 552, a 70 percent increase. Chastain's eyes flash as she relates Ali Daya's reaction to their own tragedy: "The villagers just said, 'You can't do night ops in our town.'" She repeats, "We're going to go show them some love."

FARM GIRL/WOMAN OFFICER

Chastain grew up on her family's homestead farm near Crawfordsville, farming with her brothers and sisters. "We all did it, boys and girls. I don't think there was any difference," she said. Along with the corn and beans, the Chastains raised cattle, sheep, and hogs—blue-ribbon hogs. "I showed 4-H hogs for ten years. So did my brothers and sisters," Chastain noted. "It's really what put us through college—our 4-H hogs." She went to Purdue in the mid-1970s, where, not surprisingly, she was a pre-vet student. Chastain enlisted in the Reserve Officers' Training Corps program of the very prefeminist-influenced army.

When it came time to choose between being a veterinarian or an officer, Chastain went with her heart and headed for her first posting: Italy. "I haven't regretted my decision," she said. Through her thirty-year career, Chastain has been part of the tectonic shifts in attitudes toward women in the military. The ADT will be her last mission, as she retires when her deployment ends. She will return to Avon, where her graphic-designer husband, Pete, and her dogs are waiting. After some quiet time, she is hoping they will build a house on some land they own and start a farm, her own little farm.

But her last military mission allows Chastain to merge her farm background with her military experience. She is spearheading the animal husbandry projects and also planning microbusinesses for Afghan women. "It's going to be a tough nut to crack," she said, "but we're going to try to grow some women's businesses here. Some self-respect enters into this." Women in conservative Khost Province lead tightly circumscribed lives. When in public, women are most often clothed in burqas, the loose-fitting garment that drops from a headband to cover the entire body, including the eyes, which are veiled with a fabric grill—a garment Westerners sometimes call "shuttlecock burqas." But Khost women are seldom even outside the home. Pashtun men take great pride in "protecting their women's honor," by shielding them from contact with unrelated men. In one cur-infested village, a Pashtun leader was leading the ADT through his village. "Wait here," he called as he dodged through a gate. "Let me look for dogs and women."

ALI DAYA AND THE ADT

So how does the ADT show its love? In the case of Ali Daya, we are going to spend time with an Afghan farmer, who has complained his wheat yields are declining. The team will talk to him about his irrigation, essential in this semiarid environment where access to water is critical to farming. The ag experts will also analyze his seed and check out his soil. Other ADT members will parlay with villagers about a potential irrigation project. But no one is sure of the reception Ali Daya will give the team.

In spite of the ADT's concerns, the Ali Daya villagers give them a warm greeting when they arrive. Young Afghan men crowd around the ADT and the sapper combat soldiers. The throng heads to the wheat field, where a bearded middle-aged Pashtun dressed in white tells Chastain and the ag specialists about his declining yields. In the hot sun, his Islamic skullcap flares incandescent white, a contrast to the soldiers' camouflage helmets and body armor. He has plenty of water, the Afghan says. That is not the problem. They look at the small wheat seeds he provided earlier. Then he said they were bad. Now he says they are fine. The specialists conjecture: Maybe a bad translation? There are shrugs of Who Knows? As ag expert Major Larry Temple from Muncie stalks the field taking soil samples, the sappers toss Frisbees with the young boys, who spin like tops trying to follow the discs' unfamiliar arcs. Fascinated by the smiling American woman in body armor, a throng of young men cluster around Chastain.

On the dirt road adjacent to the field, the ADT security platoon distributes pens, candy, and stuffed animals to a gaggle of children, including a small girl venturing out from her family's *qalat*. In many im-

The US government's counterinsurgency efforts against the resilient Afghan resistance were riven with dysfunction and waste. About a trillion dollars of US taxpayer money have been "poured in the sand pit," as cynical soldiers put it. I took this photo on an embattled forward operating base after a night of Taliban attacks had artillery and combat teams scrambling.

Courtesy of Douglas A. Wissing.

poverished societies, even well-meant handouts can destabilize a place. As the soldiers hand out the largess, the boys become wolfish, pushing the little girl around to get her toy. I watch her run off in tears. "They get out of control," security Specialist John Moate, a slender blond security grunt from Valparaiso says, "Makes you sick. Can't do a thing."

The trip back to Forward Operating Base Salerno is the typical tense transit across an unpredictable, asymmetrical war zone. Eyes scan for tripwires, disturbed roadbeds, suspicious tribesmen. One driver laments, "What I want to know, why can't we go back to the good old-fashioned war before IEDs?"

THE FOB

Forward Operating Base Salerno—the FOB, as soldiers call it—is a 300-hundred-acre fortified post with a couple of thousand soldiers and civilian contractors, one of the largest in Afghanistan. About a thousand tightly vetted Afghan nationals work on the base each day. It began in 2003 as a sandbagged encampment on an old government farm near the mountainous border with Pakistan. Insurgents launched so many rocket and mortar attacks on Salerno, the soldiers nicknamed it Rocket City.

One day I climb the stairs to a perimeter watchtower to talk to Major Shawn Gardner. A rangy southern Indiana farm boy, Gardner served as a ranger in Khost Province in 2002, when the U.S. forces routed the Taliban. As he watches for insurgents (and counts dogs—it was a slow day), Gardner tells about his two deployments: "It was different back then. Salerno didn't exist. Much more Spartan than now. We operated out of a *qalat* called Stormy Safe House. You can have ice cream now. There's a gym. There's hot water, a laundry! I used to do my laundry in a five-gallon bucket." Gardner calls FOB Salerno "living large."

Compared to the austere combat outposts out in the province, the FOB is a cushy place. (Support soldiers and contractors who never "break the wire"—leave the FOB—are known as "fobbits.") The KBR-run mess hall serves hot American-style meals with a daily range of ethnic choices. Fresh vegetables are flown in from Dubai. (Though it does take some adjustment to dine with heat-packing companions. "Got Weapon?" reads flyers taped to the exit doors.) The base has a twenty-four-hour gym and Green Bean coffee shop, recreation facilities, university classes, hospital, church, and mosque. With fairly reliable Internet and Skype, soldiers can survive a scary Indian Country mission, and when they return get spousal grief about a broken washing machine. It is a Little America on the Pakistan border.

Though the FOB still has a few orange and olive groves from its government farm days, a double ring of walled security now protects the highly sensitive base. The gravel runway caters to the business of war: night-landing C-130 transport planes, Blackwater-piloted STOLs (short-takeoff-and-landing planes) diving in like hungry raptors, Black-hawks heading to remote combat outposts, Kiowa and Apache attack helicopters rising like avenging demons, Medivacs "landing hot" beside trauma teams with field stretchers. The artillerymen hurl shells in all directions, sometimes as counter-barrages to Taliban rocket and mortar attacks; sometimes in support of combat missions. One night the howitzers are firing shells so heavily charged they shake the ground like immense tromping giants. Sitting in front of his barracks with a radio, one old artilleryman smiles, "Ah, that's heading to Pakistan. Somebody in trouble over there."

Most troops are now housed in hardened masonry barracks, capable of sustaining direct hits. A few disparate groups still live in tents: some medics, the road-clearing team who handle IEDs, terps in Terp Village—and visiting journalists (though the ADT blessedly ensconced me in a comfortable barracks). Because of attacks, the FOB is blacked out at night, presenting a central Asian sky ablaze with the smears and strobes of infinite stars. Soldiers are required to negotiate the darkened base with red-, blue- and green-lens flashlights. Leaving a lit building, night-blindness presents an unsettling vulnerability until your eyes adjust. However, to foil potential gropers, female soldiers are permitted to use white lights when they exit the latrines, giving the stygian base a kind of color-coded gender ID system—sort of like fireflies.

Growing up on a large, prosperous farm in southwestern Indiana's Knox County, Gardner was a high school athlete and student leader. He gravitated to ROTC while earning his biology degree at IU. Soon after 9/11, the military told Gardner to immediately report for duty to Afghanistan. But he needed to do something first. Gardner called his fiancée, Maxie, who was planning their summer wedding. "I asked her, 'What do you want to do?' She said, 'Well, marry you.'" So they did, the next afternoon. When he returned on leave, they got married again, this time in IU's Beck Chapel with Maxie in her wedding dress that got completed while Shawn was in training.

The Gardners now have two children and live in a leafy new development near Center Grove. While Gardner is busy with his ADT work, Maxie works as a pharmaceutical sales representative and is the president of the Family Readiness Group, a support organization for military families. With Shawn on missions all over the world, Maxie's learned to be self-reliant. "I bought our first house without him here," she laughed. "I think he was jumping out of an airplane." Besides his military career, Gardner has nearly completed a master's degree in systems management communications from Northwestern University, with thoughts of a PhD when he returns home.

Up in the watchtower, Gardner scans the wadis for infiltrators. Looking up from his rifle scope, he said the ADT aid mission helped him understand Afghanistan in a much different way: "It's a big change from my last trip, which was much more kinetic. This is more of a governance and development operation. It's giving me an opportunity to be with the people more—gives me a lot of compassion for the people of Afghanistan and what they go through. It's been good for my heart, it's been healing."

SHARDS OF THE WHOLE

On FOB Salerno, the whirling shards of war occasionally flicker into momentary coherence: soldiers, technocrats and diplomats in some choreographed dance, the attack helicopters rising, the transports descending, the MRAPs rumbling, the boom of artillery, the FOB's Giant Voice screeching out the attack siren; announcing another medivac full of casualties.

One day returning from the airfield, Copes and I pass under slender-leaved pepper trees filled with raucous jackdaws cawing out their territories. We talk about the battle between the U.S.-led coalition and the hydra-headed enemy. I ask about President Karzai's Government of the Islamic Republic of Afghanistan, and its reputation for corruption and poor governance. Copes talks about the emerging U.S. counterinsurgency strategy that focuses on long-term, economically sustainable missions, an approach that dovetails with the ADT multiyear commitment and the commonsense Hoosier "little money, big impact" philosophy. As we discuss the complications of asymmetrical war, where the U.S. technological might is pitted against an innovative opponent fighting on their own turf, Copes talks of the generations needed to resolve all of Afghanistan's problems. We stride out of the dappled shade into the harsh central Asian sun, turning down the graveled alleys between rows of hardened, windowless barracks, soldiers snapping salutes as we pass. Returning the salutes, Copes tells me about the essential need for patience in this clash of cultures, and the Taliban's exploitation of America's cut-and-run reputation. He turns to me and said, "You know the Taliban leaders' favorite saying? 'The Americans have the watches, but we have the time.'"

CREDITS

The epigraph was previously published in "Manufacturing Place" in *The Flatness and Other Landscapes* by Michael Martone, University of Georgia Press, 2000.

"The Last Vaudevillian: Red Skelton" was previously published in *Traces*, Winter 1998.

"Hubris: Bobby Knight" was previously published in *Nuvo*, March 1998.

"Odd Bodkin" was previously published in *Condé Nast Details*, August 1999, reprinted by *Independent on Sunday (UK)*, October 1999.

"D. C. Riddle" was previously published in *Indiana Alumni Magazine*, September/October 2007.

"Inner Vision: Amish Healer" was previously published in *Bloomington Voice*, March 1997.

"A Fair of the Heart" was previously published in *Endless Vacation*, July/August 2002.

"A Surprising Utopia" was previously published in *Los Angeles Times*, May 7, 2006.

"Architecture and Community" was previously published in *artsindiana*, November 1998.

"The Song of Indiana" was previously published in *Scenic Driving Indiana*, Falcon Press, 2001.

"'Cook Good, Serve Generously, Price Modestly': The Shapiro's Story" was previously published in *Traces*, Fall 2009.

"She's the Cheese" was previously published in *Louisville*, June 2002.

"Strange Brew" was previously published in *Indianapolis Monthly*, April 2010.

"Market Daze: Bloomington's Farmer's Market" was previously published in *Indianapolis Star*, October 1996.

"Pawpaw Redux" was previously published in *Saveur*, September/October 2001.

"Tibetan New Year Celebration" was previously published in *Bloomington Voice*, February 1997.

"Lair of the Turtle Soup: A Culinary Tradition" was previously published in *Bloomington Voice*, July 1996.

"This Rash Adventure: Ezra Pound at Wabash College" was previously published in *Traces*, Fall 2007.

"Erotica Whose Purpose Was Scholarly: Kinsey Institute Art Exhibit" was previously published in *The New York Times*, November 1997.

"Gargoyles and Other Curious Creatures" was published as "Gargoyles and Other Pagans" in *artsindiana*, May 1998.

"Crossroads of American Sculpture" was previously published in *artsindiana*, Autumn 2000.

"The Stuff of Legend: Indiana and the Empire State Building" was previously

published in *Indianapolis Star,* January
1999.

"John Dillinger's Funeral" was previously
published in *Crown Hill: History, Spirit,
Sanctuary,* Indiana Historical Society
Press, 2013.

"Twist the Tiger's Tail" was previously
published in *Traces,* Fall 1998.

"That's It: Prohibition, 1918–1933" was previously published in *Indiana, One Pint
at a Time,* Indiana Historical Society
Press, 2010.

"Black Gold Era's Luxurious Perch: Evansville Petroleum Club" was previously
published in *Indianapolis Star,* February
1999.

"Lions, Tigers, High Wires" was previously published in *artsindiana,* Summer
2001.

"Conflict and Conciliation" was previously
published in *Indiana University Alumni
Magazine,* March/April 2006.

"War Fare" was previously published in *Indianapolis Monthly,* December 2009.

INDEX

DOUGLAS A. WISSING is an Indiana-based award-winning journalist and author who uses his education as a historian and political scientist to weave complex narratives, which merge academic research with the on-the-ground reality of far-flung and familiar places. Wissing has contributed hundreds of stories to media outlets that include the *New York Times, Washington Post, Los Angeles Times, Independent on Sunday* (UK), *Foreign Policy, American Legion, Asia Times,* CNN.com, Fox.com, Salon.com, Time.com, BBC, and NPR networks, as well as tastemaking journals that include *Forbes Life, National Geographic Traveler, Condé Nast Details, ARTnews, Travel + Leisure, American Way, Saveur,* and *Gray's Sporting Life.* Through his contributions to a broad range of Indiana media that include *Traces, Indianapolis Monthly, Indianapolis Star, Nuvo, Evansville Courier, Hoosier Farmer, Indiana Alumni Magazine, artsindiana,* and his 28-part radio series on Hoosier soldiers in Afghanistan for the Indiana Public Media NPR network, Wissing's work has become known across Indiana. His work has garnered multiple awards from the Indiana Society of Professional Journalists, the Indiana Broadcasters Association and the Indiana Historical Society. He is the author of eight books.

Lightning Source UK Ltd.
Milton Keynes UK
UKOW06f0741040216

267673UK00021B/155/P

9 780253 019042